The Future of Work Series

Series Editor: **Peter Nolan,** Director of the ESRC Future of Work Programme and the Montague Burton Professor of Industrial Relations at Leeds University Business School in the UK.

Few subjects could be judged more vital to current policy and academic debates than the prospects for work and employment. *The Future of Work* series provides the much needed evidence and theoretical advances to enhance our understanding of the critical developments most likely to impact on people's working lives.

Titles include:

Chris Baldry, Peter Bain, Phil Taylor, Jeff Hyman, Dora Scholarios, Abigail Marks, Aileen Watson, Kay Gilbert, Gregor Gall and Dirk Bunzel
THE MEANING OF WORK IN THE NEW ECONOMY

Harriet Bradley and Geraldine Healy
ETHNICITY AND GENDER AT WORK
Inequalities, Careers and Employment Relations

Julia Brannen, Peter Moss and Ann Mooney
WORKING AND CARING OVER THE TWENTIETH CENTURY
Change and Continuity in Four Generation Families

Andy Danford, Mike Richardson, Paul Stewart, Stephanie Tailby and Martin Upchurch
PARTNERSHIP AND THE HIGH PERFORMANCE WORKPLACE
Work and Employment Relations in the Aerospace Industry

Geraldine Healy, Edmund Heery, Phil Taylor and William Brown (*editors*)
THE FUTURE OF WORKER REPRESENTATION

Diane Houston (*editor*)
WORK-LIFE BALANCE IN THE 21st CENTURY

Theo Nichols and Surhan Cam
LABOUR IN A GLOBAL WORLD
Case Studies from the White Goods Industry in Africa, South America, East Asia and Europe

Paul Stewart (*editor*)
EMPLOYMENT, TRADE UNION RENEWAL AND THE FUTURE OF WORK
The Experience of Work and Organisational Change

Clare Ungerson and Sue Yeandle (*editors*)
CASH FOR CARE IN DEVELOPED WELFARE STATES

Michael White, Stephen Hill, Colin Mills and Deborah Smeaton
MANAGING TO CHANGE?
British Workplaces and the Future of Work

The Future of Work Series
Series Standing Order ISBN 1–4039–1477–X

You can receive future titles in this series as they are published by placing a standing order. Please contact your bookseller or, in case of difficulty, write to us at the address below with your name and address, the title of the series and the ISBN quoted above.

Customer Services Department, Macmillan Distribution Ltd, Houndmills, Basingstoke, Hampshire RG21 6XS, England

Ethnicity and Gender at Work

Inequalities, Careers and Employment Relations

Harriet Bradley

and

Geraldine Healy

First published in 2008 by
PALGRAVE MACMILLAN
Houndmills, Basingstoke, Hampshire RG21 6XS and
175 Fifth Avenue, New York, N.Y. 10010
Companies and representatives throughout the world.

PALGRAVE MACMILLAN is the global academic imprint of the Palgrave
Macmillan division of St. Martin's Press, LLC and of Palgrave Macmillan Ltd.
Macmillan® is a registered trademark in the United States, United Kingdom
and other countries. Palgrave is a registered trademark in the European
Union and other countries.

ISBN-13: 978–1–4039–9175–1 hardback
ISBN-10: 1–4039–9175–8 hardback

This book is printed on paper suitable for recycling and made from fully
managed and sustained forest sources. Logging, pulping and manufacturing
processes are expected to conform to the environmental regulations of
the country of origin.

A catalogue record for this book is available from the British Library.

A catalog record for this book is available from the Library of Congress.

10   9   8   7   6   5   4   3   2   1
17 16 15 14 13 12 11 10 09 08

Printed and bound in Great Britain by
CPI Antony Rowe, Chippenham and Eastbourne

Contents

List of Figures and Tables

Figures

Tables

Foreword

The segmentation of labour markets has long been a major focus of concern for researchers on work and employment. The evidence base reveals systematic tendencies in advanced capitalist economies that reproduce the supply of relatively good and bad jobs. It is widely accepted moreover that social groups bearing particular characteristics are more likely to be crowded into bad jobs, while others gain access to higher paid, more secure and more challenging paid work. Within this broad area of study, explanations for the compartmentalisation of labour markets continue to diverge, and there also remain many critical issues that have been under-researched. One such issue is the labour market position of women from minority ethnic backgrounds.

This important new book by Professor Harriet Bradley and Professor Geraldine Healy, two distinguished specialists on work and employment, advances in important ways knowledge of this vitally important social and economic issue. The research on which it is based was conducted as part of the Economic and Social Research Council's Future of Work Programme, which commenced in 1998, and supported the work of more than one hundred researchers and 27 projects. The Programme set-out to generate new data, refine established concepts, and produce a theoretically grounded understanding of the changing world of work. Further information on the Programme is available at: www.leeds.ac.uk/esrcfutureofwork

Ethnicity and Gender at Work is the tenth research monograph in the Palgrave Macmillan Future of Work Series. Timely and policy relevant, it brings forward a searching account of the jobs that ethnic minority women do, the extent to which they work full-time or in 'non-standard' jobs, and the degree to which they are clustered in particular occupations and labour market segments. It looks in detail at their pay, the extent to which they are able to pursue careers, and the particular obstacles they face, over and above the discriminatory practices that most women have to contend with.

An especially novel and critically important aspect of Bradley and Healy's research design is its focus on the relationship between trade unions and ethnic minority women. What, if any, assistance do unions provide to such women? Have they sought to encourage the participation of ethnic minority women in trade union decision making processes and workplace organisation?

Drawing upon the varying experiences of 57 women from four ethnic groups (African, African-Caribbean, Indian and Pakistani), the study carefully documents the policy initiatives of four trade unions and reveals the diverse roles that ethnic minority women have within their structures. It not only highlights the currently limited participation of ethnic minority women, but also demonstrates the difference that their involvement can make to the working lives of other women. Compelling and rigorous, this book is essential reading for scholars, practitioners, union activists, indeed anyone with a stake in the future effectiveness and policy direction of the labour movement.

Professor Peter Nolan

Acknowledgements

This book presents findings from the 'Double Disadvantage – ethnic minority women in trade unions' project funded under the ESRC's *Future of Work* programme. We are grateful to Peter Nolan, Director of the Future of Work programme, for his support and encouragement.

We should particularly like to acknowledge the help of the many individuals who facilitated this project in different ways. In particular we owe a debt of thanks to: Jenny Ainsley (CWU), Manny Blake (CWU), Ruth Cross (USDAW), Michelle Emerson (CWU), Kate Heasman (UCU), Roger MacKenzie (TUC), Jenny Murray (USDAW), Silu Pascoe (UNISON), Midge Purcell (UCU), Wilf Sullivan (TUC), Leanne Venner (UNISON), Cindy Westcarr (UNISON) and the many inspiring women we met and interviewed in the course of this work.

We are particularly grateful to Nupur Mukherjee Ganguly who was the research assistant on the project (2002–4) and whose excellent interviewing skills were invaluable. Thanks also to Karen Morgan who helped us with a literature search for the project. Jorun Solheim of ISF in Oslo helped set up a research visit for Harriet and provided space – in both its senses – in which the initial chapters of the book were drafted.

We presented material from the 'Double Disadvantage' study at a number of seminars, workshops and conferences and are grateful to all those who attended and made helpful comments.

Thanks also go to the expertise of the staff at Palgrave Macmillan, including Emily Bown and Penny Simmons for facilitating the publication process.

In addition we would like to acknowledge the support of those who enrich our lives by being there, Steve, Rachel, Jason and Rebecca, and Terry, Aideen and Ciara.

List of Abbreviations

ACAS	Advisory Conciliation and Advisory Service
AUT	Association of University Teachers
BERR	Department for Business, Enterprise and Regulatory Reform
BME	Black and minority ethnic
BMJ	British Medical Journal
BT	British Telecom
CEO	Chief Executive Officer
CIPD	Chartered Institute of Personnel and Development
COHSE	Confederation of Health Service Employees
CRE	Commission for Racial Equality
CSW	Commission on the Status of Women
CWU	Communication Workers Union
DTI	Department of Trade and Industry (now BERR)
DWP	Department of Work and Pensions
EC	Executive Council
EDP	Equality and Diversity Policy
EO	Equal opportunities
EOC	Equal Opportunities Commission
EHRC	Equality and Human Rights Commission
ETS	Employment Tribunal Service
EU	European Union
EWL	European Women's Lobby
FE	Further education
FTSE	FTSE Group [owned by Financial Times and London Stock Exchange]
GLC	Greater London Council
GMB	General and Municipal and Boilermakers Union
HE	Higher Education
HESA	Higher Education Statistics Authority
HR	Human Resources
ILEA	Inner London Education Department
ILO	International Labour Organisation
LGBT	Lesbian, gay, bisexual and transgender
LRD	Labour Research Department
NALGO	National Association of Local Government Officers

NATFHE	National Association of Teachers in Further and Higher Education
NEC	National Executive Council
NHS	National Health Service
NUPE	National Union of Public Employees
NVQ	National vocational qualification
OECD	Organisation for Economic Cooperation and Development
PSI	Policy Studies Institute
REC	Race Equality Council
RRA 1968	Race Relations Act 1968
RRAA	Race Relations Amendment Act
SENDA	Special Education Needs and Disability Act
SERTUC	South East Region Trades Union Council
SOG	Self-organizing group
SLTG	Stephen Lawrence Task Group
TGWU	Transport and General Workers' Union
TUC	Trades Union Congress
UCU	Universities and Colleges Union
UN	United Nations
US	United States
USDAW	Union of Shop, Distributive and Allied Workers
WERS	Workplace Employment Relations Survey

1
Introduction

Ethnicity and gender at work: the background to this book

This book explores the position of women from minority ethnic backgrounds as workers in contemporary labour markets. What jobs do they do? Do they work full-time or in 'non-standard contracts'? Are they clustered in particular sectors or occupations? How does their pay compare to workers in other social categories? Are they benefiting from recent processes of social and economic change or are they among those losing out as neo-liberal economic policies seek to secure 'flexibility' in the highly competitive global marketplace? How do they view their jobs? Are they committed to developing careers? What problems do they face? Are they experiencing racism and sexism within their jobs and how are current governmental and organisational policies on equality and diversity addressing this? How do they combine their jobs with their family responsibilities? What can trade unions do to assist them and cater for their specific needs? How can unions work more effectively with minority community organisations and agencies? How are these women's experiences affected by their differing class backgrounds and ethnic affiliations?

We seek to answer these questions by drawing both on secondary sources, such as official statistics from Britain and other advanced industrial economies, and by presenting material from our own research studies. In particular we report findings from a study we carried out between 2000 and 2002 exploring the 'double disadvantage' of gender and ethnicity or multiple discriminations faced by women workers who were also active within their trade unions.

The research, which was part of the Economic and Social Research Council's *Future of Work* programme, was carried out in conjunction

1

with four trade unions: UNISON, the National Association of Teachers in Further and Higher Education (NATFHE), the Communication Workers' Union (CWU), and the Union of Shop, Distributive and Allied Workers (USDAW), who assisted us with their full collaboration and helped us find women to take part in the research. We interviewed women from four of Britain's minority ethnic communities: those of African, African-Caribbean, Indian and Pakistani) backgrounds. We tried to interview 15 women from each union, from a mix of ethnic backgrounds. In some of the unions it was quite hard to locate any minority ethnic women who were activists; in the end we carried out lengthy semi-structured interviews with 57 women, including three as a pilot study. We also attended meetings, workshops and union conferences for black workers, spoke with equality officers from all the unions and looked at their documents and policies on equality.

As well as this research, which is used as the basis for much of the book's discussion, we use some examples from other research carried out with young minority workers (both women and men) in London and Bristol over the past ten years and from a recent project looking at minority ethnic women's experience of workplace cultures, which we carried out for the Equal Opportunities Commission (EOC) in 2006–7.

We believe that this book is especially timely for a number of reasons. First, the report of the Women and Work Commission, chaired by Margaret Prosser of the Transport and General Workers Union, has highlighted the continuing disadvantages faced by women in the labour market, especially in regard to pay, and made a number of recommendations to address these disadvantages (Prosser 2006). Our research can bring the dimension of ethnicity into the picture. Second, the terrible recent attacks, first in New York and then in London, have led to worldwide tensions between Christian and Islamic populations, and have exacerbated racist attitudes to Muslims in Britain and elsewhere (Modood 2005). It is crucial that women from Muslim communities do not become the subject of increased discrimination as a result of these events. Moreover, at the same time, the increased focus on young Muslim men, seen to have replaced African-Caribbean young men as a 'social problem' in the eyes of the public and the police, means that Muslim women's specific needs and problems are in danger of being overlooked. Third, in the broader context, international employment relations are in the throes of some monumental changes. Especially within the European Community there is a continued trend of feminisation, with women's participation in the labour market increasing relative to men as a result of de-industrialisation and the replacement of manufacturing with service jobs (Bradley, Erickson et al. 2000; Jensen, Hagen and Reddy 1988). At the same time, the freeing up of labour mobility within the European Union (EU) alongside the processes of international migration produced by the workings of global capitalism are producing new patterns of ethnic relations and an increasing and contested climate of multiculturalism. Thus there is a need to review the changing intersections of gender and ethnicity in the labour market. Finally, the EU enjoins on its member states a 'duty of equality' in regard to pay, which has led to a wealth of new Equal Opportunities (EO) and anti-discrimination legislation. There is a general acceptance in the industrial nations of the West that social diversity is a desirable thing and is helpful to the economy. Thus governments across Europe are to varying degrees attempting to ensure that citizens, old and new, are being treated with fairness and dignity. Many organisations have developed their own programmes to address these issues, under various names such as 'Dignity at Work', 'Positive Working Environment' or 'Equality and Diversity'. Such developments have an almost obligatory nature in the public sector, where legislation such as the Race Relations Amendment Act (RRAA), the Special Education Needs and Disability Act (SENDA) and the recently introduced Gender Duty have a binding status.

Despite these developments, there is still surprisingly little research into the work and lives of Britain's minority ethnic women. Recent research (Dale et al. 2002; Ahmad, Modood and Lissenberg 2003) has tended to focus on the various British Asian groups (Indian, Pakistani and Bangladeshi), perhaps as a result of the fears of racism and Islamophobia. Partly, however, this is also to do with the increasing recognition that the different ethnic groups are very differently located within the nexus of socio-economic relations. It is no longer safe to make sweeping generalisations about racial discrimination and disadvantage. As in the case of the analysis of gender, it may well be that all minority ethnic citizens do face common problems, but there are also, as we shall see in Chapter 1, some dramatic differences. In this book we seek to explore both commonalities and differentiation. We also seek to explore how the various processes of change described above are affecting the position of the various minority groups. While there is increasing interest in the workings of the 'new economy' or 'knowledge-based economy' (Walby, Gottfried et al. 2007; Sayer and Walker 1992) we still know little about how patterns of gender and ethnic segmentation are currently evolving.

A key aim of this book, then, is to open up this field of investigation, both providing our own account of what is happening and allowing the words of the women we have interviewed, which have shaped our understanding, to be heard in their own distinctive voices. In constructing our account we are concerned to highlight the intersections of ethnicity, nationality, gender and class in these women's lives. We also relate the women's experiences to the various agencies that are involved in challenging the structures of inequality and disadvantage, We consider the role of the state, of trade unions and of the various community, voluntary-sector and private organisations that have become involved in the fight for racial justice. It is, we think, possible to contemplate the current political moment in the United Kingdom as constituting something of a revival of the tripartism (the collaboration between government, employers' organisations and unions as representatives of employees) which evolved after the Second World War but was crushed out during the Thatcher era. The Commission on Women and Work , for example, consisted of representatives of these three core groups. This provides an important opportunity for trade unions to reassert themselves as legitimate players in the political arena.

A note on terminology

The study of race relations and ethnicity has long been known as a difficult area with regard to the choice of appropriate, non-offensive and non-stigmatising terminology. In this book, which has been written within a policy context, we have followed prevailing tendencies in the equality and diversity field as much as we can, while acknowledging that the terms we use are contested. As a general descriptor we use the term 'black and minority ethnic' (BME) which is used in many research and policy contexts.

However, within the trade union movement there is still a preference to use the term 'black' as a symbolic marker of unity across non-majority ethnic groups. Thus the unions arranged 'Black Workers' conferences'. We asked all the women participants what they felt about the use of the term 'black' in this context and, while opinions were divided, with some feeling that some British Asian women felt excluded by it, the majority stated that they supported its use as a political tool and that they themselves identified as black. Therefore, when we talk about relations within the trade unions we use black, and also white to convey its converse.

There are similar issues around the term 'race' which is seen as discredited by its link with essentialist racist theories (discussed in Chapter 4). We are well aware that the notion of genetically and biologically distinct 'races' is a discredited social construct, so we prefer to speak of ethnicity and ethnic groups, concepts with cultural and political rather than biological referents. However, we do talk of race relations, racial discrimination and racialisation to convey the sense that these forms of social action derive from the fact that many people act as if race does exist. For the same sorts of reasons, the unions themselves talk of 'race equality officers' rather than ethnic equality officers. As this demonstrates, we have tried to use these terms as sensitively as possible in the way our participants employed them.

Structure of the book

Our book starts with a general review of minority ethnic women's position in contemporary labour markets, drawing primarily on statistical material. We aim to give an overview of their situation in the United Kingdom and to briefly describe some of the distinctions between women from different ethnic backgrounds. The specific positions of recent migrants and of refugees will also be given some attention, as in many cases they will experience the greatest level of discrimination.

We then set out a framework for explaining the continuance of ethnic and gender segregation in the labour market, elaborating on a number of analytic tools. Drawing on the concept of intersectionality, we seek to explore how class, ethnicity and gender come together in the context of racism and xenophobia to create patterns of multiple disadvantage. Intersectionality was defined by the United Nations as follows, following the Durban Conference against racism in 2001:

> An intersectional approach to analysing the disempowerment and marginalisation of women attempts to capture the consequences of the interaction between two or more forms of subordination. It addresses the manner in which racism, patriarchy, class oppression and other discriminatory systems create inequalities that structure the relative positions of women, races, ethnicities, class and the like ... Racially subordinated women are often positioned in the space where racism or xenophobia, class and gender meet.
>
> (UN 2001)

In Chapters 4 to 6, we turn to explore the role of the three parties in the tripartite alliance, government, employers and trade unions, in confronting racist and sexist practices in the workplace, looking at recent and current initiatives from these key actors. Here, we will begin to focus on our own research as we describe the array of policies developed by the four unions who participated in the 'double disadvantage' project.

This leads into Chapters 8 to 11, which draw on the interview materials from the study and which give prominence to the stories and voices of the activist women. We have referred to them as 'inspiring activists' and we hope that readers will be as impressed and moved as we were by the strength of commitment and the tenacity of these women in their contributions to the quest for racial equality. These chapters deal with their experiences within their workplaces, their experiences of racism and sexism at work and elsewhere, their career aspirations and the constraints and opportunities they faced. We show how their union membership and activism constituted an alternative career pattern for them, helping them to channel their energies and talents into union work.

Finally, we explore the policy implications of our research and of our wider explorations of ethnic and gender segmentation. We live in a multicultural world, in which much lip-service is paid to equality and diversity. What can we do to ensure that all the citizens in our society, regardless of their social origins, are given a fair chance to enjoy the benefits of contemporary living? A great aspiration for the activist women we interviewed was 'making a difference' in the lives of the working people they represented and in their communities as a whole. We are convinced that the remarkable women whose stories appear in this book are indeed helping to improve the working lives of others, as they themselves believed. In the words of Ginette:

> I know that I have made a difference to people. I have stopped people losing their job you know, I have stopped people getting into all sorts of difficulties. You think, I haven't done anything really, all I've done is listen, you know that sort of stuff, but you know you have made a difference.

If this book can make its own small contribution to the spread of relations of dignity and respect at work, we shall have fulfilled one of our own most important goals.

2
Ethnicity and Gender in the Labour Market

Soraya was born in Guyana, but has lived in England for 13 years, in an inner-city area in Bristol. In Guyana her grandfather was a rice farmer, and both her parents owned small shops. Soraya trained as a secretary, but when she came to England she desperately needed work and wound up peeling potatoes for £1.80 an hour in a restaurant. A friend suggested she applied for a job as a domestic in a nursing home, and thus commenced Soraya's career as a carer. Subsequently, she joined an agency and held jobs as a nursing auxiliary in numerous hospitals and care homes. She finally quit the agency for a permanent job in a school for disabled children, which she loves. She resisted pressures to train as a nurse as she believed it would take her away from the caring work to which she is committed. Soraya's husband suffers from poor health, so she provides economic stability for him and her grown-up son when he is unable to work.

Unlike Soraya, Angelique was born in this country and has lived in Bristol all her life, in the same city-centre area as Soraya, where most of Bristol's Caribbeans live. She is a lone mother in her thirties with three children (the youngest is six). Her mother was also a lone parent. While Angelique, says, as did all the Bristol mothers that we have interviewed, that her children must come first, she also described herself as frustrated and would like to have a career. She left school at 15, did a youth training course and held a variety of jobs: 'I've done a catering course; I did a cleaning job; I've done office work; I've worked in a garage doing reception; I worked in a dry-cleaning place; cleaning still again.' The longest job she held was in a primary school canteen (for three years). This pattern of 'churning' between low-skilled jobs is very typical of young people in Britain with minimal qualifications. While working at the school, Angelique discovered that she enjoyed working with children and started a course in childcare, but her funding ran out. She has done a variety of other courses (in catering, training as an educational assistant) and has enjoyed them all, but like many people trapped in a rather chaotic situation she has not succeeded in building from them into regular unemployment. She is currently unemployed.

Sushila's work history is very different from that of Soraya or Angelique. Sushila comes from a middle-class British-Indian family (that is how she defines her ethnicity). Her father was a well-to-do business man who sent his daughters to boarding school in India. Sushila, who has a BA and an MA, faced immense pressure to qualify in a high-status professional job as a lawyer or doctor (two of her sisters are solicitors). However, being rebellious, as she put it, she opted to become a social worker. Her husband is a well-paid engineer and she has a pre-school child, but she is determined to carry on working full-time and build a career. Ultimately she would like to rise to the top of her profession, but she also has aspirations to run a business.

We have started this chapter with the stories of Soraya, Sushila and Angelique, three women who were interviewed for a project on young adults in Bristol, because their circumstances are so different but also fairly typical of the range of labour market slots filled by ethnic minority women in the United Kingdom in the twenty-first century. Soraya exemplifies the experience of incoming migrants. Although she came from a property-owning family 'back home' and had office qualifications, Soraya found herself at the bottom of the labour market hierarchy, confined to 'dirty jobs' in the service sector. There is a strong association between women of colour and domestic and caring work. Although Angelique is part of the second generation of Britain's migrant population, she is also at the bottom of the hierarchy, due to her lack of qualifications. Unlike Soraya, however, she is not content with low-level jobs, saying they 'were not for me'. Handicapped by childcare problems, she has become part of the unemployed population, and the government attempts to get lone parents into work have not reached her: she told us 'the New Deal doesn't work here'. By contrast, Sushila, who is also part of the second generation, grew up within the prosperous Indian community. Although her parents, as she told us, had to struggle on first arriving in the country, this is a group of citizens who, by and large, have worked their way up Britain's occupational and social-class structure to reoccupy the professional and business slots they had filled in India and East Africa. While Soraya and Angelique live in what might be characterised as the 'Bristol ghetto', Sushila grew up in a comfortable suburb in South London and now lives in a similarly affluent area of

Bristol. She is part of a dynamic and ambitious young generation of minority ethnic women who have used their educational success to good effect in the labour market. Although many of them have had to struggle against some of the conventions of Indian family life (resisting early marriage or refusing to pursue vocational degrees), these young women are joining the cohorts of labour market 'winners' and refusing to be constrained by racist attitudes and racial stereotyping.

In this chapter, we offer a background to the stories of women such as Soraya, Angelique and Sushila, drawing on various statistical sources from Britain, the European Community and North America. By their nature, statistical materials paint a broad picture of social positioning, which can mask the kind of complexities and variations displayed in the stories of Soraya, Sushila and Angelique. Nevertheless they provide us with important information about the typical labour market positions of minority women, and highlight the differences between them and majority women, minority men and majority men. Thus we hope to show how contemporary labour markets are characterised by clear hierarchies of gender and ethnicity, and also to suggest how different minority groups tend to fill distinct slots in these hierarchies. In this way we will provide a background for discussion of women's own accounts of their experiences of gendering and ethnicising in their work and social lives, and the way they have learned to confront and overcome sexism and racism in the workplace.

Before we set out this material, however, it is important to set it in the context of three important general trends: the flexibilisation of working life, the feminisation of the workforce and new patterns of migration produced by globalising forces in the world economy. These can be seen as part of the contemporary dynamics of class, gender and ethnicity (see Bradley 1996, 1999; Bradley, Erickson et al. 2000). These dynamics are framing the contemporary development of the labour market.

Flexibility

During the past decades, the notion of flexibility has become a central and indeed essential term for any discussion of the labour market or of work relations. The use of this concept in Britain stems particularly from Atkinson and Meager's work on the 'flexible firm' (Atkinson 1984, 1986; Atkinson and Meager 1986) and was part of a debate which posited a shift from Fordism to post-Fordist production systems. Flexibility refers to the ability of employers and organisations to make rapid changes in their deployment of labour and other resources. Various strategies of flexibility have been introduced to counter the supposed rigidities of Fordist production (the mass production of standardised items – in Henry Ford's memorable phrase, the car can be any colour so long as it's black). Flexibility poses a challenge to the trade unions with their attachment to 'custom and practice' and their objections to workers crossing the boundaries of their job descriptions, and also to the supposed inability of bureaucratised companies to respond quickly to the demands of a more volatile customer-driven market. The flexible firm needed to have a high degree of suppleness – the ability to reorganise quickly if necessary.

The term was then extended to the labour market through the concepts of 'functional flexibility' (the ability to move employees around between jobs and functions), 'numerical flexibility' (tailoring the size of the labour force to cope with fluctuations in demand) and 'financial flexibility' (the use of systems such as piece rates and bonuses which allowed payment to tally better with shifts in demand and output and the ability to adjust budgets rapidly according to need). Women workers were often preferred as workers where employers were seeking flexibility, as they were considered less likely to be militant trade union members, more prepared to undertake part-time working and other forms of 'non-standard employment', and more ready to accept changes in working practices and conditions. Other vulnerable groups of workers (ethnic minority citizens, young workers) are also disproportionately employed to increase 'numerical and functional flexibility' and are less powerful to resist the introduction of flexible working practices than well-unionised white male workers. These various groups are also concentrated in services, both private and public, where numerical and functional flexibility are more commonly found than in manufacturing (strangely, since Atkinson and Meager's initial arguments were based on manufacturing and the needs of industry).

Subsequently, an additional meaning was added through the notions of flexible working and flexi-time which referred to allowing employees to set and adapt their own working hours to fit with external obligations. This is a version of flexibility which has proved to be very popular with workers, especially women with responsibilities for small children: many we have interviewed have told us they would not be able to hold their jobs without flexi-time.

There has been much criticism of the concept of flexibility, focusing particularly on lack of empirical evidence to show that there have been increased levels of numerical and functional flexibility, and also arguing that such policies were not really new (for example Gallie 1998; Pollert 1988a; 1988b). However, the term has persisted and has become almost a mantra for employers: whatever precisely they mean by it, they see it as a good thing. Research among young adults in Bristol showed that they also valued the notion of flexibility, especially in relation to flexible working hours, which helped young couples and, especially, lone mothers, to reconcile their domestic and workplace demands. Also it gave even single young adults the sense of being 'in control' of their work and leisure time. They were also broadly accepting of 'functional flexibility' as they tended to prize variability and change in their working tasks (Bradley 2006).

However, there is a very definite down side to flexibility as it has also led, not just in the United Kingdom but in Europe, North America and Australasia, to the creation of low-paid insecure, temporary and part-time jobs, which are disproportionately filled by women, minority ethnic citizens and young people. This makes all these groups vulnerable to poverty and to unemployment, as we shall see later in this chapter and throughout the book. The flexible labour market is thus disadvantageous for minority ethnic women and is deeply implicated with the simultaneous trend of feminisation.

Feminisation

One major trend which has manifested itself across the whole of the developed world since the 1950s has been the advance of women out from the household into the labour market. Especially in the last three decades, this has been accompanied by increasing male unemployment, so that the proportion of women in the labour market has increased relative to men. This trend is usually referred to as *feminisation*. In the United Kingdom in 1975 there were 9.1 million women in employment, while in 2006 this had risen to12.5 million. In 1975, 47 per cent of mothers were working, but only 25 per cent of mothers with pre-school children; by 2006 the figures had increased to 66 per cent and 52 per cent respectively. Moreover, while in 1975 only 15 per cent of mothers had returned to work eight months after giving birth, in 2006 this had increased to 70 per cent. It is clear from these figures that not only have women increased their workforce participation, but it has become the norm for mothers to return to work (Bradley 2007; Crompton 1997; McRae 1993). Women are now 46 per cent of the UK labour force. However, we should point out that 44 per cent of women and only 10 per cent of men in employment work part-time.

Feminisation is intimately linked to broader changes in the economies of the advanced capitalist societies, notably the switch from manufacturing to services. Women have always been clustered in service occupations for which they are often seen as more 'suitable', especially those jobs which involve strong elements of care work or customer service for which women are seen as 'naturally' equipped. By contrast many men, especially those from manual backgrounds, feel uncomfortable in such jobs and may resist being redeployed into them (Nixon 2006). Feminisation is also closely linked to flexibility, especially numerical flexibility. As many women are prepared to work part-time, they are, for example, employed in shops to work at the peak times of the day. In general, employers see women as more 'adaptable' than men, and will thus prefer to employ them in some of the new types of service work.

As the above discussion indicates there are several dimensions to feminisation (Bradley, Erickson et al. 2000). First, there is the overall feminisation of the workforce, the increase in the proportion of women employees relative to men. Second, there is the feminisation of occupations, as women move into areas formerly dominated by men, such as has happened in the legal and medical professions in the United Kingdom. Third, there is the feminisation of work tasks, which may ultimately be the most significant. More and more jobs are defined by skills or attributes associated with women: caring and nurturing, dealing with people, glamour and sexual attractiveness.

Feminisation has very important effects on minority ethnic communities. First, as has happened in Britain, men in settled minority communities may find that the manufacturing jobs they used to work in are disappearing. This means that some minority families may have to rethink their strategies with women becoming more involved in paid work and, for others, economically active women may move from manufacturing to service work. Second, the nature of initial migration is affected as the main areas of labour shortage change in nature. Sassen (2000) and Kofman (2005) note that globalisation has led to thousands of women moving around the world to work as sex workers, entertainers, maids and domestics, hotel and restaurant workers, as native-born reject these low-skilled, often 'dirty', and low-paid jobs. Kofman (2005) notes that 85 per cent of Filipina nurses now work abroad. Thus, as Castles and Miller (1998) suggest, migration itself is being 'feminised.'

Feminisation, then, may constitute a major shift in patterns of both gender and ethnic segmentation, opening chances for some groups of workers and closing them down for others. It is often stated that women are the winners and men the losers in these processes: however, we wish to show that things are more complicated than that. Class is a key factor in the recomposition of the labour market: both white and minority ethnic men from working-class backgrounds have seen their labour devalued. But, as we stated above, the 'new jobs' which are available to women are often insecure and poorly rewarded. At the top of the class hierarchy, qualified women, from all ethnic groups, may find that a wider range of options is open to them; but, as we shall see in later chapters, white middle-class men retain their hold over the most desirable jobs.

Migration

We have already linked flexibility and feminisation to changes in migration. Castles and Miller argue that the end of the twentieth century and beginning of the twenty-first century can be labelled 'the Age of Migration' (1998). Although people have moved around the globe ever since the commencement of civilisation and conquest, they believe that the process has increased in intensity in the last decades. They identify five trends; first, the globalisation of migration (more countries are involved); second, the acceleration of migration (the flows of migrants are increasing in rapidity and volume); third, the differentiation of migration (there is a wider range of types). The fourth trend they identify is politicisation: migration is linked to various types of national and international upheavals, and is becoming increasingly a matter of political concern (this is probably less true in Britain than elsewhere in Europe as migration in Britain has been a political battleground since the Notting Hill Riots in 1976). Intriguingly, since they were writing before the events of 9/11, Castles and Miller point to migration as increasingly a major security concern. Finally, and most importantly for this book, there has been a feminisation of migration. More women are moving for economic reasons in their own right, rather than as the dependants of men. This, of course, is linked to the feminisation of Western economies discussed above. Castles and Miller also point out that women are considered more reliable in sending remittances from their earnings to their families back at home. Dumont and Liebig (2005) report that women have accounted for over 50 per cent of immigration flows in nearly all European OECD countries.

As Morris rightly states: 'to a much greater extent than gender, racialised patterns of difference are country-specific' (2002:135). This is because the labour market position of minorities in any country will be shaped by a number of factors, which include: the past history of in and out migration, the stage of economic development at which immigrants arrived, the particular ethnic groups who constitute the majority of immigrants, the particular immigration regime of the country and the types of labour contract with which they entered (Fenton 1999, 2003).

In Britain, the pattern of ethnic relations is strongly shaped by the nation's colonial past. Until recently, the two dominant groups were from the Caribbean islands (especially Jamaica, Trinidad and Barbados) and from the Indian subcontinent (India, Pakistan and especially the Bengal region). Although there has been a long history of migration, the bulk of today's settler population arrived during the postwar period of economic reconstruction. African-Caribbeans, in particular, were deliberately recruited to fill jobs in areas of labour shortage, such as nursing and transport. Although some were well qualified, most ended up initially in unskilled work. Pakistanis and Bengalis, particularly from poor rural areas, arrived and found work in the textile and garment industries in London, the East Midlands, Yorkshire and Lancashire. As members of the British Commonwealth these groups automatically acquired citizenship rights, until these were tightened by successive immigration acts, starting in 1971. In the 1970s there was a major influx of Indians from East Africa where they had been expelled by the African rulers. Many of these were business owners and professionals who had been an important mainstay of the economies of Uganda and Kenya. As stated above, these middle-class refugees often had to take on low-skilled work in factories or transport, although shortages in the health service offered opportunities for skilled medical personnel. New migrants from these backgrounds are still entering Britain, but largely now because of rights to family unification.

There has also been a smaller but steady flow of economic migrants who have come to fill specific 'niche' needs in the labour market, two major groups being Chinese, both from Hong Kong and mainland China, and Turks. Primarily these groups have been concentrated in the restaurant and food sector, as have some of the South Asian migrants. These groups, especially the Turks and Chinese, have tended to cluster in specific areas and create an 'ethnic niche' in which their families can find employment.

More recently what some have called the 'new migrants', have joined the ranks of these long-settled people. This can be related to new patterns of international labour mobility created by globalisation and the dynamics of world politics. One important group of new migrants is a highly skilled elite who are able to sell their skills on the world market. Key occupations, for example, are computer experts, engineers and technical specialists. Other groups include medical personnel, financial specialists, executives and entrepreneurs (Castles and Miller 1998). Many work for multinational companies and find themselves deployed around the world. A particularly well-known example is the young Indian graduates recruited by computer firms in California's Silicon Valley. Many of this elite group are men. In 2007 the EU was drafting new legislation to develop a 'blue card' to speed up and simplify immigration procedures for skilled workers in order to compete for these kind of highly qualified employees with North America and Australia.

A second major group are asylum-seekers and refugees from the many trouble spots of the world, who seek rights of settlement under the Geneva Convention when they are seen to be in danger of political persecution. Of these, around two-thirds are women and children. In 2000, Britain received 4000 applications for refugee status, the leading countries of origin being Iraq, Sri Lanka, Afghanistan, Iran, Somalia, the former Yugoslavian bloc (especially Kosovans) and Turkey (mainly Kurds) (Morris 2002). Along with these people who are attempting to gain legal status, there are also in Britain, as everywhere across Europe, unknown numbers of undocumented migrants making a living in low-paid work, the informal economy or through ethnic networks. A notorious example was the Chinese cockle-pickers who were drowned in Morecambe Bay while working for a gang-master. Many of these illegal migrants are women sex-workers, either trafficked or voluntarily seeking a way to escape from poverty at home. Eastern Europe, Russia and Africa are particular sources of these women.

Fourthly, there are a growing group of mobile workers mainly from the European Union, but some from the rest of the English-speaking world (Australia, New Zealand, North America). Many of these are young people, students and graduates, taking advantage of their rights as citizens of the EU to reside and work anywhere within the Union. Others have come to study (many of whom hope to settle and work in the United Kingdom) or with temporary work permits. This is a major result of globalisation which opens up for a new generation of workers a perspective that, immigration restrictions notwithstanding, the world is their oyster, and they will travel where interesting opportunities beckon. There are also some less skilled people on temporary work permits who are exempted from normal restrictions to fill jobs where there are labour shortages which the native citizens cannot or will not fill. Thus London, for example, is full of Polish construction workers, Filipina maids and women of an assortment of nationalities working in the hotel and catering industry. In the past few years Britain has experienced a major influx of workers from the EU accession countries of East Europe, some with manual craft skills, others prepared to take on low-paid work in agriculture or factories. The impact of this migration is such that the British population is predicted to rise from 60 million in 2007 to 65 million by 2016 (Carvel 2007).

Migration and mobility, then, present a complex and shifting picture. However, the basis of labour market ethnic segmentation in the United Kingdom remains the settled groups of British African-Caribbean and

Asian citizens. As the next section will show, they occupy distinct labour market positions and most of the data available on ethnic difference relates to these larger groups.

Ethnicity and gender in the British labour market

In the remainder of this chapter we present and discuss the available information on the position of minority ethnic women in labour markets. We present this in comparison to the situation of majority women, and of minority and majority men. We wish to argue that there are four characteristic ways in which minority members *might* theoretically fit into existing labour market structures:

1. **Economic integration.** In this pattern the distribution of minority members into economic slots would be broadly similar to that of the majority population. This would mean that existing patterns of gender segmentation, which characterise all modern economies, would also be replicated among the minority women.
2. **Segmentation.** Here minority members would be clustered into distinct occupational slots, in the same way as women and men are differently located.
3. **Marginalisation.** Here the access to the range of jobs becomes so restricted that minorities must manufacture their own occupations in order to gain a living. This arrangement resembles the Hindu caste system. In Britain, as we shall see, the Chinese come closest to this pattern, which is often given the name 'ethnic niche'
4. **Exclusion.** Here minority members have great difficulty in finding jobs at all. They suffer unemployment, underemployment or are forced into crime or the informal economy. We shall see that certain groups of minority ethnic men and women are especially vulnerable to labour market exclusion.

In the material that follows, we shall be looking for evidence of these patterns and relating them to the existing patterns of gender segregation. We shall be considering the minority populations as a whole, but also discussing the very different experiences of different groups.

Labour market participation

According to the 2001 census, 8 per cent of the population was a member of a minority ethnic group, 2.34 million women and 2.27 million men

(EOC 2004). However, the distribution around the country is very skewed with a huge concentration in London, where minorities make up 31 per cent of the population. Other areas with a high density of minority ethnic citizens are the West Midlands (21 per cent), West Yorkshire (12 per cent) and Greater Manchester (9 per cent), the latter two being the old textile areas where many Asian migrants orginally found employment. The figures for the countries that make up the United Kingdom are England 9.3 per cent, Wales 2.4 per cent, Scotland 1.9 per cent and Northern Ireland 0.6 per cent (Brook 2004).

Members of minority groups are more likely to be excluded from the labour market than the white majority, both in terms of economic inactivity (which includes those voluntarily not in employment) and unemployment. According to the Commission for Racial Equality (CRE), in 2004 80 per cent of Great Britain's working-age population was economically active, but only 65 per cent of the minority ethnic working population. The minority ethnic employment rate was 59 per cent as compared to an overall rate of 76 per cent. Among specific groups the gap is much wider; only 46 per cent of Pakistanis and 42 per cent of Bangladeshis are in employment. This is reflected in the higher unemployment rates as shown in Table 2.1. In this table, as in the others in this chapter, the terminology follows the ethnic category system that was used in the 2001 census, from which much of the data is derived.

It will be seen that in all ethnic groups except the Indians and Pakistanis, women have a lower unemployment rate than men (with the

Table 2.1 Rates of unemployment in Britain by ethnic group and sex, 2004

	Women %	Men %	All %
White	4.0	4.6	4.3
Indian	5.6	4.8	5.1
Pakistani	20.2	9.7	12.9
Bangladeshi	*–	15.7	*–
Black Caribbean	10.8	12.9	11.8
Black African	13.0	12.9	13.0
Chinese	n/a	n/a	8.4
Mixed parentage	9.0	11.1	10.0

* Cell size too small

Source: CRE 2006b, from Labour Force Survey data.

rates among black Africans being virtually equal). However, this may in part relate to the fact that women are less likely to make themselves available for work because they have taken on the role of home-makers or carers. The major point, however, is the greater vulnerability of minority ethnic citizens to unemployment, with Pakistanis, Bangladeshis and black Africans being especially disadvantaged. They are three to four times as likely to experience unemployment as the white population. It is not hard to see that this means hardship for women as well as men in minority families.

It might be argued that these figures reflect the fact that minority members, especially recent migrants, are less likely to be well qualified and may have language difficulties that make them less employable. While that might be true for the older generation, especially women, it is certainly not true for the second generation. For some while now, certainly for the past ten years, levels of participation in higher education (HE) have been higher among the minority population. Table 2.2 shows this, and also some dramatic variations among the different groups

Table 2.2 is based on calculating percentages of people aged 17 to 30 who enter HE for the first time in any one year. Here it will be seen that women of all groups apart from Bangladeshis are more likely to be in HE than men in their ethnic group and that participation rates are higher in all ethnic groups, even Bangladeshi, than in the white group.

Table 2.2   Initial participation rates in higher education by ethnicity and sex*

	Women %	Men %	All %
White	41	34	38
All minority ethnic	58	55	56
Black Caribbean	52	36	45
Black African	75	71	73
Black Other	72	56	64
Indian	72	70	71
Pakistani	44	54	49
Bangladeshi	33	43	39
Chinese	50	47	49
Asian other	94	74	83
Mixed ethnic	44	35	40

* provisional estimates

Source: Connor et al. 2004.

There is a dramatic contrast between the very high participation rates of the black Africans of both sexes and their unemployment rates. Even though the unemployment rates cover all age groups, these figures suggest that unemployment cannot simply be explained in terms of different levels of qualification. This is confirmed in a recent report from the Equal Opportunities Commission (EOC) which focused on young women under 35, as part of a major investigation into minority ethnic women's labour market situation, entitled 'Moving On Up'. Under the headline 'outdated assumptions are blighting ethnic minority women's careers', the EOC stated that while young Pakistani, Bangladeshi and black Caribbean women were just as ambitious about their careers as young white women, they were three or four times more likely to have to take a job below their qualification level. Young Bangladeshi and Pakistani women seeking work were also three or four times more likely to be unemployed than their white counterparts, and black Caribbean women twice as likely. Among graduates the position was worse, with the differences rising to five and three respectively (EOC 2005).

It seems extremely likely that these figures are indicative of prejudice and discrimination, especially as the study, carried out by Connect Research, found that one fifth of the Pakistani and Bangladeshi women, who are predominantly Muslim, reported experiencing negative reaction to their dress in their workplaces. Moreover, at interview, minority ethnic women were three times as likely to be asked questions about their marriage and family plans, although such questions are in violation of the 1976 Sex Discrimination Act!

Patterns of working

One major difference between women and men's working lives is that women are more likely to be found in non-standard forms of employment, especially part-time work, but also temporary, seasonal and casual work, term-time working, job-share and so forth (see Bradley, Erickson et al. 2000). On the other hand, men are more likely to be self-employed. Is this also true for ethnic minority women in Britain?

Table 2.3 shows the high proportions of women who work part-time in each ethnic group; part-time work is highest in the white group and lowest among black Caribbean and Chinese. Perhaps particularly interesting, though, is that compared to white men at 8 per cent, most ethnic minority men are much more likely to work part-time. There is little reason to believe that this is a voluntary phenomenon: it is much more likely to be the result of the much greater difficulty minority men have in finding employment, as already seen in the unemployment data.

Table 2.3 Percentages of women and men in the workforce working part-time and in self-employment, 2002, by ethnic group

	Women PT %	Men PT %	Women SE %	Men SE %
White	43	8	6	15
Mixed parentage	40	19	–	–
Indian	38	17	9	15
Pakistani/Bangladeshi	41	22	–	22
Black African	40	26	–	–
Black Caribbean	33	12	–	14
Chinese	36	–	–	28

Source: Hibbett 2002, from Labour Force Survey.

This again makes life tough for women in minority families, given that part-time work is usually poorly paid.

A similarly interesting question is why minority ethnic women are less likely than white women to work part-time. Is this because of choice or because such work is not available to them? Dale and Holdsworth (1998) have explored this question and suggest that where employers offer part-time work, they may make it preferentially available to white women. Thus they state that full-time employment among minority ethnic women may sometimes be 'the result of discrimination rather than choice' (ibid.: 453). However, other factors are also likely to be at play, including the lack of ability of male partners to find work, or cultural values highlighting the importance of work which are very strong among Indians of both sexes and Caribbean women.

One response to labour market exclusion or limited opportunity is to set up your own business. This has long been given as a reason why self-employment is common among some ethnic groups such as Indians and Chinese, as Table 2.3 shows. It may be seen as a freely chosen option offering the potential for greater prosperity and autonomy. Alternatively, it can be seen as a defensive move in the face of racism and exclusion. Clearly, this is not an option taken by many woman as levels are generally low. There is little difference among different ethnic groups, although the rate is highest among English, Chinese and Asian (Lindley and Dale 2004).

A report by the CBI in 2006 highlighted the fact that the proportions of women and ethnic minorities among the self-employed were declining; business start-ups are dominated by white men living in London, and businesses started by men achieve quicker growth in the early stages.

The report called for greater help to be given to women and ethnic minorities and suggested that there was a failure to tap into a 'huge, untapped well of entrepreneurial potential' (Murden 2006). Certainly, the research among Bristol young adults showed that many were interested in owning their own business, including young ethnic minority women. It has often been suggested that banks are happier to lend money for start-ups to white men, so that ethnic minority women with these aspirations may fail to realise their dreams.

Patterns of segregation

We have seen that members of ethnic minorities run greater risks of labour market exclusion. What happens to them once they do get into employment? The answer is that the labour market remains clearly segmented on the basis of gender and ethnicity, causing a clustering of ethnic minority women in distinct labour market sectors.

Measuring and mapping occupational segregation is a complicated matter, especially if gender and ethnicity are considered jointly. There are various ways of trying to measure segregation across the whole workforce which are technically quite complex and analysts have sometimes disagreed about their findings as a result. However, there is a fairly broad consensus, based on the pioneering work of Hakim (1979, 1981), that the structure of gender segregation remained fairly stable across the twentieth century, with only a slight decline, but that the decline became more marked after the passing of the equal opportunities legislation in the late 1970s, and in the context of de-industrialisation, which has had marked effects on the structure of men's employment.

A very useful and informative article by Blackwell and Guinea-Martin (2005) brings us up to date with current trends. They use data from the 1991 and 2001 censuses to study changes in the 1990s. There are several key findings. Occupational segregation by sex declined more rapidly in the 1990s than in previous decades. However, it still persists and is higher than levels of ethnic segregation, with the exception of two groups: Bangladeshi and Chinese men. The decline in segregation can, in part, be explained by the continued rise of service work, in which women and men of all ethnic groups are increasingly concentrated. The measure commonly used to calculate segregation is the Gini index, which measures actual distribution in an occupation against a theoretical model of integration. A Gini score of 0 would mean complete lack of segregation and of 1 would mean that people in this occupation were all of one sex or ethnic group. The Gini index for sex segregation was 0.81 in 1971, 0.77 in 1991 and 0.72 in 2001. Sex segregation within each ethnic group also fell, with Chinese, black Africans and Indians the least internally sex-segregated, and whites, black Caribbeans and Bangladeshis the most (Blackwell and Guinea-Martin 2005:503).

Indices of ethnic segregation also fell during the 1990s for all ethnic groups but black African men (men and women are analysed separately, given the prevalence of sex segregation). The most segregated groups among men are the Chinese and Bangladeshi, the least the white and black Caribbean. Among women the pattern is similar: the most segregated group are the Chinese, followed by Bangladeshi and Indian, and the least segregated are white and black Caribbean (Blackwell and Guinea-Martin 2005:505–6).

This discussion so far has been rather abstract, and we shall now try to illustrate the points made above by looking at some data showing the occupational distribution of women and men of different groups. This also begins to demonstrate the types of work habitually associated with black and minority ethnic women.

Table 2.4 shows the general pattern of distribution of minority and majority women and men in the major occupational categories. It illustrates the point that differences between men and women are more marked than ethnic differences. Greater proportions of men are found in the top group of managers, and they greatly predominate in skilled and unskilled manual work. Women are found in greater proportions in

Table 2.4   Employment in standard occupational categories by sex and ethnicity

Occupational Group	White men %	Minority men %	White women %	Minority women %
Managers and senior officials	19	16	11	9
Professions	13	17	11	13
Associate professions & technical occupations	13	11	14	18
Administrative & secretarial occupations	5	5	22	19
Skilled trades	20	12	2	2
Personal services	2	3	14	13
Sales & customer service	4	9	12	13
Process, plant & machine operatives	12	12	2	3
Elementary occupations	12	15	11	11

Source: CRE 2006b, from Labour Force Survey data.

administrative work, personal services and sales. The greatest ethnic differences are among men, with ethnic minorities being somewhat more concentrated in sales and less in the skilled trades.

However, it is generally acknowledged that aggregated data, such as that in Table 2.4, may be misleading in masking the specificities of seg-regation. Thus, the more we move to the level of individual occupa-tions, the more likely we are to reveal the existence of segregation (Bradley 1989). This is also true if we look at the situations of different ethnic groups. Table 2.5 focuses specifically on the groups which are often known as the 'salariat' (Cheung and Heath 2004) or 'service class' (Goldthorpe 1980). Obviously, failure to gain admittance to these posts at the top of the occupational hierarchy would be an important indica-tor of ethnic disadvantage.

Table 2.5 shows, once again, that men dominate in these top posts, apart from black Caribbeans. Bangladeshi men do worse than other ethnic groups in the professions. Indian and Chinese men are the most successful in these areas, although many of the managerial posts they hold are likely to be in the ethnic business sector. The same holds true for Indian and Chinese women. As we have seen, these are the groups currently with the highest level of educational achievement and this seems to be paying off. We could say here that class can offset the effects of ethnicity,

When we interviewed black and Asian women for the *Double Disadvantage* project, we were repeatedly told that they had encountered the attitude that 'black people cannot manage'. This certainly seems to

Table 2.5 Percentages of women and men in the workforce in the salariat, 2004, by ethnic group

	Women Managers & senior officials %	Men Managers & senior officials %	Women professionals %	Men professionals %
White	11	18	10	12
Indian	12	21	13	21
Pakistani	9	15	13	11
Bangladeshi	6	14	11	8
Black African	7	12	10	18
Black Caribbean	8	11	9	9
Chinese	14	20	15	21

Source: EOC 2004, from 2001 Census.

hold good for attitudes to both black African and black Caribbean women. This is a most important aspect of discrimination which we shall be exploring fully in later chapters in this book.

Another signal of disadvantage is clustering, the concentration of groups in a small number of occupations. This is often a symptom of racial and gender stereotyping which sees particular groups as particularly suited for some types of labour and, the corollary, unsuited for others. Clustering makes ethnic groups particularly vulnerable to sectoral change in the economy. For example, black Caribbean men were in the past clustered in the motor industry. The virtual collapse of car manufacture in Britain displaced many of them from the labour market. Table 2.6 offers some further examples of clustering.

It will be seen from Table 2.6 that women are very heavily clustered in the public sector. Over half of black African and black Caribbean women employees are found in these areas, which in part reflects the history of Caribbean migration when people were recruited specifically to fill vacancies in the NHS. It also suggests that discrimination may be keeping black women out of private-sector employment.

This table highlights another area of clustering: Chinese women and men, along with Pakistani men, are very concentrated in hotels, restaurants and transport, and the Bangladeshi men quite dangerously so. Given that many of these men work in Asian-owned restaurants, coffee

Table 2.6 Employment in selected industrial sectors by gender and ethnic group

	Women Hotels, transport & distribution %	Men Hotels, transport & distribution %	Women Public services %	Men Public services %
White	25	27	42	16
Mixed parentage	31	32	40	17
Indian	31	36	39	17
Pakistani	31	52	43	9
Bangladeshi	–	81	51	–
Other Asian	27	46	42	22
Black Caribbean	20	35	54	19
Black African	23	32	52	28
Chinese	42	52	31	15

Source: CRE 2006b, from Labour Force Survey data.

shops, takeaways and taxi companies, this implies that it is not easy for these groups to find employment in white-owned businesses. One in six employed Pakistani men were taxi-drivers or chauffeurs in 2002–3 and one in three Bangladeshi men were cooks and waiters compared to one in 100 white men in each occupation (Social Trends 2005)

As we have seen, women and men continue to work in very different occupations from each other, but among women of different ethnic groups there are both common features (clustering in public sector work) and differences. Table 2.7 gives a useful indication of these. It shows the five occupations in which the greatest number of women work by ethnic group. The figure in the final column shows the proportion of women in the labour force who work in these five occupational groups combined. This shows that between a quarter and just over a third of women are found in these jobs, with black African women being the most concentrated. One in ten black African women work as nurses, compared with one in thirty-two white women and Indian women are seven times more likely than white women to work as sewing machinists and four times as likely to be working as packers, bottlers, canners and fillers (Social Trends 2005).

Overall, Table 2.7 indicates the way women tend to work in three core areas: retail, office work and care work. There are some strong similarities between the groups with sales assistant and clerk being the most common two occupations. However, there are also interesting differences. Indian women are the only group whose top five include two factory

Table 2.7 The five most concentrated occupations for women by ethnic group, England and Wales 2001

White	Sales Assistants	Clerks	Care assistants	Secretaries	Cleaners	24.15
Indian	Sales Assistants	Clerks	Financial clerks	Packers	Sewing Machinists	23.69
Pakistani	Sales Assistants	Clerks	Educational Assistants	Care Assistants	Financial Clerks	26.10
Bangladeshi	Sales Assistants	Clerks	Educational Assistants	Retail cashiers	Financial Clerks	31.95
Black Caribbean	Nurses	Clerks	Care Assistants	Sales Assistants	Secretaries	29.44
Black African	Care Assistants	Nurses	Sales Assistants	Cleaners	Clerks	36.46
Chinese	Sales Assistants	Cooks	Nurses	Restaurant Managers	Waitresses	32.12

Source: Blackwell and Guinea-Martin 2005, from census data.

occupations (packer and sewing machinists). The two black groups are more concentrated in caring occupations, and the Chinese women stand out from the other groups as working in catering jobs.

Most of the statistics we have looked at so far refer to what is known as the *horizontal* dimension of segregation, that is the clustering of different groups, such as men and women, in different occupational categories. The other and very important dimension is *vertical* segregation. This refers to the fact that within any particular occupational hierarchy (which usually takes the form of a pyramid) certain groups dominate in the top posts. These are almost always, in the United Kingdom at least, white men.

Official statistics are not particularly useful in analysing vertical segregation as the categories they use are too large. Although a category like 'managers' gives some indication of which people hold authority, the term covers a multitude of different work statuses, from the CEO of a large multinational, to the personnel manager of a department store, to somebody running a chip shop. Guards on railway trains are now referred to as 'train managers'. Only case studies of individual organisations are really helpful in this respect (see Bradley 1999). We shall be exploring vertical segregation later in the book, when we talk about our research from the Double Disadvantage project. However, here we can give a few examples. Within the civil service, 8.2 per cent of the staff were from ethnic minorities (itself a poor proportion given that the bulk of civil servants are in London), but they made up only 3.3 per cent of senior staff (CRE 2006a). There are only two minority ethnic female MPs, no minority ethnic female police chief constables, or judges in the House of Lords or Court of Appeal (Fawcett Society 2005). But in 2004 Linda Dobbs broke through one of the toughest glass ceilings when she became Britain's first black High Court judge.

The gender and ethnic gap in pay

One of the most important effects of combined patterns of horizontal and vertical segregation is difference in pay. Blackaby et al. (1998) have studied the wage differential between minority ethnic workers and found that, after having increased in the 1980s, it fell slightly in the mid-1990s to 10.9 per cent overall: the differential then was 12.4 per cent for blacks, 6.6 per cent for Indians and a shocking 30.5 per cent for Pakistanis, once again showing the sharp disadvantage faced by this group.

The difference between women's and men's pay is known as the *gender pay gap*. In 2004 this stood at 18 per cent for the average hourly earnings of full-time employees. Part-time women's average hourly

Table 2.8 Median hourly wages by ethnicity and sex
for employees aged 18 and over, 2004

	Women £	Men £	All £
White	7.06	9.30	8.00
Black	8.27	7.00	7.33
Indian	7.60	9.56	8.41
Pakistani/Bangladeshi	6.24	6.25	6.25
Mixed/other	7.58	7.60	7.60

Source: CRE 2006a, from the Low Pay Commission.

earnings were only 60 per cent of those of full-time men (EOC 2004).
There are strong cumulative effects, too, of lower earnings over a life-
time. The current pensions gap between men and women is estimated
at 43 per cent, meaning that many women will end their lives in poverty. The gender gap is also strong among younger employees, even
though, as we know, women are now better qualified than men in these
age groups. Among teenagers in their first jobs, young women earn
16 per cent less (source: CRE 2006a, from Low Pay Commission).

Table 2.8 illustrates the combined effects of gender and ethnicity.
Here we see that, predictably, Pakistani and Bangladeshi women and
men are the lowest earners and Indian men and white men the highest.
In these cases we see the impact of class locations as well as gender and
ethnicity. The Bangladeshi and Pakistani population are predominantly
working class and Indians disproportionately clustered in middle-class
positions.

It will be seen that some ethnic minority women (black, Indian) earn
more than white women. This may be partly because of their concentration in full-time work which is much better paid, as noted above. In a
well-known article Irene Bruegel (1989) analysed this issue and argued
that it was also because of the concentration of the black groups in
London, where pay levels are generally higher. The class skew in the
Indian community may be another factor. This, however, is an interesting example of the specificity of patterns of disadvantage and the
danger of over-generalisations about ethnic situations (see Modood,
Berthoud et al. 1997).

Ethnic specificity

We have seen many examples already of the way the positions of
Pakistani and Bangladeshi stand out from the rest. Only 26 per cent of

Pakistani women and 18 per cent of Bangladeshi women are economically active. We might regard these figures with a small degree of suspicion as there may be some forms of employment which are concealed here in the processes of data collection, such as working in a family business or doing homework within the illegal economy. However, it is clear that the majority of women in these two groups are excluded from the formal labour market.

Sarah Salway (2006) has written a useful piece analysing data from the Family Resources Survey to explore why this should be the case. Contrary to the suggestions of some earlier analyses (Ahmad, Modood, and Lissenberg 2003; Dale et al 2002; West and Pilgrim 1995), she found no evidence of increased labour market activity through the 1990s. These authors had suggested that aspirations were rising among young women and that those who managed to acquire HE qualifications were energetically pursuing careers. However, Salway points out that this is statistically a very small group of women so that, while it is true that they have high levels of economic activity, this makes little impression on the figures for the whole group. Here we would add that this in turn is the result of the class position of Pakistanis and Bangladeshis, who are predominantly low-skilled manual or service workers with low levels of cultural capital.

As Salway demonstrates, the bulk of Pakistani and Bangladeshi women of working age are married with dependant children. In these groups, there are virtually no women who do not marry (an important contrast with the white population). Salway suggests that, especially among the Bangladeshis, there may be a preference not to work once married. Marriage is significant in itself in inhibiting employment, even when there are no children. Thus it seems likely that very strongly held cultural norms are a strong disincentive to employment outside the home. Women we interviewed for the EOC project indicate that their husbands would only allow them to take up employment if it was clearly compatible with their household responsibilities (Bradley, Healy and Kaul 2007). These are likely to be enforced by the fact that, as most women have low levels of educational attainment, there are limited jobs that they could fill or which would be culturally seen as appropriate. The Fourth National Survey found that 73 per cent of Bangladeshis and 60 per cent of Pakistanis had no qualifications, or only qualifications below O level; only 2 to 3 per cent had degrees (Modood, Berthoud et al. 1997). Although this situation has since changed, as Table 2.2 shows, it will take some time for the effects of this to work through. Moreover, Salway points out that there is a stream of new immigrants, especially as a result of marriage, who will have no UK qualifications and whose employment options and expectations are likely to be very different from those educated in Britain. The work of Lindley and Dale (2004) highlights the fact that only 13 per cent of the British Bangladeshi population in 2002 were born in this country. Thus the second generation is a small part of the whole community and the ambitious young highly educated women who have featured in some qualitative research have a limited statistical significance. Moreover, this pattern does accord with the state of things 'back home'. In Pakistan, 50 per cent of women are categorised as contributory family workers, as opposed to 33 per cent categorised as employees and 17 per cent as self-employed; in Bangladesh a mere 8 per cent of women are employees and 11 per cent self-employed, while 73 per cent are categorised as contributory family workers (ILO 2004). While this, of course, reflects the rural structures in these countries, it is likely to shape the expectations of those not born in Britain. Monica Ali's novel *Brick Lane* poignantly highlights the stressful experience of women arriving in Britain with limited English from the villages of Sylhet.

Those who do work are very strongly clustered in certain areas: 51 per cent of Bangladeshi women and 43 per cent of Pakistani work in the public sector (predominantly education and public administration (CRE 2006a)). Pakistani women are also clustered in unskilled factory work and retail. It is difficult to find evidence of Bangladeshi women's situation as the numbers working are so small that they are often omitted from survey analysis (as, for example, from the Fourth National Survey). However Table 2.5 suggests their profile is very similar to Pakistani women's, with retail a major employment area. Given the prevalence of Asian shops in Britain's cities we would certainly expect to find many employed there.

The picture for these two groups then, is one of exclusion. However, as we said before, the picture may be misleading in that many women may be employed in family businesses or involved in irregular or casual work, but not registering as such in government data collection. Others are likely to be working in the informal economy. It is most unlikely that all these women are sitting at home twiddling their thumbs! Moreover, qualitative studies continue to show that young Pakistani and Bangladeshi women are ambitious to succeed in education and careers (Dwyer, Modood et al. 2006; EOC 2005). Dwyer et al. carried out interviews with young Pakistani women in Bradford and Slough. They state that, while the findings were still tentative, 'we found plenty of evidence of the strong commitment of young women to education, including a widespread desire…to pursue higher education and a career' (ibid.:16). This was as true of working-class as middle-class girls. Some of the quotations from their respondents suggested that they may see education as a way to escape from early marriage and 'make something of themselves'. Yasmin told them:

> You can't depend on anyone but yourself. I know lots of people whose marriages have not worked out. You need your education to get a good job so you can support yourself.
>
> (Dwyer, Modood et al. 2006)

Yet even among the higher qualified groups the employment rates are less than whites (69 per cent compared to 85 per cent), although the gap is much starker among those with no qualifications, 7 per cent compared to 48 per cent (CRE Labour Force Survey 2001).

It may be that slowly, the desire to improve their economic position (many of these families are very poor) may lead to the shifting of established gender norms. Half of Pakistani and Bangladeshi working households have incomes 50 per cent below the national average (CRE 2006b). Census data show that 19 per cent of household income in Pakistani and Bangladeshi households comes from benefits, compared to 15 per cent among black groups and around 5 per cent for whites (DWP 2002).

If we turn to the third major Asian group, Indians, we find a very different picture. As we have seen, many Indian migrants to Britain came from middle-class backgrounds; many also had good command of English and were quickly able to adapt to the British education system. Qualitative research has revealed the very high value that Indian families put on education, for both sons and daughters, and this is reflected in the high numbers entering HE (Table 2.2). Connor et al. (2004) found that, along with Chinese, Indian undergraduates were most likely to have taken the traditional A level route into HE (as opposed to going into further education first or becoming a mature entrant) and had the best A-level qualifications. Thus, it is not surprising that data from the Labour Force Survey analysed by the EOC reveal them to have the highest proportion of women in high-level managerial and professional jobs, 13 per cent (by comparison, the figure for white women is 8 per cent; information on Chinese women was not included in this report) (Hibbett 2002).

The Fourth National Survey, which distinguished Indian from African-Asian, indicated that they were spread more broadly through the occupational structure than any other groups except whites (Modood, Berthoud et al. 1997). However, both groups had a much higher proportion than others (apart from Pakistanis) in manufacturing (21 per cent of Indian women, 14 per cent of African-Asian). We suggest that this is linked to the downward mobility experienced by many families when they arrived in Britain and that this figure will diminish as class restabilisation is achieved. For example, in the 1970s and 1980s many Indian women worked in the then flourishing hosiery industry in the East Midlands. Table 2.5 shows that they continue to stand out from other groups of women by having two of their top five categories in manufacturing. Modood et al. (1997) also demonstrated that these two groups had higher earnings than white women, though less than Caribbeans and Chinese. Their data also show that among the Asian religious groups, Hindus, both men and women, earned more than Sikhs, with Muslims consistently earning the least. Among all the minority ethnic groups, the pattern of Indian employment is perhaps looking the closest to economic integration.

We have mentioned the high earnings of Chinese women; Chinese men, too, were shown by Modood et al. to be the only minority group to earn as much as whites in the survey, £336 per week for full-time employees: to give some idea of contrasts, Pakistani men earned £227 and Bangladeshi £227. Along with the Indians, the Chinese are taken to be the most success-ful ethnic minority group in Britain, although surprisingly little research has been conducted into the Chinese community. However, what has been done suggests that the nature of Chinese success is very different from Indian. Rather than economic integration, we would describe the pattern of employment as marginalisation. Here is a classic case of an ethnic enclave, with a majority of employees working in the Chinese business sector. This accounts for their economic prosperity and the very high pro-portion categorised as professionals, managers and small employers (46 per cent of men and 30 per cent of women in the Fourth National Survey). The bulk of these businesses are in the food and restaurant industry, reflecting the well-known ubiquity of the Chinese takeaway. Table 2.4 showed that 52 per cent of Chinese men and 41 per cent of Chinese women worked in hotels, transport and distribution (CRE 2006b). This explains the quite distinct pattern of Chinese women's employment in Table 2.5, with three of the top jobs being cooks, restaurant managers and waitresses.

While this type of employment brings security and stability to the family, it is very hard work for them and can be limiting and constrain-ing for young people, as described in an article on a project set up to help the Chinese community in Manchester with parenting:

Guo-quiang Lam, 46, works eight hours a day in his Chinese takeaway business, helping in the kitchen and delivering food. His wife Ying works as the chef: she spends two hours every afternoon preparing food and keeps the takeaway open from 5 pm to midnight. When their daughter, Yuet-ching, aged 11, comes home from school they are just getting ready to open the shop. Yuet-ching helps with kitchen work and food wrapping. It gets busier at the weekends and they work at a faster pace. They have no social life to speak of. When they're not working, they try to recover from work and catch up on sleep.

(Pai 2006)

Cheung and Heath (1993) in their important analysis of the returns on educational investment among different ethnic groups in Britain found that the Chinese were the only minority group not to suffer an 'ethnic penalty'. However, this apparent success must be set against the facts of life within a restricted range of employment options and high levels of the 'self-exploitation' often associated with self-employment. It remains to be seen whether second- and third-generation young Chinese will be able to enter the full range of good employment opportunities merited by their high educational achievements.

Cheung and Heath state in their paper, which deals only with first-generation immigrants and was based on 1980s Labour Force Survey data, that the lack of ethnic penalty among the Chinese and its presence among Indian, Pakistani and West Indian men 'suggests strongly that discrimination along the lines of skin colour is likely to be an important part of any story' (1993:164). To some extent this is confirmed when we turn to the next two groups, black Caribbeans and black Africans. It says something in itself that the term 'black' was chosen as the official census category for these and the rather mysterious 'black other' group. Interviews with black women, both African and Caribbean for the *Double Disadvantage* project, indicated that colour-based racism was indeed a common, even an everyday, experience for this group of women, and was of a different degree to the discrimination experienced by Asians, though they too had suffered it.

However, the picture is made more complex in the black Caribbean group by the distinct divergence of the fates of women and men. As Table 2.2 shows this is the group with the sharpest distinction in HE participation between the sexes, 52 per cent for women and 36 per cent for men. There has been concern for a long time about the low levels of attainment of Caribbean boys in school and their embracing of an aggressive anti-school and street-wise culture. There is a major problem of unemployment, drug-taking and criminal behaviour among a substantial group of young Caribbean men. Black Caribbean boys are three times as likely to be excluded from school as whites; and only a quarter of them achieved five or more A*–C GSCEs as opposed to 40 per cent of girls (Botcherby and Hurrell 2004).

By contrast, research into girls' education has long shown that young Caribbean women strategically used school success as a way to provide for their futures, given the realities of marriage and childbearing among poor Caribbean families (Fuller 1982; Lees 1993; Mirza 1992). Girls were trained by their mothers to be independent and work-oriented, given the centrality of mothers in Caribbean families, where men were quite frequently absent. Thus Caribbean women with young children are most likely to be working full-time compared to other mothers: 33 per cent of lone mothers, 39 per cent of partnered mothers with children aged 0–4 and, 43 per cent of partnered mothers with children aged 5–15; the figures for whites are 16, 20 and 27 per cent, for Indians, 19, 26 and 37 per cent and for Pakistanis and Bangladeshis 6, 6 and 8 per cent (Lindley and Dale 2004).

The tables above show that black Caribbean and black African women are particularly associated with caring work and very likely to work in the public sector: 39 per cent of them are found in education, health and social work compared to 31 per cent of white women (Botcherby and Hurrell 2004). We have seen that they have relatively higher earnings than white women, though that may be the result of having no choice but to work full-time.

Black Africans are a diverse group (from Somalian refugees to West African nobility) and little research has focused on their experiences. We have seen that they are highly educated, but there is a major problem of an 'ethnic penalty', that is, that their occupational status does not match their educational investment (Heath and Cheung 2004). We interviewed a woman with a PhD who was working on a supermarket cash till, and trained teachers who could not find employment in schools because their overseas qualifications were not recognised. However, shortages in the NHS open up some secure and well-paid work for them: two of the most common occupations for black African men are medical practitioners and software professionals.

Altogether, the position of these two groups is especially complex. Black Caribbeans are in many ways the most likely to get assimilated to British culture. Rates of intermarriage with the white population are high and English is their first language. However, there remains, we would argue, a terrible legacy from the colonial past and the history of slavery which has scarred race relations and leaves these visible minority groups especially vulnerable to racist stereotyping. Various studies have found that they are more likely than other groups to report racism

(Brown 1984; Heath 2001; Smith 1977). We shall return to the issue of 'colour racism' later in the book. Now, however, we conclude this survey with a brief comment on the position of ethnic minority women in Europe and the United States.

The European picture

It is, of course, not possible to set out full details of the position of minority ethnic workers in Europe, as each country is so very different. This chapter has already highlighted the very different experiences of specific ethnic groups, thus indicating that the position of the minority populations will be very diverse in each country, according to patterns of migration and settlement. There are also major problems around comparability of statistics. Different countries use different categories, for example classifying people as 'native-born' or 'foreign-born' rather than on the basis of ethnicity. In these countries, nationality is often viewed as the key issue rather than ethnicity: in Sweden, for example, the various groups of migrants are referred to as 'new Swedes'. This is done with a good liberal intent of inclusion, but can be ethnic-blind and thus overlook the particular problems faced by certain ethnic groups, such as Muslims, recent refugee groups and the more visible minorities. Thus, for example, Somali refugees in Norway have particularly poor labour market prospects

With so very many different ethnic groups involved, it becomes extraordinarily difficult to develop meaningful categories for national comparison. The European Women's Lobby (EWL), which was formed in 1990 to promote women's rights across the EU, states in a recent briefing that it will use the term 'black, ethnic minority and migrant women' in its discussion, and goes on to explain that this term covers 'among others ... women refugees, asylum seekers, Roma women, women from indigenous minority ethnic groups, coloured women, newcomers and long-term immigrants' (EWL 2006a). Obviously this is a highly heterogeneous group about whose position it would be difficult to generalise – except that they are all disadvantaged!

There is also a problem about the limited availability of statistics. The French, with their very strong policy of assimilation and secularism, do not permit the collection of data on ethnicity. Countries which have only recently experienced significant levels of migration may also have very limited data. In many European countries the study of ethnicity is a relatively recent academic interest, as until recently migration was not seen as an important social concern. The ILO, although providing very good information on gender, does not collect statistics on ethnicity or race. Moreover, the level of illegal immigration across Europe is considered to be very high, given that the borders are much more easily crossed. In addition, the recent influx of people from East Europe and of refugees from around the world means that the situation is highly dynamic and changing.

All we can do here is give a few general comments to indicate some commonalities across the European Union. Lydia Morris in her study of European migration (2002) analyses three different scenarios which can help us bring some order into this rather chaotic picture. First, there are countries with a colonial past, such as the United Kingdom, which tend to have relatively settled groups with citizen rights. Second, there are countries, such as Germany, which have solved their labour shortage problems since the Second World War by bringing in 'guest-workers' who had only temporary residence rights. Third, there are countries where there has not been much of a previous history of in-migration, such as Italy, where most migration is of the 'new' type; EU citizens, illegal immigrants, refugees and short-term permit holders.

In some countries, such as France, Holland and Portugal, the pattern of ethnic relations is very much shaped by the colonial past; in France the major immigrant groups were from North and West Africa. In the Netherlands, the main groups are from parts of East Asia, such as Indonesia, Vietnam and China. As in the case of Britain, Asian groups have tended to create ethnic enclaves especially in restaurants and catering. Across the whole of Europe groups from Africa are among the most disadvantaged and are often unemployed or working in the illegal or informal economy. The situation of Algerians, Tunisians and Moroccans in France is similar: here there is a particular problem for women, as they are often the target of religious discrimination, because of their choice of clothing. Employers often discriminate against those who wear veils.

For the same reason, there is a problem about women in the 'guest-worker' scenario. This is found especially in Germany and Austria. This type of migration, in contrast to the contemporary pattern, was male-dominated, as migrant men were brought in to fill labour shortages in manufacturing after the Second World War. The major groups involved were Turks, people from the former Yugoslavia and North Africans. Although many have subsequently gained residency and citizen rights, they are still highly vulnerable to unemployment and are at the bottom of the labour market hierarchy. Women came in as family members rather than workers and are also likely to be excluded and marginalised.

As stated before, the third groups, the 'new migrants' are a mixed bag. However, it is clear that in contrast to the colonial and guestworker scenarios, women are centrally involved in this form of migration. The EWL estimate that there are some 12 million female migrants in Europe, making up over half of the migrant population. They state that these women are concentrated into a few occupations, which on the whole are characterised by poor working conditions and insecurity: 'domestic work, "entertainment" (sometimes prostitution), helping in restaurants and hotels, illegal clothing companies, assembly lines in labour-intensive manufacturing plants' (EWL 2006a). Across Europe 500,000 women are trafficked annually, with the average age of entry into prostitution being 13 or 14. Prostitution has developed into a mass and generally acceptable industry over the past decades: in the Netherlands in 1981 there were 2500 prostitutes. Since legalisation, that figure has increased to over 20,000 (EWL 2006b). In the run-up to the 2006 Football World Cup in Germany, thousands of prostitutes were brought into the towns to cater for male spectators and team members. A distinctive group of female migrants are the Thais, who come in as marriage partners in countries including Sweden, Denmark and Finland (Kofman 2005).

The work of Heath and Cheung (2006) has highlighted that across Europe, those with the highest ethnic penalty are those from Muslim groups. Thus, for example, in the Netherlands in 1998 only 7 per cent of Turks (women and men) and 6 per cent of Moroccans were in jobs classified as higher or scholarly level, compared to 33 per cent of the Dutch, while 21 per cent of Turks and 23 per cent of Moroccans were unemployed compared to 6 per cent of Dutch (Institute for Migration and Ethnic Studies 2006).

Hochschild has provided an interesting account of what she calls 'global care chains', movements around the globe to accommodate care needs. Thus, if a British or American woman employs a woman from a third-world country, then she herself must employ somebody to look after her own children or get a family member to do so (Hochschild 2000). This highlights the link of women to care and housework. Wherever you are in Europe, if you stay in a hotel you are likely to find ethnic minority women cleaning your room; and the domestic association has led to such women being employed across Europe as maids and nannies by rich middle-class families. Dumont and Liebig (2005) report that across Europe immigrant women are four times more likely to work in the household sector and twice as likely to work in hotels and catering than native-born women. Bridget Anderson's work has highlighted the appalling conditions and sometimes downright brutality and abuse faced by these women if they are live-in servants (Anderson 2000). Dumont and Leibig (2005) show that across Europe foreign-born women have lower labour market participation rates and that growth in their employment has been in low-skilled work. Without doubt, these are the positions at the very bottom of the gendered and ethnicised occupational hierarchy to which recent migrant women often find themselves confined across Europe.

Segregation in the United States

There are some similarities between the United States and the United Kingdom, in that both have a long history of immgration, large settled populations of former migrants, and a strong legacy from colonial history and slavery. However, a difference in the United States is the very large group of Hispanic or Latino citizens who came from (and are still coming from) Central and South America. African-Americans and Hispanics are the largest ethnic minority groups. There is also a group known in the literature as Asians, but confusingly this American usage of the term is different from the English usage. While for us it refers to the population who came from the Indian subcontinent, in America it refers to the East Asians: Vietnamese, Koreans, Japanese and above all Chinese. The term 'Asian miracle' is often used in relation to these groups (Woo 2002) who have done extremely well in terms of educational achievement and occupational success. Their situation has some similarities to those of the Chinese and the Indians in the United Kingdom. Their success is reflected in their earnings, as shown in Table 2.9. Here we see that, while the gender pay gap is actually greater than in the other ethnic groups, their weekly earnings are the highest (indicating, of course, the great height of the Asian men's weekly earnings).

Table 2.9   US earning statistics for women

	Gender pay gap	Women's median weekly earnings
White	20%	$584
Black	11%	$505
Asian	24%	$613
Hispanic/Latina	17%	$419

Source: US Bureau of Labor 2005.

In terms of occupational segregation, the picture has some similarities with the United Kingdom. Women are clustered in services, especially retail and administration. About one-third of women work in these occupations. Gender segregation at an occupational level is marked, as in Britain: in 1998 women were, for example, 98 per cent of secretaries, 95 per cent of receptionists, 89 per cent of nursing aides, 84 per cent of elementary schoolteachers and 78 per cent of waitresses (Walsh and Wrigley 2001).

It is not possible to make a direct comparison with the United Kingdom as the categories used in the census are different. Table 2.10 shows where women are clustered, but in industrial terms not occupational (that is, women may be working in these industries in clerical or managerial occupations, which is why manufacturing appears in the table). Compared to men, women are less likely to work in production occupations, especially white women. Only 4.1 are employed in these occupations, compared to 8.6 per cent of Hispanic/Latina women and 7.6 per cent of Asian women.

The most interesting ethnic difference shown in Table 2.10 is the concentration of black or African-American women in public services and caring occupations. Once again we see the strong association of 'blackness' with care work, especially of a heavy or dirty kind. Duffy (2005) has made an interesting study of American women's involvement in service work, distinguishing between nurturant and non-nurturant reproductive services. This shows white and black women over-represented in nurturant

Table 2.10   The five most concentrated industrial areas for women by ethnic group, USA 2004

White	African American	Asian	Hispanic
Education	Non-hospital Health services	Manufacturing	Retail
Retail	Education	Retail	Accommodation & food services
Non-hospital health services	Retail	Accommodation & food services	Manufacturing
Manufacturing	Hospitals	Education	Education
Accommodation & food services	Public administration	Non-hospital health services	Non-hospital health services

Source: US Bureau of Labor 2006.

and Hispanics in non-nurturant labour. The former includes teaching and nursing, and also the category of attendants in hospitals and nursing homes, where there is a major clustering of black women. Non-nurturant jobs are cleaning, catering and so forth. Duffy suggests that the historical trend has been 'to concentrate women of color in the back-room jobs of reproductive labor' (2005: 80). Similarly Harrington (1999) has suggested that the current conditions are creating a new low-wage servant class, constituted largely of ethnic minority workers. New migrants are also likely to find themselves in these low-paid jobs: 9.8 per cent of foreign born minority women are in cleaning and maintenance as opposed to 2.3 per cent of US-born (Bureau of Labor 2005).

The profiles of Asian and Hispanic women as shown in Table 2.10 are on the face of it rather similar, and reflect their employment in private services (shops, hotels and catering). In the case of the Asians, this probably reflects their success in the small-business sector. Hispanic women tend to occupy the least rewarded and low-skilled jobs of the non-nurturant kind mentioned above.

However, a major difference from the United Kingdom and Europe is the success of women in breaking through the 'glass ceiling' into managerial and professional jobs, especially white and Asian women. This success has been marked since the 1980s as detailed in the report, *Changing America*, which was prepared as part of the President's Initiative on Race in 2006. Among white women 38.6 per cent work in these occupations, and among Asians 43.8 per cent. This is in marked contrast with black women (30.6 per cent) and especially Hispanic women (22.4 per cent).

The data shows that Hispanic and Latina women are at the most disadvantaged by processes of gender and ethnic segregation. Their position has some resemblances to that of Pakistani and Bangladeshi women in Britain in that they come out worst on most measures. However, a difference is that their participation rate is much higher (66 per cent in 1997), although it is lower than that of black and white women (both 77 per cent). Hispanic women, like black women, have a higher unemployment rate (7.6 and 9.8 per cent respectively) compared to white (4.7) and Asian (4.4) (US Bureau of Labor 2006), while the percentage of women aged 16 to 24 who are not in education or employment is highest among Hispanics (26 per cent), compared to black women (22 per cen)t and white women (8 per cent). The report suggests this may relate to the raising of children; as in the United Kingdom, these groups are likely to marry and have children at an earlier age than whites. This fact of late entry (if at all) into the labour market sets them behind white and Asian women in the race to the top.

Conclusions

This chapter has provided an overview of the position of ethnic minority women in the UK labour market, with a brief sketch of their situation in Europe and the United States. We have noted that at the aggregate level gender segregation is more marked than ethnic segregation. However, if we look at the positions of particular ethnic groups there are marked differences between them, caused by the specific intersections of ethnicity, gender and class that frame their entry into the labour market. We have shown how different ethnic minority groups are inserted into the UK labour market in different patterns, using the framework of economic integration, segmentation, marginalisation and exclusion.

Overall, ethnic minority women occupy less advantaged positions in the gendered and ethnicised occupational hierarchy. The second generation are doing somewhat better than the first in terms of access to top jobs and levels of earnings, but not in terms of their vulnerability to unemployment (Heath 2001). On almost every measure, Pakistani and Bangladeshi women are doing worst. We can see these groups as suffering from social isolation which cuts them off from the socio-economic currents affecting the rest of society. This disadvantage is exacerbated by the current political climate where the 'war against terrorism' engenders Islamophobia and subjects Muslim communities to stigmatisation and intense external and internal pressures.

It is not all gloom, however. As we shall highlight in subsequent chapters, many minority women are energetic, determined and resilient. With increasing levels of qualifications and skills, they are increasingly well-equipped to confront the racism and sexism of the labour market. We started this chapter with the stories of three minority ethnic women. We close with another which illustrates how young women are taking advantage of the opportunities offered by the 'new economy'.

Aysha was born in Africa, grew up in London and has a degree in hotel and catering management. Reflecting the internationalisation of the labour market, Aysha has worked in Holland, Luxembourg, Belgium and Germany. She was building a successful career in hospitality and the luxury hotel sector, but as she stated: 'I like people and I wanted to work with people, not just the executives.' Thus she moved into recruitment, employed as a recruitment consultant 'where you earn a lot of money'. But then she decided to shift into the welfare to work area in order to work with black young people, since, like so many ethnic minority women (as we shall explore in Chapter 11), she felt strongly committed to her community and wanted to give something back to it.

She now works for a recruitment agency in a public/private partnership which is currently financed with government funding. She is their operations manager, and is working with unemployed people who have particular difficulties in finding jobs, such as single parents, people with criminal records, drug addicts and minority ethnic youth. Notably successful in her job, Aysha said that 'my dream has always been, empowering people, developing people'.

There are many more Ayshas out there, and in this book we shall stress the tremendous potential of ethnic minority women for contributing to the success of the UK economy and helping to transform society. Before we tell more of the stories of the women we have interviewed, however, we shall consider the role employers, the state and trade unions can play in addressing the patterns of gender and ethnic segregation discussed in this chapter, while in the following chapter we consider the explanations which may account for these patterns of difference.

3
Gender, Ethnicity and Class – the Case for Intersectional Analysis

The contemporary labour market position of minority ethnic women was explored in the last chapter. It is clear that black and minority ethnic women are disadvantaged in a range of ways despite their often high human capital. How do we explain this? This chapter offers a number of key theoretical and conceptual approaches that go some way to understanding how inequalities are reproduced in the labour market. Critical concepts we draw on include: the nature of intersectionality, the importance of history in the social construction of inequalities; inequalities in organisations; segregation – both horizontal and vertical; the cycle of reproduction of segregation; the importance of 'career'; 'choice' and inequality regimes. These concepts will be of value in shaping the discussion at different points in the book. We argue the importance of the interrelationship of structure and agency in understanding both the transformation and the reproduction of gendered and racist practices. The prioritising of identities at moments in time will intersect with agency and structures in influencing both transformation and reproduction. The importance of levels of analysis from the macro to the micro to the self, and the impact of historical factors at these levels, will enable an understanding of the uneven and sometimes contradictory developments in both transforming and reproducing a sexist and racist order.

We believe that an intersectional analysis provides a stronger purchase on ethnic relations than a poststructuralist approach to difference which puts the emphasis on discourse and identity. Such an approach allows the interrelationship of structure and agency at different levels of analysis to emerge.

Importantly, this chapter will be informed by key writers on gender, ethnicity, work and organisation. Work and organisation are at the heart of this book. This is not to say that social relations that emerge from home and other structural influences outside the workplace are

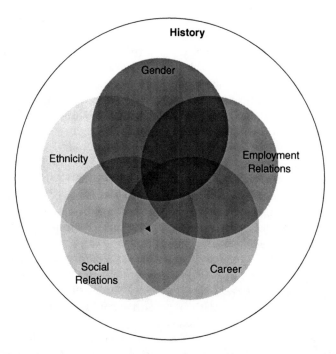

Figure 3.1 Diagrammatic representation of the key themes and their intersections

irrelevant. On the contrary, these are crucial, but it is how they play out at the level of work and organisation that is our main focus.

Figure 3.1 presents graphically the key foci of the chapter and the intersections: between them.

An intersectional approach

We begin by setting out our position. We argue for the importance of an intersectional approach. We seek not to prioritise gender, ethnicity/race or class. Rather, we situate women in their context and thereby aim to understand how at a moment in time ethnicity may be the dominant form of explanation, whereas at other times and in other contexts, it will be gender. But the key task is to understand the intersection between these various dimensions of social difference and to understand how this process provides new insights. Class relations and processes remain fundamental to all analyses as it is crucial to maintain the material basis of analysis. In this book, the way class is played out through hierarchies is particularly important (see Acker 2006; Cockburn 1991). However, as

Holgate et al. (2006) argue, a sole focus on class may fail to uncover the myriad of social processes that position workers in the labour market and the workplace. This is not to suggest that that we lose sight of the importance of the capitalist dynamic in social relationships; rather, we believe that it frequently shapes the complexity of social relations. It is, however, to suggest that this needs to be understood without losing sight of the complex interrelationship between agency and structure as expounded by critical realist and structuration theorists (see Archer 1995; Giddens 1979; Layder 1993). The realist approach offers a layered or 'stratified' model of society which macro (structural, institutional) phenomena as well as the more micro phenomena of interaction and behaviour and the importance of history at different levels (Layder 1993:7). Thus a realist methodological approach has the potential to provide the tools to understand the complexity of gender relations (Healy, Hansen and Ledwith 2006:206). An intersectional approach may be a way forward to achieve this in the field of inequalities. Thus we would caution against ownership of the intersectional concept by poststructuralist thinking and argue that a richer analysis takes account of the interrelationship of agency and structure, giving insight into the reproduction of inequalities, as well as the less frequent changes in their patterning.

What is intersectionality? It refers to the way that individuals often do not suffer a single form of discrimination, but are subject to a number of discriminatory forms at once:

> Intersectionality is an integrated approach that addresses forms of multiple discrimination on the basis of racism, racial discrimination, xenophobia and related intolerance as they intersect with gender, age, sexual orientation, disability, migrant, socio-economic or other status. Intersectional discrimination is a form of racism and racial discrimination which is not the sum of race PLUS another form of discrimination to be dealt with separately but is a distinct and particular experience of discrimination unified in one person or group.
> (United Nations 2001)

The above quotation emphasises that discrimination resulting from both racism and sexism may lead to a different form of discrimination rather than a simple increase in disadvantage. We have shown elsewhere that the term 'double disadvantage' is only a partial account of what is in reality multiple forms of discrimination (Bradley 2007; Bradley, Healy and Mukherjee 2002). Thus, intersectionality relates to the way in which 'multiple forms of subordination interlink and compound to result in a multiple burden' (Kanyora 2001). Bradley (2007) argues that the key points of an intersectional approach are threefold. First, looking at a single aspect of disadvantage may lead to distortions and also mask other forms of oppression, second, in any given context different social dynamics will be in operation together, and third, the intersection of differences may produce the most extreme cases of exploitation and discrimination.

We owe much of contemporary thinking on intersectionality to black feminists. Collins (2004) states that while different socio-historical periods may have increased the saliency of one or another type of oppression, the thesis of the linked nature of oppression has long pervaded black feminist thought. She goes on to say that minimising one form of oppression may still leave black women oppressed in other equally dehumanising ways (Collins 2004:109). Indeed, it is also argued that black feminists have possessed an ideological commitment to addressing interlocking oppression yet have been excluded from arenas that would have allowed them to do so (Davis 1981). Intersectional approaches go some way to redress the valid claims that feminist concerns may be conflated to 'white feminist concerns', and we might further add to 'middle-class feminist concerns'. When the attention has been focused on 'getting on', those with access to material and social resources are white middle-class women and most likely to benefit from a middle-class feminist agenda. Thus an intersectional approach is more inclusive and, as Bradley (2007) states above, directs our attention to the most extreme forms of exploitation.

This raises the question of which type of inequality is most important in an intersectional analysis. Can we say that class, race and gender have equal claims for analytical attention? What are the dangers in such an approach? By giving priority to gender, Bhattacharyya et al. warn of the dangers of seeing 'a reaffirmation of an uncritical individualism, the denial of class advantage, the subordination of group identity...an entirely untenable heralding of the end of racism' (2002:4). They argue against a universalist perspective, particularly with respect to feminism, as from this stance all other social structures and divisions become insignificant beside the bigger experience of being a woman, rendering all the women the same at some level and 'thus able to intuitively understand all other women and their concerns across the globe' (Bhattacharya, Gabriel and Small 2002:90). When we consider the different experiences of women around the globe, and indeed also within one country, the commonality between women who are rich and those who are poor and unable to access resources is weak. In these cases, women from the more developed and less developed world's points of common reference are solely that which binds them as women. This may create some bond, but does not give them an active and common group identity. Being a woman is not sufficient analytically and veers to essentialism.

Accepting the importance of these arguments, we take the view that gender relations remain important in an intersectional approach, but that these must be considered alongside class and ethnicity. Following Cockburn (1991), we consider that woman should not be considered as a unitary category; rather women have identities formed in gender processes that vary according to whether they are black or white, whether they are lesbian or heterosexual, and whether or not they experience disabilities or practise a particular religion (see also Bradley, 1996). Further, these different relations may take prominence at different moments in time and under different conditions. At the same time we would argue that underpinning these relations is the nature of the capitalist endeavour, which provides the structural conditions against which gender, class and ethnic relations play out, intersect, reproduce and, from time to time, transform.

At the end of the chapter we shall return to the issue of intersectionality through the lens of Acker's (2006) concept of inequality regimes. But, first, we acknowledge briefly the importance of historical factors that continue to shape contemporary thinking.

History

How do we seek to understand the significance of history in the lives of black women? Marx stated that men make their own history, but not in the conditions of their choosing. With more than a nod to Marx, Bradley (1999) and Walby (1997) both emphasise the importance of action in historical analysis. Bradley states that 'Of course as we know, women and men make history under constraints, under conditions not of their choosing: but they can and do, make history' (1999:226). Whereas Walby's view is that 'women's individual agency is found in the myriad ways in which women actively choose options within the constrained opportunities available to them – women act, but not always in circumstances of their choosing (Walby 1997:7).

Accepting, then, the importance of history, do we start by looking at historical forces shaping the domination of women in general or do we look at the forces which shape racism and therefore affect black and minority ethnic (BME) men and women alike? We shall seek to provide an overview of both these approaches in order to understand how different histories intersect with race, ethnicity and gender. Inevitably, our discussion is partial. Women are not a homogeneous group and neither are minority ethnic women. Their historical experiences are hugely varied and reflect patterns of colonialism, slavery and migration.

Chapter 2 identified the different patterns of work of different BME women. History and culture are central to our understanding of these patterns in contemporary society. It is clear that in Britain and the United States, black women have a high attachment to full-time work. It is suggested that the centrality of paid work is a consequence of black women's status under slavery, British colonialism in the Caribbean and economic migration of black women to Britain from the Caribbean during the postwar era (Reynolds 2001). Reynolds argues that what connects each of these distinctive historical moments to each other is that black women in each of these instances are socially positioned as workers. She goes on to explain that

> Black women irrespective of a mothering status were expected to work alongside their men folk. Slavery, where black women acted as free labour, first removed women's (also black men's) 'human' status and instead conceptualised them as 'mules' and 'work-horses' ... Black women were not only constructed as human chattel but they were judged purely on their reproductive labour capacities. Work to emerge from the United States, exploring the implications of colonial slavery, illustrates the dichotomous relationship of man/woman, work/home and dominant/subordinate. Dominant ideological patterns of Western societies were not applicable to the slavery experiences of black men and women.
>
> (Reynolds 2001:1049)

This view is not uncontested. Nnaemeda (1997 quoted in Reynolds 2001) identifies a high work activity among black women also in pre-slavery societies.

Reynolds affirms that colonial history was pivotal in decisions of British citizens in the Caribbean, Pakistan, India and Cyprus to migrate to Britain, the 'motherland'. So often we read and watch old footage of how the 'motherland' needed people to come to work in her factories, hospitals and buses. Thus the historical conditions were shaped by the economic necessity of the 'motherland'. By implication, such necessity would ensure a friendly welcome would await such migrants. It was not just the cold weather that cooled the optimism of migrants who had often travelled half way round the globe, but also the frostiness of their reception by the British population. The signs that stated 'Room to let – no blacks, no Irish, no dogs' were symbolic of the treatment that the migrants would find in the streets, the offices, shops and lodging houses of the 1950s and 1960s. This is well described in Andrea Levy's (2004) novel 'Small Island' where she captures the daily experience of the Caribbean migrant in a way that academic texts fail to do; the emotions, the abuse, the personal pride, the contradictions and the struggle all emerge through the eyes of the two main characters. For example, the female character (Hortense, a teacher) has just arrived in England to join her husband (Gilbert). She is judgmental about what she perceives to be the uncivilised behaviour of the English. This is in contrast to the low opinion she (rightly) feels the English have of her. Despite her high standards and education, she is perceived as inferior, to be avoided and at best tolerated. Such contradictions are inherent in migrant social relations.

In the following quotation, Andrea Levy records, though the lens of Hortense, the attempt by a white woman (Queenie) to befriend Hortense and the way this attempt is both saturated in the racism of the 1950s and the perceived occupational hierarchies between the two women:

'I could show you around the shops, if you like. Show you where to get things' ...
'Thank you', I said.
But this excited her. 'No, don't thank me. It's no trouble. Be nice to have some company'. I was nodding and smiling like a half-wit while all the time opening the door so this woman might leave me in peace.
'Do you have pictures ... films ... where you come from?' she wanted to know. What this woman think Gilbert spill me from a bottle?
'Of course we have films – cinema' I told her ...

The conversation went on and Queenie needed to check 'Can you understand what I'm saying?'
'Of course' I said quietly.
'Good well give me a knock and I'll let you know when I'm ready to go out.' She then took her hand and placed it on my arm. She leaned in too close to me to whisper, 'It's all right. I don't mind being seen in the street with you. You'll find I'm not like most' ...

Now why should this woman worry to be seen in the street with me? After all, I was a teacher and she was only a woman whose living was obtained from the letting of rooms. If anyone should be shy, it should be I.

(Levy 2004:230–1)

Different conditions shaped Caribbean migration as opposed to migration from South Asia. While Caribbean women tended to come with their partners or come alone, South Asian women were more likely to follow their menfolk. Phizacklea (1990) shows how the immigration laws, intended to reduce immigration to Britain, paradoxically led to an increase in dependants arriving in Britain. The labour migrations from the Indian subcontinent were male-led; the men were 'target workers' and the expectation was that they would return home to buy land, a business and so forth (which does sometimes happen). However, Phizacklea (1990) argues that the introduction of restrictive immigration legislation for Commonwealth citizens in 1962 resulted in the possibility of men not being able to return to Britain if they left. This prompted many men to encourage their wives and children to join them. Whilst this historical event was a particular spur for women's migration, the pattern of male-led migration continued. The traditional settlement patterns expected from historical experiences of migration may be disrupted with respect to some communities, when there is a cultural expectation to seek wives (or husbands) from the country of origin. However, it should be clear that much contemporary migration is now female-led and has been for many years. This is particularly the case with the health industry and the migration of nurses (see Kingma 2006).

Employment relations and inequalities in organisations

Employment or industrial relations have at their core power relations. Such power relations and the way they play out in organisations are central to the subordination of different groups. We begin this section by mapping some of the key studies that influenced our thinking on equality and segregation in organisations. The late seventies and early eighties were highly productive in terms of insightful empirical studies of equalities in organisations and conceptual developments that have stood the test of time (Cockburn 1991; Collinson, Knights and Collinson 1990; Jenkins 1986; Jewson and Mason 1986). It is on this work that we draw as well as more contemporary developments.

One of the most valuable accounts of sex segregation in organisations is that of Collinson, Knights and Collinson (1990). They seek to explore the asymmetrical power relations of the labour market and recruitment process by focusing on the forms of control and resistance which were found to characterise sex discrimination in selection. Seeking to reflect the changing and dynamic nature of the social practices which constitute the labour market, the book draws on empirical material to reveal how sex discrimination can be *reproduced, rationalised* and *resisted* by those in positions of domination and subordination within the recruitment process. Their research was conducted in the United Kingdom in the early 1983–5. It nevertheless is remarkably fresh in its insights. Despite the narrow focus of the work on recruitment and its exclusive focus on gender, we contend that its theoretical insights have a wider use and may be of value in understanding the intersection of gender and race/ethnicity.

Unsurprisingly, Collinson et al. found that, despite publicly subscribing to equal opportunities, a substantial number of employers were still 'managing to discriminate' on the grounds of sex through a variety of recruitment practices. They identified a 'vicious circle' of job segregation, which we have adapted to update and include ethnicity (see Figure 3.2). They argued that a set of practices, including informality in recruitment channels, criteria, procedures and the setting of interviews, preoccupations with domestic responsibilities and their different valuation according to sex, along with assumptions around geographical mobility all facilitated the reproduction of job segregation (Collinson, Knights and Collinson 1990). These were taken-for-granted practices that rarely required explanation but when they did, different types of rationalisations were recorded. These were: to deny employer responsibility by blaming women and society; to state that they (the employers) were seeking to control production effectively; and that their practices were socially beneficial (ibid.). For Collinson et al., the plausibility of these ideological rationalisations is grounded not only in vested economic interests in the perpetuation of job segregation, but also in the 'partial truths' on which the vicious circles are based. Partial truths are highly selective and exaggerated accounts of the social and material realities of production and reproduction (ibid.). Indeed, we would go further and suggest that partial truths far from being 'partially true' are indeed distortions of reality and as such may indeed be vicious in their consequence. Such distortions are very much in evidence in the lives of the women in our study, particularly when they seek career development or resist sexist or racist behaviours (see Chapters 8, 9 and 10).

Collinson et al. conclude that the persistence of the contradictory vicious circles of job segregation is therefore based, in particular, on the partial truths embedded in gender and managerial ideology and the preoccupation with gender and hierarchical identity which they reflect and reinforce. To explain the way in which job segregation is

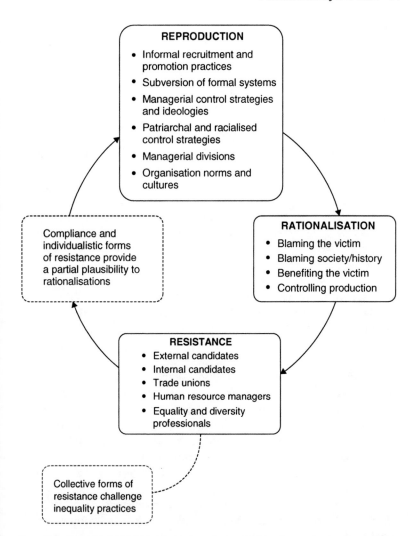

Figure 3.2 The vicious and discriminatory circles of job and organisation inequalities
Source: Adapted from Collinson, Knights and Collinson (1990: 194).

routinely reproduced, rationalised and resisted in the recruitment process, they were concerned to develop the analysis of power inequalities
in the labour market, by focusing on human agency and the subjective
preoccupation with the security of self (Collinson, Knights and
Collinson 1990). Thus their study shows how it may be in the self-interest
of the selectors to discriminate. For those who witness discriminatory

behaviour, and whose moral and professional senses (e.g. human resource managers) are alerted to the unacceptability of this behaviour, it may be in their self-interest to remain silent or to collude in discriminatory rationalisations. Indeed, it may be against their career interests to challenge ideological rationalisations that are embedded in the dominant structures of power. As Young (1990:206) argues 'everyday judgment of and interaction with women, people of color, gay men and lesbians, disabled people and old people is often influenced by unconscious aversions and devaluations.' She goes on to argue that evaluators often carry unconscious biases and prejudices against specially marked groups. These are all played out in the vicious circles of segregation.

For our work, this is a useful framework that addresses the perennial challenge of reconciling the relationship between structure and agency. However, despite its value, it has major shortcomings. For example, there is a major neglect of ethnicity in the analysis. The authors attributed this neglect to the funders (the EOC) (Collinson, Knights and Collinson 1990). This very much reflects the public policy strategy of dealing with race and gender discrimination as disconnected issues. It is only recently that the EOC has enthusiastically embraced and supported work on the intersection of sex and race (e.g., Bhavnani 2006; Bradley, Healy et al., 2007; EOC 2007c).

Jenkins (1986) distinguished between *acceptability* and *suitability* in recruitment and selection. We would also apply these ideas to promotion. *Suitability* is the person's technical ability to do the job, whereas *acceptability* is the likelihood that the person will 'fit' into the organisation; thus this notion intrinsically embodies subjectivity and partiality. These concepts are valuable in understanding the way that subjectivity permeates management recruitment and promotion decisions. The notion of acceptability is reinforced by decisions based on stereotypical assertions and the unconscious biases and prejudices identified by Young (1990).

Stereotypes are dangerous enough when consistently used, but the reality of stereotypical behaviour conveys a form of 'double-speak' (Healy 1993). Indeed Cockburn argues that men engage in a coherent and consistent discourse of gender differentiation:

> On the one hand, women were described as more diligent and industrious: 'you can rely on the girls, they work harder', they were nicer than men in middle management, women were less autocratic, gave orders more 'sweetly', they 'charm the birds out of the bloody trees', they had more sympathy with staff feelings and related better to the public. Men also indicated a repertoire of negative representations of

women and, significantly, they were critical of women only in relation to authority. Two themes emerge, firstly that women were not capable of authority and secondly that they turn into nasty people when in authority. On the first count, women 'lack a bit of judgment' and get a bit emotional', 'are not cut out for it', find it difficult to be ruthless enough and so on. On the second count, women in top jobs are 'bossy', 'pushy', 'absolute bastards'.

(Cockburn 1991:68)

Such gendered differentiation is also racialised. In our various empirical studies, we heard of the impact of stereotypical assumptions on people's careers (Bradley, Healy et al. 2007; Healy and Oikelome 2006). Common views conveyed to BME women are that black women cannot manage, that Asian women are not interested in careers, that they are passive and subject to the demands of husbands and families. We discuss these issues fully in Chapters 8 and 9.

Collinson, Knights and Collinson's study is some 25 years old and given that some 40 years of equality legislation have passed (see Chapter 4), we should expect some major positive changes to practices in the intervening years. Sadly, as we shall see in later chapters, findings in studies undertaken at the begin of the 21st century echo many of their 1990 findings at the level of the organisation, despite major changes in public policy (Bradley, Healy et al. 2007, Healy and Oikelome 2006).

How to challenge the undoubted inequities in organisations has exercised many minds. One argument is that it is important to equip BME women with skills and resources to combat the discriminations they face; the deficit model. This is a liberal and individualistic approach and does not seek to challenge the structures that are outside the resources of any individual. Whilst these approaches help women learn to 'play the game' and in some cases to succeed, they leave in place the structures and policies of the game itself (Kolb, Fletcher et al. 2003). This approach reflects the liberal approach outlined by Jewson and Mason (1986), traditionally based on bureaucratisation and formalisation of procedures within organisations.

This is in contrast to Jewson and Mason's (1986) account of the radical approach, which emphasises direct intervention to achieve equality of outcome rather than just equality of opportunity. A radical approach supports positive action and positive discrimination, such as targets or quotas, to tackle deep-seated inequalities. For Cockburn (1991), the radical approach is not sufficient. For her, the analysis requires both a short and a long agenda. The short agenda seeks to promote opportunities for current groups of employees. The long agenda demands exploration and eradication of the deep-rooted structures that underpin occupational hierarchies, such as class-based reward systems or the devaluation of 'women's work'.

Indeed, legislation in the United Kingdom has persistently but inter-mittently flirted with more radical approaches and ultimately failed to embrace a radical equality agenda as we shall see in Chapter 4. The United States has been bolder in adopting positive action policies, but eventually this led to a backlash. We return to this and some of the conceptual thinking outlined in this section when we address employer strategies in Chapter 5.

Do black women 'choose' their careers?

Chapter 2 mapped the dominant occupations where women work and it is clear that there are distinctions by ethnicity. An important question to ask relates to women's 'choices'. Do black women choose to do the work they do or do they do the work that is available to them? Do they choose to work in the organisations where they work? What are the constraints they face in these choices? Do women choose organisations where they believe they will not be rejected? Are they committed to the work they do? Are they rejected by other organisations?

Thus choice and career are inextricably linked, as indeed is the importance of commitment in the context of career. We take Sikes et al.s' view that the 'adult career is a product of the dialectical relationship between self and circumstances' (Sikes, Measor and Woods 1985:2). Thus we do not use career as a hierarchical concept, referring to steady steps up the occupational ladder. Rather it embraces the different changes in paid and non-paid work over the life course including family formation.

In the sociological literature, debates on women's lack of commitment to work as a central life goal (Hakim 1991) are well trodden. In its crudest form, the debate identifies two kinds of women, self-made women (com-mitted) and grateful slaves (uncommitted). The latter are concentrated in the secondary, part-time labour market yet demonstrate high levels of job satisfaction. Hakim's argument (Hakim 1991, 1995, 1996) is based on the view that women 'choose' to accept low-status work because they have a less committed prior orientation to work. The methodological and philo-sophical weaknesses of this argument have been critically exposed (Devine 1992; Ginn, Arber et al. 1996). These critiques have been from a gender perspective. If we include ethnicity in the argument, then this approach is further weakened, since we find that black Caribbean women are highly committed to work as we have seen from Chapter 2 and the earlier sections in this chapter. Yet, their experiences of racist behaviour lead to lower levels of job satisfaction (Shields and Wheatley Price 2002).

It is women's different career patterns, involving combinations of career breaks and part-time working that are at the root of assumptions about women's commitment. The careers of women with caring responsibilities, which reflect the dominant domestic division of labour, tend not to fit the continuous, hierarchical model of career. Halford, Savage and Witz (1997) argue that the bureaucratic hierarchical meaning of career has been remarkably resilient to change and that this particular meaning has been socially sanctioned and constructed to convey material rewards, power and status to those who pursue it, as well as marginalising and disempowering those who do not, or cannot. Again, whilst black Caribbean or South Asian women often find themselves in occupations that offer hierarchical development, the bureaucracy, despite its claims to objectivity, does not work to their advantage.

The notion of 'commitment' is a social construction and we need to recognise its multiplicity of meanings, as well as its subjective, contradictory, temporal, frequently gendered nature, and its association with subjective perceptions of 'career' (Healy 1999). To this we would add that this concept is also ethnicised. The concept itself is not unproblematic; Becker (1985) argued that the term has been used to describe a great variety of social-psychological mechanisms, such a variety that it has no stable meaning and Guest (1992) sees it as a difficult and rather elusive concept. We draw on it as, despite these valid criticisms, it is a concept that is widely used in everyday life and used as a key rationalising concept to include or exclude people from career opportunities (Healy 1997). The gendered and ethnicised assumptions shaping the 'partial truths' on commitment to work tend to emphasise women's broken careers and ignore the impact of discrimination on commitment to work. Indeed, such concepts imply a necessary association with an unbroken attachment to work rather than recognising that people's attachment to work may indeed wax and wane as circumstances, both internal and external to work, alter.

Women's commitment is often viewed in relation to their mothering role (either actual or expected), thus confusing assessments of commitment to work with assumed competing domestic commitments. Indeed, rational choice theory leads Gary Becker to argue that married women economise on the effort expended on market work by seeking less demanding jobs (1985). The 'evidence' of women's lesser commitment is, however, weak; Marsden et al. argue that research in the area reveals 'inconsistent conclusions' (1993:374), although when job attributes, career variables and family ties are simultaneously controlled, women tend to exhibit slightly greater organisational commitment. Bielby and Bielby provide further evidence of women's work commitment by showing that on average, women allocate more effort to work than do men (1988:1031). Further, we have already seen the high level of attachment of many black women to the labour market.

Although Hakim recognises that there is no sharp boundary line between the 'self-made women' and the 'grateful slaves', with many women switching between groups at some point in their lives (1991:114), she does not attempt to provide insight into the processes of 'switching' nor the consequences, nor does she seek to illuminate the complexity of experience of women from different backgrounds, ethnicities and so on. Rational choice arguments also present women as a homogeneous group. As we argue, it is impossible to understand women's behaviour and 'choices' without insight into their class and ethnicity. Reynolds's (2001) study of black women questioned the extent to which Caribbean women's high work rate was the outcome of 'choice'. Indeed, historically and culturally black mothers in Britain, along with black mothers in the Caribbean and the United States, have been constructed as workers. Reynolds showed that historical and cultural factors, through the experiences of slavery, colonialism and economic migration, framed black mothers' economic labour capacity for work as primary status (ibid.: 1061). In addition her study revealed that the high rates of unemployment for black men and the lower rates of pay for black men and women compared to their white male and female counterparts, actively encourage a high proportion of black women towards full-time paid work in order to make up for this economic shortfall. Thus full-time work may not be a preference; rather, it is the result of economic necessity and at best could be described as a constrained choice.

In the case of women from the Indian subcontinent, Phizacklea showed that the conditions of women's migration gave them little choice but to work in family business or for a relative (1990:95). Whilst the gendered effects of immigration legislation has since changed (by reducing the rights of men), it did result in large numbers of women entering Britain following their menfolk and thus becoming dependent on them for employment chances. Immigration rules thus strengthened patriarchal controls and sponsorship within the South Asian communities and limited women's 'choices'.

The implication of rational choice arguments is that if women and black people invest in human capital to the same extent as white men, they will have the same opportunities. This is clearly fallacious and the reason lies in the consequence of the intersection of race and sex discrimination. The outcome of such race and sex discrimination was presented in Chapter 2. Despite greater opportunities, and women's increased level of qualifications, we know that the pay gap is remarkably resilient in Europe and in the United States. In 2007, the UK Equal Opportunities Commission (EOC) found that the despite some advances, the indicators show worrying gender gaps across all areas of life, and at the current rate of progress change will be painfully slow (EOC 2007a).

Inequality regimes

We end this chapter by drawing on Acker's concept of inequality regimes. For the reasons outlined in this chapter, we see this as a more valuable and inclusive approach than that of gender regimes (Connell 1987; Walby 1997). The analysis of gender regimes may be seen as overly deterministic stressing male power, thereby neglecting women's agency. Along with Pollert (1981) and Westwood (1984), we take the view that women are not passive recipients of dominant ideologies. Rather, they are active agents in the reproduction and transformation of the structures they face. The structures of class, race/ethnicity and gender are immensely powerful and provide the conditions for racism and sexism to thrive. They provide the conditions for constrained action, but action it still is, so that subsequent behaviours are not wholly determined, rather they work, as Mouzelis (1989) states, within 'variable degrees of freedom'.

We see Acker's (2006) analysis of inequality regimes as a useful way forward. Acker states that such regimes are embedded in all organisations. Acker defines inequality regimes as 'interrelated practices, processes actions and meanings that result in and maintain class, gender and racial inequalities' (2006:443). She conceptualises inequality in organisations as 'the systematic disparities between participants in power and control over goals, resources and outcomes, workplace decisions, such as how to organise work, opportunities for promotion and interesting work, security in employment and benefits, pay and other monetary rewards, respect and pleasures in work and work relations' (ibid.). In other words, inequality is built into organisational dynamics at all levels. As such, we argue elsewhere (Bradley, Healy and Forson 2007) that investigating inequality regimes in organisations poses particular challenges because of their minutiae, and the indiscernible, fluid and changeable nature of such regimes. Inequality regimes are therefore complex and multifaceted. In fact, Acker isolates six interconnected components of inequality regimes: the bases of inequality; shape and degree of inequality; organising processes that produce inequality; the visibility of inequalities; the legitimacy of inequalities; control and compliance. We see these components as interacting and operating at different levels, with the first two in particular operating at the macro-social as well as the institutional level of the organisation. Notwithstanding this complexity, we think that Acker's approach offers a way forward in understanding the intersection of gender, race, class and other bases of inequality.

Indeed for Acker (2006), the first component relates to the *bases for inequality*. We agree that in general the main bases of inequality are gender, race/ethnicity and class. However, Acker also argues that sexual orientation may be a particularly important base, and we would add that religion too has an important part in understanding the bases of inequality (Bradley, Healy et al. 2007). Thus Acker recognises the importance of gender regimes as independent explanatory factors, but suggests that such regimes cannot be understood without understanding the intersection with class and race/ethnicity regimes and fundamentally with capitalism. In contrast, in a plenary at the 2007 Gender Work and Organisation conference held at Keele University, Walby drawing on macro data saw gender regimes as separate from capitalism.

The second component relates to the *shape and degree of inequality*. Understanding the wider context of hierarchy is central to this component, which Acker characterises as the steepness of hierarchy. A second aspect of this component is the degree and pattern of segregation. These aspects have resonance with what we more often characterise as vertical and horizontal segregation, as discussed in Chapter 2. This showed how white men dominate the hierarchies across a range of Western countries and how there are different patterns of segregation between women and men; and within groups of women, differences in segregation patterns between women from different ethnic groups. Chapters 8 and 9 will show the processes that lead to these patterns of segregation at the level of the organisation.

The third component is *organising processes that produce inequality*. Organising processes of inequality regimes include the requirements of the work, recruitment and selection, training, promotion and wage setting. These clearly relate to the work of Cockburn and of Jewson and

Mason discussed earlier in the chapter. Many of the organising processes that produce inequality and the way these processes may be challenged are explored in later chapters.

The *legitimacy of inequalities* is the fourth component. If equalities are not seen as important to the powerful stakeholders within the organisation, equality strategies have little chance of claiming legitimacy, despite legislation. Legitimacy of inequalities is reproduced at different levels in the organisation. The legitimacy of equality policies lies not only in the rhetoric around such policies but also in the degree of enforcement undertaken. In constantly having to challenge stereotypical images of themselves, BME women often find that their efforts only serve to reinforce their otherness and further legitimise the inequalities they experience. Too often policing of such micro-interactions and relationships falls outside of the formal structure of equalities of an organisation and so it is left to individual women as we shall see in later chapters. Further, we note that it is still rare to incorporate equalities into performance management

The fifth component identified by Ackers is the *visibility of inequality*, that is, the degree of awareness of inequalities in organisations. Patterns of visibility and invisibility vary with the basis for the inequality (Acker 2006b:11). Our previous work has demonstrated that the visibility of inequality varies with the emphasis that is put on equality policy and practice and further that visibility will vary with the presence and influence of key individuals (Bradley, Healy et al. 2007).

The sixth and final component is *control and compliance*. Organisational controls are primarily class controls. They also draw on power derived from hierarchical gender and race relations and impede changes in inequality regimes (Acker 2006). Indeed, controls are created and recreated in interactions between workers, between workers and supervisors, and between managers and supervisors in which expectations of ethnic-, gender-, and class-appropriate behaviours are covertly or overtly expressed, then complied with or opposed (Acker 2006b).

Where there is compliance, in a pluralist society, there will, however, also be resistance. Trade unions are a key collective agent of resistance in organisations and their influences can thread through these various components of inequality regimes. They will come to the fore in the challenge to control or compliance. Equally, their history suggests that they, too, have been agents of discrimination, protecting white men's influence and material well-being against the perceived dangers of women and black workers' encroachment into the labour market, as will be discussed in Chapters 6 and 10 and 11.

Conclusion

The field we have charted in this chapter is wide and complex. The analytical tools available do not provide an easy solution to the investigation of the intersectionality of inequalities in organisations and our society. Rather they enable us to get some purchase on a complex and worthwhile project. The following chapters will show how well they stand up to the challenge we have set.

4
Challenging Discrimination, Sexism and Racism: the Role of the State

In this chapter we consider the role played by the government in promoting policies which challenge discrimination. Early theorising on the state, including its welfare arm, tended to portray it as patriarchal and imperialist and, above all, capitalist. It was seen first and foremost to serve the interests of 'Big Business' and to help it exploit women and racialised minorities by using them as cheap sources of labour. The British state was described as patriarchal by feminists in the decades after the war, in that its security policy was predicated upon a view of the family which saw men as breadwinners and women as dependants, thus reinforcing male power and authority in the family (Barrett 1980; Wilson 1977). Other feminists also pointed to the failure of the British state to protect women from domestic violence and rape (Edwards 1981; Smart 1984). Amina Mama (1984), in a powerful critique of the British state's approach to black women, pointed to the way the state tended to pathologise black families and present black women's fertility as a threat, leading to attempts to limit their reproductive capacities through the use of contraceptives such as Depo-provera.

However, subsequent analysis presented the relationship as rather more complex. A view derived more from the position of Max Weber recognised the state, both national and local, as the focus of contestation, where different groups lobbied to get their interests represented. This is not to say that the state was neutral, more that outcomes represented the interplay of different interest groups. For example, in the United States, feminist activists, especially lawyers, developed a very powerful lobbying presence during the 1960s, and as a result America took the lead in anti-sexist legislation (Gelb and Palley 1982). In Australia a group of feminist activists were able to make their way into the state bureaucracy and to become involved in policy-making from the inside, earning the name of 'femocrats'. While such moves were slower to develop in Europe and the United Kingdom, where feminism took a more grass-roots form, as the European superstate evolved feminists were also able to gain important positions as advisers and commissioners within the EU bureaucracy, leading to the development of stronger policies on gender equality. Scandinavian states, who prided themselves on their egalitarian nature, played an important role here. Borchhorst and Siim (1987) took a more critical line on this; they argued that in Scandinavian countries and Denmark there had been the development of a kind of benevolent state paternalism, which freed women from dependency on men, but could trap them into dependency on the state. Certainly, we know that in the United Kingdom and elsewhere there has been a 'feminisation of poverty' whereby women, especially single parents and the elderly, are especially likely to be dependent on state benefits for their economic livelihood.

In this chapter we briefly survey the role of the state and its impact on policies of equality and diversity. We start by looking at the history of legislation on sex and race equality, and then consider current initiatives, especially the Race Relations Amendment Act 2000 and the Gender Duty introduced in 2007. We highlight problems in the state approach by looking at the limits of legislation. The contribution of the EU is also considered. We end by considering New Labour's latest approaches to the issues of equality and diversity. Finally, we suggest ways in which the role of legislation might be strengthened, especially in relation to the state's attitudes to the private sector.

Initial state interventions: race relations and sex discrimination legislation

We think it is fair to say that the initiation of anti-discrimination legislation on employment in Britain was forced upon the government, rather than primarily motivated by commitment to equality. The development of the race relations legislation in the United Kingdom (often seen as a model for Europe) has always been bound up with panics over immigration; successive Race Relations Acts were linked to laws which progressively controlled and limited entry of non-white people into Britain. The first moves to develop such laws were a direct result of the Nottingham and Notting Hill disturbances or 'race riots' in 1958, which abruptly brought to the fore the issue of relations between white and black communities. This and other agitations around the impact of postwar immigration led to what

Colin Brown describes as 'the twin-plank policy of keeping out further migrants but giving fair treatment to those already in Britain' (Brown 1992). The first major act to curb immigration was the Commonwealth Immigrants Act of 1962. This was followed by the Race Relations Acts of 1965 and 1968, the latter covering employment and housing.

Legislation on discrimination against women had a rather different genesis. American feminists had taken the lead in fighting for legislation against sexist discrimination, and feminists in Britain had been campaigning for similar laws in Britain to the American Equal Pay Act of 1963 and the Equal Employment Opportunities Act of 1972 (interestingly these acts covered both sex and race discrimination). However, it is taken to be the EU and its 'social chapter' which pushed the UK government into passing the Equal Pay Act and the Sex Discrimination act in the 1970s. Improvements in these acts have also been subsequently driven by the EU. It is only recently, and partly due to the increased number of women within Parliament (Blair's babes as they were rather offensively nicknamed), that the government seems to have taken a more proactive lead in positively espousing the notion of diversity and championing the causes of women, ethnic minorities, disabled people, elderly people and victims of other kinds of discrimination (religious minorities, gays and lesbians).

The third Race Relations Act in 1976 is taken to be the crucial piece of legislation since it set up a monitoring body (a key aspect of the American laws). It made discrimination in employment, education and the provision of services and facilities unlawful. The Commission for Racial Equality (CRE) was set up to monitor the Act and was empowered to carry out investigations. Local Race Equality Councils (RECs) were subsequently formed in many places to supplement the CRE's work at local level. While the legislation was important, as with sex discrimination legislation the onus was on the individual to prove discrimination by bringing a case to an industrial tribunal. Not only is this a very stressful process for the complainant, it was and is difficult to prove discrimination; for example, a person may suspect that their ethnicity was the reason for not getting a job, but as there is often no written account of the discussion of a recruitment panel, this is hard to prove. Moreover, people quickly learned, following the Act, that overt, spoken racial prejudice was illegal: but this does not prevent people making decisions on the basis of racist views. Unspoken prejudice remains common, but is very hard to prove.

A very similar analysis can be given of the initial legislation on gender discrimination, which, however, took the form of two separate laws: the Equal Pay Act (EPA) (1970) and the Sex Discrimination Act (SDA) (1975).

Both were not implemented until 1976, giving time for employers to 'get their house in order', or, conversely, to give them time to think of ways to evade the Acts, for example by devising ways to ensure that men's jobs and women's jobs could not be described as 'similar'. The EPA specifically addressed the issue of the longstanding 'gender pay gap' by stating that men and women must be paid alike for 'like work' or work 'of equal value'. This wording, of course, opened up a legal minefield of debates as to what counted as 'equal value' and subsequent amendments, made under pressure from the EU to make the legislation more effective, changed it to 'work rated equivalent' under a job evaluation scheme. This brought an opportunity for trade unions to be involved with job evaluation as a way for pressing for gender equity and resulted in some notable victories for various groups of women, such as the Ford women machinists (who worked on car seats) or the speech therapists. In general, however, the burden of proof still fell on women, who had to find a suitable male comparator and take an equal pay case to the tribunal.

The Sex Discrimination Act was more general in scope, covering all other types of discrimination apart from pay (such as recruitment or promotion). It was very similar to the Race Relations Act in covering employment, education and provision of services and facilities. It also set up a watchdog body, the Equal Opportunities Commission (EOC), with similar powers to the CRE. Until recently, the EOC was judged to be rather less active and effective in fighting for equality than the CRE; being less likely, for example, to institute a general investigation into an organisation where there were allegations of sex discrimination or to issue anti-discrimination orders. The success of both commissions can be seen to be influenced by the people chosen to head them: Sir Herman Ouseley and Trevor Phillips as CRE heads have been more outspoken critics of UK social relations than some earlier EOC directors: however, recently Joanna Foster and Jenny Watson have publicised the work of the EOC more aggressively. To be fair to both commissions, their activities have been handicapped, especially in the early days, by lack of substantial budgets to carry out research and investigations. This in turn reflects the low priority given by Conservative governments to equality issues during their period of government in the 1970s and 1980s. The return of New Labour in 1997 has seen more attention given to equality and diversity, as we shall see.

The current legislative context

A different type of climate for the equality agenda was signalled by Tony Blair's government when it signed up to the EU Social Chapter (which the Conservatives had refused to do under the Treaty of Maastricht). This brought gains for part-time workers who had to be treated *pro rata* in the same way as full-timers. Labour also introduced the National Minimum Wage. Both these moves have clearly been beneficial for women workers. Another important legislative change was the passing of the Race Relations (Amendment) Act 2000 (RRAA).

A crucial influence on this was the Stephen Lawrence Inquiry and the MacPherson Report, which had found the Police Service guilty of institutional racism in handling the murder of black teenager Stephen. The subsequent enquiry and report, brought about largely by the brave and insistent campaigning of Stephen's parents, Neville and Doreen, was a spur to action against racism in the public sector. The important aspect of the RRAA was that it placed a positive duty on public-sector organisations *actively* to promote racial equality. This pioneering piece of legislation has since been followed by a number of similar Acts in relation to disability, gender and age.

The RRAA obliges public organisations to prepare a Race Equality Plan, to monitor it and to assess its impact. New policies and plans are to be subject to consultation. Organisations have to publish details of their policies, monitoring and assessment annually, and every three years they must carry out a full review. They also have to train staff in relation to specific activities (such as recruitment and selection). Thus the responsibility for working against racism has been shifted from the individual sufferer to the organisation. However, a crucial limitation is that, unlike the Race Relations Act, the RRAA does not apply to private-sector organisations (which, however, are still covered by the earlier legislation). As is often the case, the government was here using the public sector to act as an exemplar of good practice, a model employer, and hoping that these practices would 'trickle across' to the private sector.

The principles of the RRAA have been applied to other aspects of discrimination, with legislation which presses organisations into taking a more proactive and accountable approach to inequalities in the workplace. The Disability Discrimination Act of 1995 forbade discrimination against disabled people, defined as those with physical or mental impairments which have a long-term and adverse effect on their ability to perform work duties. The DDA obliges employers to make reasonable adjustments to allow access to disabled people and enable them to participate. There are special obligations on educational institutions to this effect. In December 2006 a duty to make proactive efforts to end discrimination against disabled people was introduced into the public sector.

In 2007, the government introduced a Gender Equality Duty for the public sector which mirrors the duty in the RRAA. Organisations have to develop a gender equality plan. They are obliged to promote equality, rather than just avoiding discrimination. They will be required to review their provisions and to make action plans for promoting opportunities for women. These plans must define goals that must be implemented within a three-year period. They are also required to consult with stakeholders and to carry out impact assessments.

The Employment Equality (Age) Regulations 2006 are an important step forward and potentially may have significant impact on women since they are more likely to suffer indirect discrimination because of age. Recent legislation has also focused on newly championed aspects of inequality and discrimination. The Employment Equality (Sexual Orientation) Regulations of 2003 made it unlawful to discriminate on grounds of sexual orientation in the areas of employment and training. As with the race and gender legislation, this covered the three aspects of direct discrimination (including harassment), indirect discrimination and victimisation. An equivalent piece of legislation, the Employment Equality (Religion or Belief) Regulations, was also passed in 2003. This relates to the arguments put forward by Modood (2005) and others that religion (and most specifically Islam) is now the main basis of racial prejudice rather than skin colour. Although we do not agree entirely with this position, it is true that since the terrible events of 9/11 and 7/7 Islamophobia has become a strong current in the United Kingdom, with adverse effects for Muslim women, as we shall see in subsequent chapters.

Another very significant recent change was introduced in another amendment to the 1976 RRA passed in 2003. This was designed to make the RRA more effective, by shifting the onus to employers to prove that different treatment was not on racial grounds: therefore 'if the employer cannot provide an adequate explanation for the treatment in question then the tribunal *must* decide that racial discrimination has occurred' (Brown, Erskine and Littlejohn 2006:13). This alteration in the burden of proof is likely to make it less easy for employers to practise evasive strategies, which was a key finding in an analysis of sex discrimination cases by Chambers and Horton (1990).

At the time of writing, the UK Government is seeking to introduce a Single Equality Act that will bring together the different equality 'strands'. This will also include a single equality duty which will ultimately replace the existing duties on which consultation is currently taking place. There are great fears that employers will be able to choose on which 'strand' to concentrate and thereby give less attention to other strands. This has the potential to weaken the recent strengthening of the law. Although the aims of simplifying a complex set of laws are laudable, if they remove the few teeth in the existing law, then we must have concerns. The consultations are ongoing as we write, so it is possible that our concerns may be premature.

The role of the European Union

Recent changes in UK law are influenced by the role of the EU in pressurising member states into addressing gender inequalities. Stratigaki (2000) argues that the EU and its constituent bodies (the European Community, the European Commission and the European Court of Justice) have been major players in the fight for gender equality and women's rights. We would not disagree with this judgement, although we would note that it has been much less impressive in the fight against racism. Certainly the passing of the SDA and EPA tallied with Britain's entry into the EU in 1973 (though we should note that it also coincided with the rise of the active and campaigning UK Women's Liberation Movement in the 1970s).

The EU enshrined the principle of equal treatment from the start, with the commitment to equal pay being an article in the initial 1957 Treaty of Rome. Since then numerous initiatives and directives on gender equality have been adopted, including a social action plan which covered gender equality developed in 1974 (just after Britain's accession to the EU) and a number of Council Directives, notably on equal pay (Directive 75/117/EEC), on equal treatment for men and women in access to employment, training and promotion (76/207/EEC) and on equal treatment in social security matters (79/7/EEC).

There has also been an important development in EU policy on gender which is explored in the useful collection of papers *Gendered Policies in Europe* (2000), edited by Linda Hantrais. Hantrais and her collaborators note the shift in orientation from the notion of equal treatment to the need to reconcile family and working life. This idea of *reconciliation*, which we are more familiar with in the United Kingdom in the guise of 'work-life balance', was enshrined in the Employment Guidelines issued by the European Council in 1997. This followed increased concern about the provision of childcare and the employment of mothers, both in the EU and its member states.

Indeed, in the United Kingdom the 'problem' of 'working mothers' (i.e., mothers taking on employment outside the home in addition to the large amount of work they carry out within it!) has been a longstanding preoccupation and policy dilemma. 'Working mothers' have been blamed for everything from rising divorce rates to teenage delinquency to young men's lower school achievements. The latest manifestation of this kind of moral panic, occurring while we were writing this book in 2007, is research claiming that childhood obesity is linked to mothers' employment, as children consume more 'junk food'. In the main the Conservative preference has been to advocate that women with young children should stay at home, an attitude espoused strongly by the right-wing press. However, the New Labour approach has been to encourage labour market participation as the major solution to social exclusion (Levitas 1998), so they have encouraged young mothers, especially single parents, to find jobs, while pressurising employers to adopt 'family-friendly' policies and flexible working. Thus in 2003 a piece of legislation gave all women with dependant children the right to demand flexible hours (although employers are not obliged to comply). This is rather typical of UK law: successive governments, both Conservative and Labour, have fought shy of compulsion, especially in the private sector, preferring to couch laws within a framework of guidance, best practice and voluntarism and being reluctant to levy large fines from infringers.

The limits of legislation

Indeed, the British anti-discrimination laws have been subject to considerable criticism since initiated, on both practical and theoretical grounds. Most feminists felt the EPA and SDA did not go far enough and were too full of 'get-out' clauses (such as the view that different treatment was permissible where there were 'genuine occupational differences'). In particular they felt that the enforcement mechanisms were insufficient and that the legislation 'lacked teeth' (Coote and Campbell 1982). Linda Dickens describes the early approach by the government (especially the Thatcher regime) as 'grudging and minimalist' and often linked to de-regulatory initiatives (Dickens 2006:1). Lustgarten and Edwards state that the effect of the RRA in diminishing racism was 'minimal at best' (1992:270). While the legislation provided some individuals with compensation for discrimination (although, as we shall see, such victories were often Pyrrhic), its broader effects were strictly limited.

Practical issues

The Equal Opportunities Commission itself described the Equal Pay Act in a report of 1990 as 'paradise for lawyers, but hell for women' (quoted

Bagilhole and Byrne 2000:129). As noted, it is very stressful for claimants to undergo the process of making a case and going through the procedure of an Employment Tribunal; they often fear victimisation; they find it difficult and time-consuming to find suitable representation (Aston, Hill and Tackey, 2006). Support from trade unions and lawyers is not always very good; and the process in the past was often extremely lengthy and slow, though the Employment Tribunal Service (ETS) has currently set targets for processing cases more quickly.

However, success rates, especially in race cases, are low, reflecting the difficulty of proving discrimination, especially race discrimination. Statistics from the ETS for 2005–6 illustrate this: 115,000 claims were put in to the service in 2005–6, resulting in 29,750 judicial cases. Of 24,217 jurisdictions made under the Sex Discrimination Act, 17 per cent were successful at tribunals and 4 per cent were dismissed. Prior to the tribunal 40 per cent were withdrawn and 13 per cent were settled through the ACAS conciliation service. Of 3430 race discrimination cases, only 3 per cent succeeded in tribunals and 18 per cent were dismissed, with 42 per cent being withdrawn and 33 per cent settled by ACAS (ETS 2006). Claims under the EPA are easier to make in terms of proof and evidence, with 33 per cent being successful. While these outcomes look bleak, many of the withdrawn and conciliated cases may, of course, represent satisfactory outcomes for complainants through out of court settlements. However, qualitative research carried out by Aston et al. (2006) found that those who had withdrawn or settled the case before tribunal regretted having done so.

It is, of course, in employers' financial interests to ensure such settlements, as the costs of tribunals may be very high. In 2005–6, the maximum award in a race discrimination case was £984,465 and the average was £30,361. For sex discrimination cases the maximum was £217,961 and the average £10,807 (ETS 2006). It has been estimated that tribunals (including all the other types of cases, such as unfair dismissal) cost employers £210 million a year, with lawyers' fees being the major cost (Personnel Management.com: 2006). 'Paradise for lawyers' indeed! Moreover, high-profile discrimination cases which often find their way into the press are seen by large firms as very bad for their public image.

However, in the main, even if tribunals are costly to employers and they wish to avoid them, the experience is a great deal more unpleasant for claimants. A useful account of this is offered in the report by Aston et al. (2006), who carried out in-depth interviews with 40 BME claimants. The report offers a depressing picture. The majority of claimants, whatever the results, felt unsatisfied with the process. Tribunals were experienced as intimidating and definitely not 'user-friendly'. Claimants often felt pressured by representatives (barristers or TU reps) to settle or withdraw. They were very conscious of the power imbalance between themselves and organisations which were able to pay expensive lawyers and produce numerous witnesses. Those who represented themselves because of concern over costs or inability to find support were more likely to lose their cases and struggled to cope with the legal context, with its adversarial framework and its arcane jargon and conventions. As one unrepresented black claimant stated:

> They fail to tell you that you will be subjected to lies, legal arguments you've never even contemplated. I was led like a lamb to the slaughter, It was an arena set to fight against a trained gladiator. I thought they were in cahoots with the respondent.
>
> (Dickens 2000:49)

Research shows that where there is assistance from the EOC or CRE cases are more likely to be successful, but such assistance is rare; in 2001–2 the three equality commissions supported 300 cases out of the 20,000 going to tribunal (Dickens 2000).

The composition of the tribunal panels has also been a matter of concern, as the Aston collaboration demonstrates. A black claimant described her concern at being faced with 'on the bench three white men, all looking like the employer' (Aston, Hill and Tackey 2006:82). This is an important issue as the study also shows that the Chair of the panel, in particular, has the key role in the proceedings. Many claimants claimed that they felt the Chair was hostile to them, even racist. A linked study shows that what is particularly crucial in the judgement is the *perceived credibility* of the claimant (Brown, Erskine and Littlejohn 2006). We know from our own research into ethnicity that cultural differences in body language can be misinterpreted by those lacking in cultural intelligence as indicating that a person is shifty, dishonest, rude or confrontational when this is absolutely not the case.

Given all this it is not surprising that the BME claimants experienced a whole range of negative effects both during the legal process and after it: these included stress, anxiety, serious ill-health (including heart and stroke problems), depression, worsened relations with colleagues and subsequent victimisation at work (no chance of promotion). Many faced subsequent unemployment and financial loss. This is the more saddening as an interesting finding was that the majority of claimants described their key motivation as desire for justice and apology from employers, not money:

> I wanted to speak for the downtrodden, those people who are being discriminated against. It wasn't remuneration *per se*. I wanted those cowboy employers to be brought to book.
>
> (Aston, Hill and Tackey 2006:39)

This accords strongly with our own research, for, as will be discussed in Chapter 11, BME women expressed a very strong commitment to general ideas of equity and social justice.

Political and theoretical issues

The negative experiences of Aston et al.s' sample is indicative of much deeper problems which underlie the legislative approach. There is a major problem in using the individualistic framework of the tribunal system to address a collective problem, that of gender and ethnic segregation. In this respect the UK legislation is much weaker than the US laws which allow a class action to be taken on a behalf of a group of workers, so that the judgement effects 'existing, future and potential employees'. This not only takes the pressure off the individual claimant, but allows a collective solution to the collective problem. Stamp and Robarts (1986) in their review of the UK laws for the National Council of Civil Liberties (NCCL) argue that such a system could and should be introduced in the United Kingdom.

However, there is likely to be resistance to this as, up till now at least, successive governments have been wary of taking any initiatives that would rouse the opposition of employers. This is the problem at the core of state policy: governments may espouse an egalitarian stance, but only as long as it doesn't interfere too greatly with profits or markets. The espousal of neo-liberal economic policies, vigorously promoted by the Thatcher regime, but also a central plank of Blair's approach, is fundamentally at odds with ideas of state intervention and regulation of the economy. As Bagilhole and Byrne put it, there is a prioritised commitment to 'a relatively low-cost, low-tax unregulated labour market':

> New labour's 'third way' might be interpreted by cynics as support in principle for family-friendly measures, such as flexible working time and childcare, but only if they don't cost too much.
>
> (Bagilhole and Byrne 2000:136)

This is why the race, gender and disability duties introduced in the 2000s are not applied to the private sector. Under considerable pressure from organisations like the CBI, governments continue to believe that private-sector organisations should be allowed freedom in order to compete successfully in the global arena.

Instead of legal compulsion, the government hopes that the private sector will voluntarily espouse equality and has encouraged it to do so through initiatives such as 'Opportunity 2000' and 'Race for Opportunity'. In its more recent pronouncements, the government has taken to using the rhetoric of *diversity*, especially in relation to the 'business case' with which it hopes to persuade employers in the private sector that it is in their financial interests to open up opportunities to women, BME people and other formerly discriminated groups. The business case focuses on the rapidly changing global economy and the need to appeal to clients and customers of diverse nationalities and backgrounds; and on the competition for talent and the need to identify and employ the best people for the job. However, the 'managing diversity' approach is seen by critics as a weakening of the EO agenda. In an influential article Kandola and Fullerton (1994) set out what they saw as the key differences between the two approaches: EO concentrates on removing discrimination, sees it as a problem of disadvantaged groups, and favours positive action schemes, with HR managers seen as the key agents in taking EO forward. By contrast, diversity policy focuses on maximising employee potential (following the business case), sees it as relevant to all employees, rejects positive action, favours a voluntaristic approach and seeks to make all managers responsible for promoting diversity. In effect, the switch is from the idea that 'some people are disadvantaged at work' to that of 'everybody's different'! Thus again the liberal framework of individualism triumphs over any sense of the need to address the structures that create collective forms of disadvantage.

The way forward

Having painted rather a gloomy picture, we suggest that the replacement of Tony Blair by Gordon Brown in 2007 has opened the way for potential reform, given the stronger attachment of the new Prime Minister and his team to issues of social justice. There are also important changes which are already in progress.

It has long been acknowledged that the existing legislation is confusing, messy and not always consistent. One issue is that a BME woman facing discrimination at work may have to choose between using the

RRA or the SDA in her appeal (though claims based on multiple grounds are allowable). The Single Equalities Bill that is planned for 2009 offers the chance for a thorough overhaul of the legislation and a more integrated approach, such as is already in place in the United States and Northern Ireland.

This move is linked to the forming of a new watchdog body, the Equality and Human Rights Commission (EHRC) to replace the three existing equality commissions. This body will deal with all aspects of discrimination and allows for a more intersectional analysis to be applied in understanding inequalities.

There is debate about the likely impact of this development, which was very fiercely resisted by the CRE and the Disability Rights Commission. The selection of Trevor Phillips to head the EHRC might have been a tactical choice to bring the CRE, whose opposition was most vocal, on board, but each commission fears that its own area of activity may be overshadowed and downgraded. A team of social scientists from Bristol, who offered comments on the proposed changes, suggested that the new commission should be organised as a federal structure, with a champion for each of the areas of inequality; however, as yet little has been revealed about the organisation of the EHRC. On the positive side there are advantages to having a single, better-funded body: the EHRC could have stronger powers and benefit from operating within the broader human rights framework. Moreover, the framework of intersectionality, set out in the previous chapter, implies that we can actually tackle discrimination more successfully if we explore how different facets of inequality work together to create specific inequality regimes.

Whatever happens with the EHRC, there is a general agreement among the critics that the legislation needs to be strengthened and made less protective and more proactive (Bagilhole and Byrne 2000). Dickens (2006) points to the need for compulsory pay audits, which have been voluntarily adopted by many public-sector organisations. Stamp and Robarts (1986) argue strongly for the adoption of positive/ affirmative action on the American or Northern Ireland model. The latter was developed following the passing of the Fair Employment Act in 1989 to counter discrimination in employment on religious grounds.

Affirmative action differs in form and content in its application. However, the principle underpinning it has commonalities. A key point is that affirmative action moves from the principle that people should be treated equally to the principle that some groups are disadvantaged in their histories, their material conditions and the cultural context they inhabit, and therefore the dominant culture must make adjustments to allow disadvantaged groups to reach their potential and make a full contribution to society. Indeed, Young (1990) argues that some of the disadvantages that oppressed groups suffer can be remedied in policy only by an affirmative acknowledgement of the group's specificity. Affirmative action, whilst of importance in the US equality picture for public organisations, has experienced a considerable backlash which has been influential in the growth of diversity management.

In the United Kingdom, there is a tendency for people to confuse positive action (which generally involves setting goals and targets and developing programmes to fulfil them, such as training or novel methods of recruitment) with positive discrimination (the setting of quotas for the employment of women, ethnic minorities and so forth). There is popular hostility towards quotas which arises from a widespread espousal of meritocratic values and the employment of the 'best person for the job': who judges whom is the 'best' and how the 'best' is defined are questions that are rarely raised, so strongly rooted in our society is the ideology of meritocracy.

We would certainly favour the adoption of positive action programmes, as they are seen to have born results in the United States and Northern Ireland, and in initiatives developed by individual organisations in Britain which will be discussed in later chapters (see also Bradley, Healy et al. 2007). But the most important development we would like to see in the coming years is the extension of the equality duties to private and voluntary sector organisations. For that to happen, however, will, as we have seen, require a real shift in politics away from neo-liberal orthodoxy and voluntarism.

Conclusion

As Dickens states 'state intervention is critical to an equality agenda, because the market tends to produce discrimination, not equality' (2006:305). While we have been critical of legislation and the motives of the state in this chapter, we too see legislation as a necessary foundation for the promotion of equality. Despite the deficiencies we have noted in the legislation, gender and ethnic inequalities, while persistent, have diminished or altered in form since the passing of the original Acts in the 1970s. In the case of gender, the legislation has produced a 'climate of equality' (Bradley 1999) which makes overt gender discrimination and sexism much more unacceptable. Although the impact of the RRA on racism has probably not been so great, those we have interviewed have compared their experiences favourably with those of their mother and fathers, the 'first generation' of commonwealth immigrants. In their view, forms of racism have become less overt (except perhaps among the oldest white citizens), although new subtler forms of prejudice may be difficult to cope with, as later chapters will show. There are signs, though, that both sexism and racism are less common among younger adults who have grown up in a multicultural society, where ethnic intermarriage is increasingly common, and who have imbibed the idea that equality of the sexes is a desirable thing.

There is still much work to be done in pressurising the state to be more active in promoting equality. Hantrais (2000) in her account of policy change in the EU emphasises the key role of activist women within the Union's power structures in pushing the equality agenda against the reluctance of some national governments. This work is crucial, as is the work of NGOs, including trade unions which will be discussed in Chapter 6. If New Labour has a much stronger record on equality than its Conservative predecessors, there is still a problem posed by its business-friendly approach. Moreover, the individualist framework within the British legal system means that legislation is inherently limited in scope: indeed, Lustgarten and Edwards argue that the law can only act as a 'stick' to prevent people misbehaving and thus change 'longstanding habits' for the better (1992:288); it cannot, they state, be creative in promoting equality. This can only be done through example and good practice, through 'winning hearts and minds' and through education. We take a slightly less gloomy view, and suggest that law can be a useful tool for activists, including trade unions, in promoting equality. But the existing laws need strengthening and extending, the Employment Tribunal system needs a thorough over-hauling, and the laws need consolidating and integrating to make them more familiar and comprehensible to the public. This is probably not a task that should be left to lawyers! The role of the EHRC in the future will be crucial in ensuring positive change.

5
Employers: Agents of Transformation?

Introduction

Employers are central to any discussion on inequalities. They and their agents have the hierarchical power to influence if not determine the shape and degree of inequalities in their organisations. This important component was identified in Chapter 3 by drawing on the work of Acker (2006). Employers set the standards of behaviour, monitor those standards and have the power to punish or condone those who do not conform to the set standards. In most countries the employers are the authors of the rules in the workplace. To some extent as we saw in Chapter 4, this authorship is mediated by government intervention through legislation. In rarer cases, trade unions may be joint authors of organisational rules through collective bargaining and more recently through partnership agreements.

Yet as Chapter 3 has shown, employers have high degrees of freedom in the way that they act and often this results in what Collinson et al. (1990) characterise as vicious circles of segregation underpinned by discriminatory partial truths. Whilst rules may be recorded, they may not be implemented or enforced. Further and importantly, there may be a set of unwritten rules and behaviour shaping the norms and values of an organisation that may encourage and collude with discriminatory practice. We begin with these points as it seems to us that organisational norms and values lie at the heart of the success or failure of equality initiatives. Furthermore, the norms and values that legitimate racism and sexism are embedded in society and subsequently reproduced in organisations.

How did we reach this position? We begin by reflecting on the part played by the organisations in the postwar era (late 1940s on) in the way that racist and sexist practices became embedded. Following this historical reflection, we then introduce a typology of equal opportunities organisations and locate the findings from the Workplace Employment Relations Survey (WERS) 2004 within the typology to understand how far organisations have progressed. This chapter also includes a discussion on the debate between equal opportunities and diversity management and introduces some specific case study examples of policy and practice relevant to the women in this study.

Shape and degree of inequalities in organisations

The demand for labour has been central to employers' strategies in influencing one of the components of inequality regimes, that is, the bases and the shape and degree of inequalities in their organisation (Acker 2006). The state of the British economy in the postwar era created a huge number of job vacancies in essential services and manufacturing. This prompted invitations to British citizens from the then British Empire to come and work in Britain, but it also led to the institutionalising of racist segregation practices, many of which continue today.

It is useful to remind ourselves how discrimination in organisations worked in the early years. This allows us to consider the extent to which the world has really changed. It also offers a good example of Collinson et al.s' (1990) 'partial truths' in the interrelationship between economic demand for cheap labour and a labour supply prepared to work for low wages and do unpleasant work due to economic necessity.

The impression given in much contemporary literature is that employers have only demanded women's labour market activity in the last two to three decades. This is clearly a nonsense. Working-class women's economic activity has always been in demand and such women have always worked in one form or another. Further, the gendered demand for labour has long been a part of employers' labour strategies.

The gendered nature of early work is well spelt out in Bradley's (1989) sociological history of the sexual division of labour. Whilst this demonstrates that men and women do very different kinds of work, it also clearly shows that working-class women played a significant role in the economic activity of their own and their families' lives. Prior to the Industrial Revolution, women worked on the farms and created cottage industries in their homes. These economic activities were rarely 'counted' in the official statistics. Even today, women's economic activity in rural communities may not be captured by statisticians and the same is true of some of the contributions made by women to family businesses in British Asian communities.

A second impression given in contemporary literature is that the 'business case' as a rationale for diversity management has only just been discovered. In fact, the business case has long underpinned labour market strategies which worked to the detriment of women and migrant workers. Thus the business case in the way labour was employed and rewarded shaped the patterns of inequality we know today. We may conclude that the business case faces two ways: the upbeat assessment of its value in contemporary equality and diversity discourse overlooks the perceived economic benefits of discrimination reaped by employers in the past and the present.

Employers, who were unable to fill vacancies, often because they offered poor pay and conditions, sought to employ successive groups of migrant workers. This pattern has been reproduced in different ways across different waves of migration. Similarly, as the labour market provided new opportunities for men, the jobs they vacated were often filled by women. Thus the demand for labour was a critical factor in racialising and gendering certain occupations. First-generation migrants were fitted in to lower level work that their white counterparts rejected in favour of more lucrative and higher status work. We see this process today in the case of the 'new migrants' discussed in Chapter 2.

Hierarchies were built into what might be perceived on the surface as similar work in manufacturing. We give an example of a textile factory, observed by the authors in the early seventies, where the different types of production work were gendered and racially segregated. The sewing-machine work was allocated to the white and occasionally Asian women. This was seen as the most pleasant of production work. The (extremely) noisy spinning work was allocated to the Caribbean women. The department manager stated that 'these women can cope with the work, they don't mind', attributing essentialist characteristics associated with the 'work-horse' to the Caribbean women (see Reynolds 2001). Those were the days of neither ear-muffs nor face masks to protect against the noise and dust. The paper-making was seen as the most skilled work and was the province of white men. The unskilled heavy work was carried out by Pakistani men (separated by region – this was prior to the formation of Bangladesh). When there was an economic downturn and white men began to ask for jobs, the manager stated that he did not want the white blokes, they didn't do what they were told 'like the Pakis do'. The office workers were white; the managers were white males, although there were two influential white women in personnel and marketing. Applications for office work from black workers, identifiable by names, were sifted out of any short-listing process by departmental managers. The porters were white men, as were the garage mechanics. Women were not entitled to enter the pension scheme, but men on the same level were. Women were not allowed to wear trousers, although mini-skirts were acceptable. Pay was very low but could be enhanced by shift premiums or by overtime. The Pakistani men were told about the low rates of pay when they arrived for the job interview (sometimes with an existing employee as translator) and were also informed that overtime was plentiful with some men working up to 80 hours per week. Thus the rationalisations for the different forms of segregation abounded and included, for example: Caribbean women don't mind noisy and dirty work; Pakistani men are compliant; women don't need pensions as they will be looked after by their husbands; it is not acceptable for women to wear trousers – thus rationalisations emerge which sought to justify both sexist and racist practices.

We offer this vignette as an example of the shape and degree of inequalities and the fineness of ethnic and gender segregation in British factories in the 1970s. It came to be understood that this was the way things were and it was clear where you would be placed if you applied for particular work and with whom you would work. These patterns of segregation did not emerge by accident; they reflected the gendered and racialised assumptions of the day and were reproduced in management strategies. Indeed, these patterns shaped recruiting practices, so that 'word of mouth' led to the reproduction of the ethnic composition of particular departments. It may seem like a by-gone age, but these practices and traditions are passed on, inculcated and reproduced in different situations and in different forms. They become characterised as the workplace culture; 'the way we do things here'. It is evident from this vignette that the stereotypes associated with particular ethnic groups were strong and reinforced in the work that they did. Their work began to define both who they were and what their attributes were in the eyes of the management, and no doubt future employers. Further, they learnt the attributes of the 'good worker' as compliant and prepared to work under unpleasant conditions without complaint; their alternative was to leave, or to resist (as we shall see in Chapter 6). Thus, Collinson et al.s' (1990) 'vicious circle of segregation' played out in the above and other organisations.

However, the benefit of an historical perspective shows that whilst partial truths associated with racist and sexist practice may remain resilient over time, historical perspectives allow us to capture change. For example, what seemed an entrenched rule that women were not allowed to wear trousers to work in the early part of the twenty-first century seems ludicrous and scarcely believable. Whilst such change was welcome, the central question to ask is how is the power balance altered as a result of such change. Women wearing trousers may be a metaphor for women's power, but the removal of the trouser ban has had little effect on the shape and distribution of gendered power relations.

The above vignette also captures Acker's (2006) account of the shape and degree of inequalities in this organisation; a pattern that was no doubt replicated throughout the country, particularly in the big cities and the northern textile towns. Yet it does not capture the discriminatory experi-ence emerging from the social processes in these organisations nor the relentless and unrewarding nature of much of the work undertaken, nor the hatred that would sometimes be meted out to visible migrants in the streets. In those days, racist sexism and sexist racism were direct, unsubtle and unambiguous. And what of today? Chapter 8 will explore the way that sexism and racism (and its intersection) is experienced, rationalised and reproduced in Britain. Employers' strategies are the main focus of this chapter and it is to these that we now turn.

Employer action on equality and diversity

It is evident that employers continue to exclude particular groups. A contemporary analysis provides some harsh facts on the UK labour market. Wrench and Modood (2001) report that:

- Longitudinal surveys show that ethnic minority school leavers across Britain are having less success than whites even when other factors, such as educational attainment, are held constant.
- Discrimination tests show that people can be rejected at the first stage of application simply by having an Asian name or coming from a non-white ethnic background.
- Gatekeeper studies show how some employers operated according to ethnic stereotypes and prejudices, and sometimes took account of the racist preferences of their white workforce.
- Research on employment agencies identifies further routines of exclusion. For example, agency employees anticipate the rejection of ethnic minority candidates by their client employers and thus avoid submitting them to employers, thereby perpetuating the processes of exclusion.
- Interviews with ethnic minorities themselves showed that an aware-ness of potential discrimination can itself constrain their job-seeking behaviour.

Our own work would confirm many of these concerns (see Bradley, Healy et al. 2007; Healy and Oikelome 2006), arguing that there is a wide gap between policy and practice. We shall return to this later in this chapter.

Employing organisations have choices in the way that they deal with the shape and degree of inequalities in their organisations both now and in the past. Yet, as we shall see, they are unlikely to challenge these patterns without being required to do so; even then the steps they take may be minimal.

The previous chapter has discussed the role of the state in seeking to eliminate discrimination. Such legislation was designed to challenge these early patterns of inequalities. The second Race Relations Act 1976 and the Sex Discrimination Act 1975 introduced important concepts of indirect discrimination and were accompanied by codes of practice which were not legally binding, but might be used in evidence in legal proceedings. The laws also allowed for positive action with respect to an acknowledged disadvantaged group and included exceptions to the law under the concept of Genuine Occupational Requirement. In many ways, given the shape and degree of segregation in Britain at the time, these acts were shaped in the liberal paradigm, but even within these constraints, their potential to challenge discrimination was never fully realised. Indeed, their weaknesses soon became the object of demands for further reform from the EOC and CRE. These laws never went as far as those in the United States nor the later legislation passed in Northern Ireland, both of which introduced different forms of affirmative action and the ability of appellants to take class actions.

The codes of practice (which may be used in evidence in a tribunal case) in many ways set the parameters for the content of the drafting of the multitude of equal opportunities policies in organisations. Thus equal opportunities policies also tend to reflect what Jewson and Mason (1986) call the liberal approach, as described in Chapter 3, and which is ensconced in legislation. On balance, the codes tended not to go beyond this to a radical agenda or indeed to adopt Cockburn's (1991) long agenda. Yet these early codes set the scene for organisational policy development and offer potential resources to challenge discriminatory practices.

Legal compliance is important in influencing the strategies of many organisations. Whilst we may complain that the law is without teeth; nevertheless, it may act as an incentive for good practice. As we saw in Chapter 4, the economic costs from tribunals may be high: we argue elsewhere that there is also the reputational damage which may be a major factor for many high-profile organisations (Bradley, Healy et al. 2007).

The law sets out the framework, but it is up to employers, trade unions and employees to observe the principles of the law. Indeed, much of the diversity management discourse suggests that organisations go beyond the legislation. We would question this. Walsh (2007) sees the objective of EO policies as ensuring equal access to job opportunities by eliminating differential treatment based on an individual's social group identity, such as their sex, race, age or disability. Our work reveals that policies take many shapes and forms; they may be highly sophisticated and detailed or simple statements of intent (Bradley, Healy et al. 2007). Further, we show that there may not always be a relationship between the complexity and sophistication of the policy and the fairness of the workplace practice. Straw (1989) identified three levels of EO policy: EO as equal chance (non-discrimination); EO as equal access (fair procedures) and EO as an equal share (outcomes and positive action). It is the third Straw sees as ideal, since at this level not only is access and representation gained, there is representation at every level and it includes particular measures taken to provide opportunities not previously available.

In reality there is considerable variation in the nature and scope of policies and this variation reflects the differences between organisations. Healy (1993) provides a typology of organisations according to their approach to equal opportunities. This is an analytical construct for understanding different organisational approaches. It is not a series of inevitable steps through which an organisation must move; rather it is a continuum which allows the dynamic nature of organisational practice to be exposed showing both improvement and deterioration in practice. The types of organisations are:

1. **Negative organisation.** A negative organisation will not have an EO policy nor will it have knowledge of legislative requirements; it will make no claims to provide equal opportunities and the institutional belief is that such policies are not necessary as the organisation does not discriminate. Alternatively, the negative organisation may consciously discriminate.
2. **Minimalist/partial organisation.** This organisation will have an espoused equal opportunities policy. It will tend to focus on informality as the method of management. Its recruitment methods will emphasise acceptablity rather than suitability, and equal opportunities will have a low priority and profile. There is no attempt to assess outcomes.
3. **Compliant organisation.** The compliant organisation will take a more self-conscious and professional approach to equal opportunities. It will be careful to fulfil its legal obligations; it will have developed a

formal approach backed by training. Policies and procedures will reflect accepted 'good practice' as set out by the statutory agencies. Assessment of outcomes will be partial. EO take their place alongside other strategic developments and their level of priority will depend on their significance to the organisation at a particular moment. The focus is likely to be on the contribution EO principles make to solving labour shortage problems rather than on resolving problems of discrimination.

4. **Comprehensive proactive organisation.** The proactive organisation will have a dynamic approach to equal opportunities. It will have many of the characteristics of the compliant organisation. The proactive organisation will carefully assess outcomes in relation to a workforce audit and develop future strategies accordingly. Positive action approaches will be a feature of this organisation and EO retain a high priority alongside other strategic develolpments. Resolving problems of discrimination will be of equal importance as the labour market dimension. The implementation of EO practices will be 'with enthusiasm'. The organisation will measure the outputs of EO both quantitatively and qualitatively.

WERS 2004 allows us to consider how organisations fare according to this typology. The Workplace Employment Relations Survey is a national survey of workplaces jointly sponsored by the Department of Trade and Industry, the Advisory Conciliation and Arbitration Service (ACAS), the ESRC and the Policy Studies Institute (PSI). It follows on from earlier surveys which were conducted in 1980, 1984, 1990 and 1998. The purpose of the surveys has been to provide large-scale, statistically reliable evidence about a broad range of industrial relations and employment practices. The methodology has changed over the years, but currently the survey collects information from managers with responsibility for employment relations or personnel matters; trade union or employee representatives; and employees themselves.

WERS sheds light on changes in the coverage and scope of EO policies and practices in British workplaces since 1998. Drawing on Walsh (2007), we summarise the changes below:

- There has been a growth in the proportion of workplaces with a formal written EO policy or a policy on managing diversity. By 2004, nearly three-quarters (73 per cent) of workplaces with ten or more employees had a formal written EO policy, compared with just less than two-thirds (64 per cent) in 1998 (Walsh 2007:237).

- Just over a quarter of surveyed workplaces (26 per cent) did not possess formal written EO policies, and, as might be predicted, they tended to be smaller, private-sector workplaces, with no union presence.
- There has been an expansion in the incidence of EO policies in private-sector workplaces (from 55 per cent in 1998 to 68 per cent in 2004.
- The scope of EO policies has also been enhanced. The findings show that, in 2004, almost two-thirds of workplaces (64 per cent) had EO policies that referred to equality of treatment or discrimination with respect to particular criteria, most commonly sex/gender, race and disability.
- EO policies are increasingly being refashioned to reflect the new criteria of religion, sexual orientation and age, with policies covering these grounds distinctly more prevalent in 2004 than in 1998.
- EO policies were more common in larger workplaces, especially those with at least 100 employees and those which were part of a larger organisation.
- Furthermore, EO policies were almost universally prevalent in the public sector, reflecting the various legislative pressures and targets imposed on public-sector organisations which compels them into being compliant organisations (Healy 1993).
- There was also a higher incidence of EO policies in workplaces with an HR specialist (92 per cent of workplaces compared with less than one-half of workplaces without a specialist). Indeed, the WERS 2004 team found that the presence of HR specialists was positively related to the provision of EO policies quite independently of the effect of workplace size. It appears that HR managers play an influential role in the enactment of a wide variety of equity-based employment policies.

As the typology indicates, having an EO policy is not sufficient. Nevertheless, after 40 years of equality legislation, it is quite shocking that at least a quarter of British organisations may be classified as 'negative' EO organisations without even a nod to equality.

The issue of the equality implementation gap between policy and practice has been a recurring concern in ours and others work (Bradley, Healy and Mukherjee 2002; Bradley, Healy et al. 2007; Creegan, Colgan et al. 2003; Healy and Oikelome 2006). Furthermore, based on an analysis of WERS 1998, Hoque and Noon (2004) assessed whether policies were 'substantive' or merely 'empty shells': and conclude that on balance, the 'empty shell' argument is more convincing.

Nevertheless, the written documents take on a life of their own. As Ahmed (2007) argues, the documents are taken up as symbols of good performance, as expressions of commitment, and as descriptions of organisations as 'being diverse'. She concludes that such documents work to conceal forms of racism when they get taken up in this way. Thus the existence of a myriad of policies provides a public face for an organisation's approach to equality that may have little substance in practice. Nevertheless, we argue that policy documents are important as they may provide the tools for resistance to strategic inaction. Thus texts can provide a crucial resource for individuals and trade unions in their attempts to ensure that organisations comply with their own policies. Further, where texts are the outcome of collective decision-making through negotiation and consultation, Healy (1997) argues that they become important tools in the practice of industrial relations. But for this to happen, it is necessary for key actors to challenge disadvantage and draw on available power resources, of which the texts or documents may be only one. We shall see examples in the next chapters of how BME women activists used policies in this way. However, where the endless writing of policies becomes an end in itself, the texts, as Ahmed argues, get in the way of the practice. The title of Ahmed's paper is particularly telling: 'you end up doing the document rather than doing the doing' (Ahmed 2007).

WERS 2004 is also valuable for assessing the extent to which such policies have been operationalised and the extent to which organisations may be classified on the continuum between negative and proactive organisations. The assessment of outcomes was an important aspect that took an organisation beyond the minimalist/partial type. Using monitoring as one measure of this, WERS 2004 found:

- Only a minority of workplaces – less than one in four – sought to monitor or review their procedures to identify indirect discrimination with respect to gender, ethnicity, disability or age (Kersley, Alpin et al. 2005).
- One-fifth and one-quarter of all workplaces monitored and reviewed procedures relating to recruitment and selection and only one in ten workplaces did so with respect to promotions.
- Few reviewed relative pay rates (5 per cent for ethnicity and 7 per cent for gender).
- There was a much greater likelihood of managerial monitoring in larger workplaces, as well as in workplaces that were part of a larger organisation and in unionised workplaces.

- Public sector workplaces were more inclined to engage in EO measurement than those in the private sector (27 per cent compared with 14 per cent).

These findings are cause for concern. The majority of organisations has not sought to identify the shape and degree of inequalities and therefore must be unable to identify where action is needed. On the above measures, most organisations would fall into Healy's (1993) minimalist/ partial EO organisational type.

A distinguishing characteristic of the comprehensive organisation is the use of positive action strategies. Again drawing on WERS 2004 findings, we find such usage very limited:

- Only 18 per cent of British workplaces had procedures to encourage applications from groups such as women, ethnic minority employees, older and disabled employees or the unemployed.
- Only 4 per cent sought to target four or more groups.
- There was a greater likelihood of targeting in workplaces with formal EO policies and in the public sector.
- The incidence of special procedures to attract applications from ethnic minorities has actually fallen in the public sector (especially the health sector) despite the legal requirement to promote race equality.

This assessment of WERS suggests that few organisations could be classified as comprehensive proactive organisations. This has serious implications for those who are disadvantaged. The British workplace is a long way away from the long agenda envisioned by Cockburn (1991).

Towards managing diversity?

The discussion so far has been in the context and language of equal opportunities. Yet there has been a discursive turn from equal opportunities to diversity management. This has led to a polarised debate between the equal opportunities and the diversity management approaches. Indeed, these are frequently presented as competing approaches and the view often conveyed is that diversity management has usurped the equal opportunities approach, which from this perspective is seen as old fashioned and less relevant. We take the view that this polarised picture is damaging and unhelpful to understanding what the dynamics of inequality are. It becomes a distraction to overcoming the gap between policy and practice. Arguably, diversity management is presented as an alternative to the backlash to the equal opportunities approach and as a fresh new approach that embraces everyone. We consider this debate because we fear that its approach will lead us still further from a radical or long agenda approach to challenging inequalities and discrimination in organisations.

The meaning of the term managing 'diversity' is contested both in the United Kingdom and the United States (Liff 1999). For some diversity is seen as simply a broader version of equal opportunities. Kossek and Lobel (1996), for example, consider diversity to be not only derived from differences in ethnicity and gender but it is also based on differences in function, nationality, language, ability, religion, lifestyle or tenure. For others, diversity is not only a difference in degree but also in kind from equal opportunities.

Some writers describe the two as ideal types in terms of the old paradigm (equal opportunities) and the new paradigm (managing diversity) (Wilson 1996; Wilson and Iles 1999). These paradigms are shown in Table 5.1.

To show a paradigmatic change and demonstrate the 'new' concept, it is often seen as necessary to discredit the 'old' concept. Yet such a demonstration often attributes the old with a distorted view of reality as Table 5.1 might portray. With respect to equal opportunities and its link to legislation, it is not difficult to point out the failures: the continued reality of racism and sexism, the gender and ethnicised pay gap, the lip-service that is paid to the equalities debate. All of this is without question. However, to put this at the door of an equal opportunities approach *per se* is reifying a concept that rests on agency at all institutional levels. We would argue that in all organisations, there are both external and internal

Table 5.1 Equal opportunities and managing diversity compared

The old paradigm: equal opportunities	The new paradigm: managing diversity
Externally driven	Internally driven
Operational	Strategic
Diversity perceived as a liability	Diversity perceived as an asset
Group focused	Individual focused
Concerned minimally with process	Concerned with outcomes in EO
Perceive EO costs money	Accept 'business case' for embracing diversity
Supported by narrow positivist Knowledge base	Supported by wider pluralistic Knowledge base

drivers for equality initiatives, that equality approaches will have both strategic and operational elements and the balance on both these points may well be the result of legislative pressures. Perceptions of liability are central to both approaches, arguably the equal opportunities approach focused on the individual as well as the group, and of course the diversity approach claims to focus on the individual but also focuses on the group; differentiating between process and outcome is an arbitrary distinction and does not reflect the reality of some early EO approaches; there is no evidence that EO costs money and diversity makes money – both may be relevant to solving a labour supply problem; the importance of a pluralist knowledge base is not necessarily the prerogative of the diversity approach, nor is a positivist knowledge base the monopoly of the EO approach. In short, a straw concept may have been built in order to shift the discourse and the emphasis of approach.

The Chartered Institute of Personnel Management (CIPD) is the professional body for human resource specialists and influences the content of the training of human resource and equality specialists. We compare Straw's (1989) *Equal Opportunities* text with Daniels and Macdonald's (2005) text on *Equality, Diversity and Discrimination*; both texts aimed to develop professional expertise in the Institute's examination and by implication their subsequent professional practice. The comparison does reveal a difference in language, with Straw (1989) focusing on equality, whereas Daniels and Macdonald (2005) engage explicitly with the diversity concept. Yet despite a difference in language, the substance of both books is geared to building competence and understanding of the legislation; it is accepted that such competences are critical tools for effective human resource management. Today's students will no doubt 'talk the talk' of diversity, but their practices may have a significant continuity with those adopted some 16 years earlier.

Much of the comparative discussion rests with emphasis in the managing diversity approach on the business case; by implication this was of little concern to those who advocated the EO approach. Yet within the EO approach, Straw (1989) claimed that the overwhelming reason why EO policies were now centre stage was because in the current climate they made good business sense. The climate to which she referred was the changes in the mid-eighties in Britain of the structure of employment from manufacturing to a growth of the service sector, the impact of demographic factors due to the decline of the number of young people and other social factors. Straw argued that there was greater public pressure for change, resulting from greater public awareness of the social results of discrimination through media coverage; this included the rise in feminism, inner-city riots, racial harassment and physical abuse capturing the headlines. For Straw, morality remained central but this was accompanied by concern about the human wastage involved. Collins (1992, 1995) set out to provide guidance to employers and managers, but no mention was made of diversity. Yet the business case underpinned many of the texts, including the importance of compliance. Despite this, Greene, Kirton and Wrench (2005) argue that scholars tend to equate the EO approach very much with the moral case. The reality is that advocates of equal opportunities have always drawn on the business case as well, in its various forms, in order to convince those most resistant to change.

The danger comes when the managing diversity approach is stripped of any moral underpinning and rests exclusively on the business case. What happens when there is no evident case for diversity? This is the major concern of those who mount a critique of the diversity paradigm (Kirton and Greene 2006; Noon 2007). Whilst the pragmatic use of the business case may serve to achieve difficult ends, ultimately we can never lose sight of the social justice principles which must underpin the values of equality and diversity.

Both approaches are concerned with process and outcome. The managing diversity approach may stress outcome in its discourse, yet the evidence for major change in outcomes is yet to be found (Kirton and Greene 2000; Noon 2007). Indeed, the recent evidence from WERS 2004 (discussed above) underlines this.

Equally the individual focus of managing diversity is found wanting. For example, Foster and Harris (2005) found in their study of diversity management in retail that line managers, familiar with the value of demonstrating a common approach in their decision-making as the key means of defence against claims of discriminatory treatment, regarded a diversity management agenda concerned with recognising and responding to individual differences as more likely to lead to feelings of unfairness and claims of unequal treatment. This would seem a particularly telling point since our previous research has shown the pivotal role the line manager can play in both enabling and resisting equality initiatives (Bradley, Healy et al. 2007; Healy and Oikelome 2006). Indeed, we argue that the translation from top-down to local implementation which goes beyond the necessary compliance approach is focused at this level, and it is here that the 'implementation gap' may be most acute.

Kirton and Greene (2006) examine the perception trade unions have of the managing diversity discourse. They demonstrate that the main concern expressed by unions was that the upbeat rhetoric of the diversity discourse diverts attention from the realities of discrimination and disadvantage. Their research also reveals that introducing the diversity discourse might help unions to refresh a flagging commitment to 'equal opportunities' by providing a 'new look' for equality, whilst not losing sight of old inequalities (Kirton and Greene 2006:445). This research is important since it indicates that unions were pragmatically adopting the diversity discourse, exploiting the lack of stability in the diversity concept and knowingly seeking to reshape it in their relationships with management.

Notwithstanding the inherent similarities in the two approaches, we should acknowledge some of the fundamental concerns with the overall approach to challenging inequalities through managing diversity. It is widely recognised that managing diversity as a discrete concept was originally adopted in the United States, where the dominant perspective on equality was that of affirmative action (as discussed in the previous chapter), whereas in Britain it was the more benign 'positive action'. That managing diversity was a response to affirmative action in the United States (Gilbert, Stead and Ivancevich 1999) resonates strongly with those who are committed to overcoming inequalities. If affirmative action had some strength and delivered some results, why should it be replaced by a less strong tool, the more individualistic managing diversity? It raises the question as to the extent to which managing diversity was introduced as a response to the backlash against affirmative action in the United States and therefore as a way to render it powerless.

The discourse on diversity seeks instead to show the claimed benefits of this 'new' and 'more effective' approach, rather than the political and difficult realities associated with the challenging of inequalities. In doing so, it depoliticises the equality process and seeks to remove power from any organisational analysis. Further with its focus on the 'unique individual' it looks for individualist rather than structural explanations for disadvantage. Whilst we argue that the notion of a paradigmatic shift is questionable, the focus on the individual rather than the group has the potential to lead to a contradictory series of practices which may further intensify patterns of discrimination.

Nevertheless, it is quite clear that the EO approach has been limited in its impact. The question must be whether the lack of progress lies with *the nature of the approach*, or the *power dynamics* around those who seek to implement such an approach. These same power dynamics may embed the discursive turn to diversity by privileging only those individuals who are seen to benefit an organisation in its 'war for talent'. This leaves the most vulnerable at the mercy of the market, indicating that a literal shift to managing diversity is a step back in challenging inequalities.

Employer policy and practice – case study examples

We focus in this part of the chapter on the kind of organisations where the women in our study worked. As explained in Chapter 1, the women in this study were all trade union members and therefore worked in organisations which recognised a trade union. As we have seen, organisations that recognise trade unions were more likely to have made some progress in equality and diversity. The firms which recognised the unions in our study (CWU, NATFHE, UNISON and USDAW) were in the following sectors: telecommunications, postal, universities and colleges, health and local authorities, and retail and warehousing. A brief assessment of the kind of equality policies and practices adopted by such organisations suggests that the language of both equality and diversity is evident. As a basis for this, we looked at a random selection of organisations' websites and their statements about equality and diversity posted in August 2007. Of note is how few policy statements relate to the intersectional nature of equality and diversity, therefore black and ethnic minority women tend not to be directly addressed.

CWU members are employed in telecommunications and postal work. Thus they face polar opposites in their two main employers: BT which is considered one of the most progressive organisations in the field of equality and diversity, and the Royal Mail, which has been characterised as an organisational dinosaur with respect to equality (Jenkins, Lucio and Noon 2002). Jenkins argued that the power relations between the actors in the Royal Mail remain resilient and that the processes that have sustained postal work as a gendered job continue to segregate men and women's work at the level of the workplace.

BT uses the language of equal opportunities and sameness and concern for groups on its website in order to publicly promote its approach to equalities:

> We are an equal opportunities employer. Our policies clearly state that everyone should have the same opportunities for employment and promotion based on their ability, qualifications and suitability for the work in question.

> In this, we're ahead of current legislation. We make sure that no job applicant or employee receives less favourable treatment because of

their race, sex, religion/belief, disability, marital or civil partnership status, age, sexual orientation, gender identity, gender expression or caring responsibilities. Where possible, we will also take positive measures to recruit any under-represented minority group.

USDAW members work in retail and warehouses. Using Tesco, again a unionised employer, as an example of the retail sector, we find a combination of what is perceived as EO and diversity language. Thus the business case is crucial, but so is the focus on sameness and need to consider categories by group. The very positive messages in these statements suggest an employer who is serious about equality and diversity issues:

Everyone is welcome

Our success depends on people and we're all different and diverse. We believe we can't afford to be complacent around diversity issues and are continually working on initiatives to attract people from all backgrounds.

We aim to employ people who reflect the diverse nature of society and we value people and their contribution, irrespective of age, sex, disability, sexual orientation, race, colour, religion or ethnic origin.

We also try and make sure everyone can work in a way that suits their circumstances – we support flexible working, offering part-time roles and encouraging job-sharing opportunities and shift-swapping where possible.

University and college academic staff is represented by the Universities and Colleges Union, formed from the merger of the Association of Universities Teachers and NATFHE (our case study union). The support staff is represented by another of our case study unions, UNISON (see Chapter 6). Universities and colleges each deal with their own equality and diversity strategies, but they do have an employers' organisation, Equality Challenge, that seeks to provide a resource on equality and diversity for the higher and further education institutions it represents. Again we see a mix of both equality and diversity language, but the group approach dominates:

Its mission is to realise the potential of all staff and students whatever their race, gender, disability, sexual orientation, religion or age, to the benefit of those individuals, higher education institutions and society. Its strategy is to:

- develop an authoritative system for identifying and measuring equality and diversity in the higher education sector, and to assess the impact of equality initiatives
- support higher education institutions in implementing effective equality practices and ensure practices is correct
- disseminate the many examples of excellent practice in individual institutions for the benefit of the whole sector
- develop programmes that support sustained institutional change in relation to equality and diversity

Thus we can see that all these employers make recourse to a rhetoric of equality *and* diversity, although, as we shall see in Chapter 7, this does not necessarily translate into genuine equality of opportunities for all their employees. As we know, there is clear evidence of men dominating the hierarchies of universities and that universities' equality strategies are limited (Bradley, Healy et al. 2007; Deem and Morley 2006; Healy, Ozbilgin and Aliefendioglu 2005).

This can be seen in the case of our final example, which we present in more detail. This is the health sector, where UNISON is one of the main trade unions. We decided to choose one sector to study in greater detail as it allows us to consider the range of strategies a complex organization might adopt. We choose the health service since it is a major employer of women and black and minority ethnic workers and it is part of the public sector and therefore subject to more stringent legislation on equality and diversity than its private-sector counterparts. In addition, we should say that the health service has taken equality and diversity very seriously in the range of initiatives that have been adopted.

Nevertheless, it is evident from a range of studies that the health service has deep-seated problems with respect to discrimination and disadvantage (Lemos and Crane 2000; Oikelome and Healy 2007). It is an organisation that is hugely complex in its patterns of inequality. Its hierarchies are riven by status difference which range from highly qualified and skilled professionals to lowly paid ancillary workers. Thus the shape and degree of inequalities is particularly complex, with BME staff occupying both the highest levels and the lowest in the organisation. Problems of discrimination and disadvantage tend to be located in occupational silos within the larger organisations. Thus even highly qualified professionals may face structural barriers within their professional career structures (Oikelome and Healy 2007).

Part of NHS planning over the next ten years is the recognition that modernisation and reform is taking place within the context of a diverse, multicultural society and one of its key challenges is to ensure that services meet the needs and aspirations of all in an increasingly diverse society. It also needs to deliver on the Race Relations Amendment Act (RRAA). Thus legislation is a key driver. This has led to several Initiatives such as Positively Diverse, Improving Working Lives, The Vital Connection, Leadership and the Race Equality Action Plan.

Together these provide a comprehensive programme of initiatives aimed to ensure among other things, strong community links, positive action strategies, indicators and monitoring arrangements, targets, board training on equality and diversity and the encouragement and mentoring of black leaders. The most potentially contentious of these strategies is positive action, which is often criticised both by those who fear they will lose out and by the potential beneficiaries who do not want to be seen as receiving special favours. Notwithstanding these concerns, Healy and Oikelome (2006) argue that positive action is an important tool that can have an important effect on people's careers and lives. For example, the provision of health services needs to be informed by the different health needs of ethnic minority communities. It is noteworthy that the NHS is taking a proactive response with respect to its advice on positive action, that is, it is legal and, in certain circumstances, encouraged by the Department of Health. This is because positive action, according to the website:

- seeks to support groups in society which have been disadvantaged in the past
- helps to address some of the imbalances which still exist between staff in the NHS and the communities we serve
- can bring real benefits to organisations by widening recruitment channels and consequently broadening the experience, knowledge and ideas influencing the organization.

Thus we see a range of initiatives which in their totality and their interrelationships may be quite difficult to grasp, but which do provide a battery of techniques aimed at tackling equality and diversity from different perspectives at different levels. Indeed, arguably, we see action that reproduces a liberal approach, but does go some way to engaging with more radically based initiatives and analytically places the NHS towards the proactive organisation end of the continuum. However, until their impact is clear, this may be an over-optimistic assessment. Whilst the initiatives have not been fully evaluated, their introduction offers grounds for hope; we wait to learn how they work in practice.

Healy and Oikelome (2006), also analysed the NHS good practice database (http://data.ali.gov.uk/goodpracticedb/frameset) with respect to 16 trusts across England, to determine the extent to which the initiatives in the respective trusts are seeking to change either the culture or the individual. Their purpose in highlighting this distinction was, first, to recognise the importance of both approaches. We argue elsewhere that both approaches are essential (Bradley, Healy et al. 2007) It is, however, also to acknowledge that whilst individuals' relationship with the organisational culture is critical and may work to shape that culture, equally the individual may work to achieve their own career interests in relative isolation. Initiatives that focus on the individual may improve individual careers and contribute to a more representative workforce and increase the number of role models. All of this will go some way to challenging the culture, as there is clearly an interrelationship between it and the individual. However, it is also important to put resources into tackling the culture, as this investment may be more sustainable in the longer term. Indeed, it is the transformation of cultures wherein lies part of the solution to the 'implementation gap' ((Bradley, Healy et al. 2007; Healy and Oikelome 2006). We are reminded of Liff's (1999) concern that an individual focus may leave the culture untouched.

The analysis revealed that the majority of the initiatives are seemingly focused on changing the individual (e.g., mentoring, personal development, training). Interestingly, projects which focused on cultural change were in the minority, but appear to have greater impact (Healy and Oikelome 2006). Healy and Oikelome outline a particularly interesting example called a 'Diversity Action Partnership: Making Diversity Training a Two-Way Process'. This was described as 'a novel training method, which used Diversity-Training-as-Theatre which included staff in active and significant community collaboration, providing a unique opportunity for large-scale exposure, interaction, and valuable integration opportunities between staff and their communities.' The outcome of this initiative in terms of challenging attitudes and behaviour was that this method had 'impact' and represented *'the best training event they'd ever had'* (Healy and Oikelome 2006). A more conventional example was in a trust where 'following the introduction of the new policy, the percentage of Black and minority ethnic staff increased from 3.9 per cent to 4.7 per cent and staff awareness of the policy rose from 30 per cent to 62 per cent over a year'. The trust was able to link this outcome (through monitoring recruitment, specific questions in the annual staff survey, collecting feedback from staff throughout the organisation, and monitoring claims of discrimination and harassment) with the fact that the strategy focused on training middle managers to understand and appreciate why valuing staff and having a good equality and diversity policy are so important. This point is significant, especially in the light of this and other research which pinpoints middle managers being the major obstacle in preventing reforms planned at the top from cascading down to the staff for whom they are intended (Healy and Oikelome 2006). These examples suggest that when employers use creative strategies they may often reap benefits and, further, that the importance of following through and monitoring the introduction of new initiatives in different ways is crucial. So often a good idea is introduced and not followed through nor monitored for outcomes.

The example of the health service provides insight into an organisation which shows evidence of commitment to challenging discrimination and disadvantage, whether this is in the workplace or in service delivery. However, the above discussion has been based on employers' public statements and monitoring outcomes. As such, we might expect some bias and at the minimum some filtering of the data allowed in the public domain. Nevertheless, the detailed exposition of this example leads to a final consideration of organisation culture. For us, change in organisational culture is not simple, straightforward and inevitable; it will always be constrained by existing power relations within an organisation and the desire by many of those in authority to restrict access to knowledge and organisational resources. Whilst we recognise the realities and constraints of organisational life, the need for cultural change is nevertheless immense.

The above examples demonstrate the ease with which organisations move between equal opportunities and the diversity language; between sameness and difference, between individual and group. Given what we know about the shape and pattern of discrimination and its resilience, the importance of group disadvantage remains central to any meaningful initiatives on equality and diversity with respect to gender and ethnicity.

Yet the central question for this book is, what are employers doing to help BME women in their organisations? Many of the initiatives that we have discussed potentially benefit individual men and women of minority groups. Indeed, it is difficult to find initiatives specifically related to minority women. Sometimes such initiatives emerge with respect to gendered occupations; for exmple, teachers and social workers. In our work for the EOC we found that positive action remains a central mechanism to combat disadvantage. With respect to women, Tower Hamlets' positive action schemes include the encouragement of Bangladeshi and Somali people to train as social workers and occupational therapists; similar schemes are in place to train teachers and teaching assistants (Bradley, Healy et al. 2007). Thus, these schemes are encouraging women from underrepresented groups to take advantage of professional development opportunities. In the same study, we noted how technology is used to encourage young women and men from different ethnic groups. Sometimes this could be by means of images of young women and men from different ethnic groups, thus giving the message that the organisation is inclusive in its recruitment strategies. Further, technology and printed material allows images of women in religious dress working in positions of responsibility. Again important messages are conveyed pictorially.

The importance of networks emerged in our various studies. Such networks allow access to influential and supportive people who may become future sponsors. Further, the importance of role models was a recurring theme in our EOC Study:

> When I see a black person in a top position it motivates you, okay, you can get there as well.
>
> (Caribbean woman)

In our various studies, when BME women are seen to succeed, they become particularly important role models. This in itself can cause them difficulty in that they are often used as committee members, speakers at public events and the like in order to demonstrate the diversity of an organization. If they are one of very few, this puts an unacceptable demand on their time.

Concluding comments

The above picture does not lead us to have high expectations that employers will be agents of transformation. Whilst we have noted good practice, overall the picture is one of limited action, which is not centrally driven by the belief in social justice.

In the above discussion, groups are presented as characterised by, for example, their ethnicity or their sex. Black and minority ethnic women are the centre of this book, and of course these categorisations mean that potentially they would fall between the categories and become invisible in both. We do not suggest moving away from the importance of group identities, but believe that it is necessary to refine them. This does not take us to the individualism inherent in the diversity approach. Instead, it brings us to an intersectional approach as a more fruitful way forward.

Chapter 3 considered intersectionality theoretically, whereas Bradley et al. (2007) also explored the practical implications of this approach. The United Nations and other agencies have increasingly used the concept of 'intersectionality' in the analysis of inequalities and the development of EDP. As discussed in Chapter 3, intersectionality issues arise when an individual does not suffer a single form of discrimination, but is subject to a number of discriminatory forms at once. We argue elsewhere that critical to the task of addressing inequalities and improving BME women's experiences of work is uncovering the ways multiple discrimination converges to create and worsen experiences of disadvantage in the workplace. We also draw on the (United Nations 2001) framework and suggest that an 'intersectionality proofing' framework might have several distinct components:

1. Data collection and audit, including attention to culture.
2. Contextual analysis: using the data to diagnose what particular problems exist, with a strong focus on how multiple disadvantages may be displayed (e.g., are Asian women in lower positions than Asian men?).
3. Review existing policies, initiatives and systems of implementation and alter them if they are not being effective.
4. Determine priorities, in consultation with the relevant groups of employees (different groups of women may experience different types of problems so each group should be allowed to voice their concerns).
5. Identify leaders and champions to take implementation forward and raise its profile in the organisation.
6. Implementation of intersectional policy and initiatives with action to embed it throughout the organisation.
7. Monitor the outcomes and publicise achievements.

The above may seem familiar to those involved in implementing equality and diversity policies. But the key difference is that throughout the above processes, the differential impact of the shape and degrees of inequality (Acker 2006) in an organisation are explored, rather than conflated into broad categories of sex or ethnic origin. However, we must also recognise that implementation of action along these lines seems a distant dream, if the progress identified by WERS 2004 is an indicator.

The earlier chapters have shown the differences in the shape and degrees of different women's lives. In the forthcoming chapters the importance of intersectionality will be brought to life through the stories of the women in this study on their working lives. In the meantime, this chapter suggests that whilst employers have the potential and the power resources to be agents of transformation, their record in general has to date been unimpressive. We therefore turn to the other key actor in the frame, the trade unions.

6
Towards Transformation: Trade Union Strategies

In 2000, Britain's largest trade union, UNISON, issued its own charter for black women. Such charters have become popular as part of a move to make trade unions appear more democratic and inclusive and thus appeal to new potential areas of membership. The TUC produced its first Charter for Women in 1979. The TUC and its constituent unions have made some real efforts to follow the precepts of the charters they have introduced.

UNISON has been renowned for taking a strong line on democracy and representation. As part of its reformed structure after the merger of three unions, COHSE, NALGO and NUPE, to form this new 'superunion', UNISON adopted principles of fair representation, proportionality and self-organisation. Proportionality means that representation on union structures should reflect the composition of the membership (e.g., if 60 per cent of members are women, the union should target having 60 per cent of the seats on its National Executive Committee filled by women) (see Kirton and Healy 1999). Self-organisation refers to allowing specific groups of members to have their own forms of representation. Thus UNISON set up a National Black Workers' Committee and a structure of black workers' groups at regional level, along with similar structures for women, disabled members and gays and lesbians. The charter is interesting, though, as it cuts across this structural arrangement, referring to a group disadvantaged on two axes: gender and ethnicity. It is thus an excellent example of policy reflecting the notion of intersectionality, discussed in previous chapters.

The Charter was produced by the National Black Members' Committee Women's Caucus, and read as follows:

Acknowledge my **Visibility**.
Enable me to **Participate**.

Empower me to contribute.
Respect **Me** and my culture.
Promote a **Black** perspective of **Awareness** and **Understanding**.
Emphasise your experience but **Empower** me to **Speak** for myself.
Respect me as an individual and not a stereotype of a 'perceived' typical **Black** woman.
Develop my individual **Skills** and **Abilities** to aid the decision-making process.

The charter states that it is designed to serve as a set of criteria for the union and the National Women's Committee in relating to them and to 'acknowledge our contribution as black women' in 'developing motions, policies, strategies and procedures'. These contributions, they indicate, are political, social, economic and personal.

UNISON's approach is indicative of ways that in the last decade unions have tried to develop new strategies to encourage BME workers to join unions and to cater more adequately for them when they are members. This has not always been the case, as we shall see. However, currently, trade unions can be seen as playing an important role in promoting the equality agenda. Moreover, this is a key site where issues of intersectionality can be explored as unions confront the structural problem of how best to cater for the specific needs of women, of BME workers, of disabled workers, but also to consider how these various needs may or may not be interrelated.

We start this chapter with a brief account of how a concern with racial discrimination evolved in the trade union movement, focusing on how unions have had to confront their own racism. We then survey the current situation, emphasising the variability of provision within different unions. Finally, we look at what is being done by our four case study unions. The chapter also serves to introduce these four unions to the reader. The chapter stresses the important work being done by the unions but also highlights some dilemmas which face them.

Little acorns: racism and anti-racism in the trade union movement

Unions have had a long and often conflictual history of engaging with the organisation of women workers. In the nineteenth century, women were often considered as secondary workers, working for 'pin money' as the old adage had it, by male workers and they faced discrimination and exclusionary techniques in some male-dominated unions. There were various experiments in separate unionism (women-only unions, the National Federation of Women Workers), but the general trend as the century progressed was to incorporate the women into male structures. Many suffragists also espoused the cause of equal union rights for women, and women's contributions to the 'war effort' in both the world wars forced a gradual, if sometimes grudging, acceptance of women members as equally important. This history has been explored in great detail elsewhere (Boston 1987, Braybon 1987, Bradley 1989, Kirton 2006) and will not be rehearsed further here. By the 1950s, however, while women were now an accepted part of the union movement, the organisation of BME workers had hardly been considered. However, the postwar immigration of commonwealth citizens, mainly from the Caribbean and the Indian subcontinent brought many BME workers into unionised jobs. Once again, the 'race riots' of the late 1950s brought tensions between the communities to the fore.

In a useful survey of unions' early responses to migrant workers (which was how they tended to be conceptualised in those days) Phizacklea and Miles (1992) distinguished three possible stances: to oppose further immigration and demand controls (as migrant workers are viewed as competition for jobs); to try and exclude them from the skilled and best-paid jobs (just as men had done with women in the nineteenth century); or to adopt an anti-racist and anti-colonialist politics and seek to include BME workers within the movement. All three stances have been displayed by British trade unions. Phizacklea and Miles point to the widespread nature of overt racism among many working people during the postwar period, which has been discussed in earlier chapters: this led to some exclusionary responses. For example, in 1954 the TUC General Council endorsed immigration controls and in the 1960s it initially declared opposition to the extension of the Race Relations Act to employment in 1968. However, these racist moves were opposed within the movement both by an active minority of white workers (often young left-wingers) and by BME workers themselves.

The second stance, excluding black workers from certain jobs, was practised by some local union branches during the postwar decades. In a number of notable cases, black workers demanded equal rights and access to jobs with their white co-workers For example, in the case of the Bristol Bus company where TGWU members had voted in 1955 to ban the employment of black conductors, local activists, including Bristol University students, organised a boycott against the company in 1963 (Dresser 2007). At Mansfield Hosiery Mills in 1972 and at Imperial Typewriters in 1976, both in Leicester, Asian workers struck because they were excluded from skilled jobs: in both cases the unions initially refused to support the strikers even though they and the companies were in breach of the RRA 1968. In 1977, the CRE carried out an investigation at British Leyland when 'the machine tool setters held a meeting refusing to accept the employment of black fitters' after which a black applicant was refused a job (Phizacklea and Miles 1992:38).

The irony in all this was that black and Asian workers were actually very likely to join unions, more so than some of their white co-workers. There was a strong tradition of Labour politics and trade unionism within the Caribbean islands which migrants brought with them to Britain's factories and hospitals. Community organisations, such as the Indian Workers' Association, also urged their members to action. This trend was still evident in 1997 when the results of the Fourth National Survey of ethnic minorities in Britain were published (Modood, Berthoud et al. 1997). The researchers found that workers from all minority groups except Pakistanis and Bangladeshis had higher levels of union membership. This was true both for men and for women. The highest levels of membership were among black Caribbean workers. This was not just a passive and protective type of membership either. BME workers were prepared to engage in industrial action (Lee 1987). For example, in the famous and long-lasting strike at Grunwick film processing company from 1976–8, Asian women workers took the lead. This could be seen as a key turning point, as members of other unions, such as the postal workers, took secondary action in support of the women and mass picketing was supported by a variety of union and anti-racist groups.

Given the positive attitudes of BME workers to union organisation, despite their experience of racist responses from some co-workers and shop stewards, it was clearly in unions' interests to consider the needs of BME workers, especially during the 1980s when union membership began to decline. Moreover, vigorous campaigns had by now been waged by various anti-racist groups, such as the Anti-Nazi League and Rock against Racism. The Labour Party, before its defeat by Margaret Thatcher's regime, had softened its politics on immigration and was espousing the new political approach of multiculturalism. However, some unions, especially those representing manual workers, took what Phizacklea and Miles label a 'colour-blind approach'. They quote a response by the TGWU to a Greater London Council (GLC) survey asking unions about activities used to encourage minority ethnic members' participation:

All members are equal, therefore no problems. To have it separate means we are fighting the race issue rather than the class issues.

(Phizacklea and Miles 1992:42)

As Phizacklea and Miles note, such 'colour-blindness' may be a cover for racism; and at the very least it may be an excuse for not doing anything about the 'race issue'. The same, of course, applies to 'gender-blindness' which has also been a common response over the years.

Big oaks: trade union initiatives and the equality agenda

There have been massive changes since the GLC survey was carried out. In 1981 the TUC launched its Black Workers' Charter and subsequently it has worked hard to persuade its member unions to develop policies and structures for race equality. In 1987 Gloria Lee noted the failure of many unions to take it seriously, stating that persuasion without compulsion is ineffective unless 'there is a nucleus of people within the union who show some commitment to issues of race' (Lee 1987:151). There is also an important role for black activists who, as will be demonstrated later in the book, are not prepared to take discrimination lying down.

However, many unions did begin, albeit slowly, to establish black members' committees, black members' conferences and reserved seats for black members on NECs. Equality officers might take race equality as part of their brief, or specialist race equality officers might be appointed. Unions also started to target black workers with publications and training courses. The response of different unions was varied and uneven, reflecting the composition of their membership, the occupations they organised, their political stance, the way they defined their priorities and their geographical location. Some unions such as NUPE and NATFHE took a lead in developing quite radical strategies, while manual unions were more likely to drag their feet.

It was in their interest to provide good services for minority employees, since research still shows that some groups of BME workers are more prone to join unions than white workers, although overall there is lower union density among minority ethnic workers, reflecting the fact that some groups (Chinese, mixed heritage) are much less unionised. Figures for union density on the DTI website for 2006 show the overall level among all employees at 28.4 per cent, down from 29 per cent in 2005. The decline in membership is, of course, a long-term trend, giving a strong motivation for trade unions to reach out to newer constituencies. Density was higher among women than men in all ethnic groups except the mixed heritage group. Density was highest among black women (36 per cent), followed by white women (29 per cent) and Asian women (28 per cent). Black men (30 per cent) had higher density than white men (27.5 per cent) and Asian men (22 per cent) (DTI 2007). Some of this may be due to the concentration of black workers (both of Caribbean and African descent) in the public sector, where three in five workers are union members, as opposed to one in five in the private sector, but it also reflects the culture and traditions mentioned in the previous section. Moreover, black and Asian women we interviewed emphasised the need for union membership, as they perceived themselves as more vulnerable and more in need of support and protection than their white co-workers.

Despite their higher membership rates, black workers continue to be underrepresented in the power structure of trade unions. A Labour Research Department survey in 1998 found that only 2 per cent of paid officials and 4 per cent of the total number of workplace representative were black, and only a quarter of the latter were black women (LRD 1998). Moreover, the equality provisions for black workers can be seen as more restricted in their effects than those for women. For example, Kirton and Greene (2002) point out that most women's conferences are women only, while black members conferences are often open to white delegates: a motion put to the TUC Black Workers' Conference that it should be open to black delegates only was rejected. Kirton and Greene also note that race committees were more likely than women's committees to be of purely advisory status.

At the time when we started our research for the *Double Disadvantage* project in 2000, a set of developments had occurred which gave real stimulus to both unions and employers in revisiting and enhancing their race equality strategies. This was the publication of the Macpherson Report in 1999, following the enquiry into the murder of black London teenager Stephen Lawrence by white youths in 1993, and the failure of the Metropolitan Police Force to handle the crime properly and bring its perpetrators to justice. We should state that trade unions had supported Stephen Lawrence's parents' campaign to set up this committee of inquiry in the first place. The resulting report emphasised the prevalence of racism and racial stereotyping within British institutions and organisations and highlighted institutional racism within the police force. It defined institutional racism as 'the collective failure of an organisation to provide an appropriate and professional service to people because of their colour, culture or ethnic origin' and stressed the role of 'unwitting prejudice, ignorance, thoughtlessness and racist stereotyping' in leading to discrimination and disadvantaging of minority ethnic citizens. The report stated that 'it is incumbent on every institution to examine their policies and the outcomes of their policies and practices to guard against disadvantaging any section of our communities' (Macpherson 1990).

Following the Macpherson Report, the TUC set up the Stephen Lawrence Task Group to consider the role of trade unions in relation to racism and anti-racism. This was seen as a high-level and prestigious group, with many general secretaries among its members. The Task Group produced a report on actions that needed to be taken, including equality audits; unions must realise that their own structures and practices might not be innocent of institutional racism. One of our four case study unions, CWU, was engaged in carrying out such an audit while we were researching.

The Macpherson report must also be seen as a major influence behind the passing of the Race Relations (Amendment) Act in 2002, compelling public-sector organisations (such as the police) to develop visible policies to help minorities and to take steps to implement and monitor these policies. While it is doubtful whether all public-sector organisations have effectively implemented the race duty enshrined in the RRAA, this must be seen as a crucial milestone, signalling the public unacceptability of racism. As a long-time black activist and union campaigner told us: 'we are now pushing at an open door.' It thus opened the way for concerned and progressive unions to work to develop appropriate structures to help their BME members secure the promised equality. Certainly, we found it had provided a great boost to anti-racist activity in our case study unions.

The case study unions

In choosing unions to participate in our study, we had several criteria to consider: we wanted unions with a high proportion of woman members; we wanted unions covering occupations and jobs where BME women were known to work; we wanted to include women from a range of sectors, occupations and class backgrounds; and we needed to choose unions whose members worked in London and Bristol where we hoped to carry out the bulk of our interviews. We also felt it necessary to choose unions which had taken initiatives in equality, as we wanted to uncover examples of good practice rather than focus on difficulties or failures.

UNISON was an obvious choice given its very strong reputation on self-organising and equality: moreover, it had been much researched before so a lot of information was already available. UNISON organises

Table 6.1 Representation, gender and ethnicity in the case study unions

	Total membership	Female membership %	Black membership %	Women at conference %	Women in executive %
CWU	300,000	21	7	n/a	6
NATFHE	65,000	47	4	n/a	25*
UNISON	1,300,000	72	10	58	62
USDAW	310,000	60	5	44	53

n/a: not available
* at least 25 per cent
Source: SERTUC, March 2000.

a wide range of occupations, but in particular covers the Health Service and Local Authority employment, where many BME women work. For a second professional area, we chose NATFHE, as education is another popular minority ethnic choice, and NATFHE is a progressive union which had a longstanding record on catering for black members. We knew something of its ways, as one of us was a current member and the other had been a member in the past. USDAW was chosen as retail is a major employer of BME women; one of us had attended a TUC Black Workers' conference in Cardiff and met the USDAW delegation there through a former student, who helped us with access to women activists. We had a more difficult time finding a fourth union covering manual workers; but one of us had had previous contact with the CWU which organises communications workers, including postal workers and telephone engineers.

These four unions were prepared to co-operate with us and we felt that they covered a good range of occupations, as well as representing rather different union cultures and being at different stages in developing equality structures and strategies. In each of them we tried to interview 15 activist black or Asian women: we met our targets in USDAW and UNISON, but it was harder to identify suitable activists in the other two: we interviewed 11 women activists from each. Table 6.1 shows the gender and ethnic composition of the four unions as estimated by SERTUC at the time we were carrying out our research.

CWU

The CWU was chosen to represent the more traditional male-dominated union sector. As Table 6.1 shows, women are in a minority. It was formed out of a merger between the Union of Communications Workers, which mainly organised postal workers, and the National Communications Union, which mainly organised telecommunications workers. The Royal Mail and BT still provide the main bulk of the CWU's members though it also tries to recruit from other telephone companies, cable TV, the Alliance and Leicester Building Society and Girobank. The occupational groups which it represents include: engineering, computing, clerical, mechanical, driving, retail, financial and manual skills. Though it is a strongly male-dominated union, as we shall see one or two women have risen to leadership positions within it.

NATFHE

NATFHE, before its merger with AUT, recruited academic and academic-related staff in a range of educational institutions. In the university sector it organised mainly the post-1992 or 'new universities' which used to be polytechnics. It also organises teachers in colleges of further education (FE). The merger to form UCU occurred because it seemed illogical to have two unions organising academics in universities, but there is currently concern that the FE sector's interests may be marginalised. After the merger, the popular Paul Mackney, who led NATFHE at the time of our research, stood down and Sally Hunt of AUT was elected General Secretary. NATFHE described itself as a professional association, but this professional role was interrelated with its key trade union role. It has had a longstanding good record on equality issues and was the only union to have had a black president.

Black members in NATFHE face subtle forms of discrimination in colleges and universities, where they are often in a tiny minority, because at about 4 per cent of the teaching force, black staff are under-represented in both further and higher education. There are other grounds for discrimination, which NATFHE is also concerned to combat – for example, religion or belief, age or appearance. The pay gap identified by the Bett Report (1999) and the increasing use of agency staff and part-time staff create negative conditions for women in the education sector. A high percentage of black women employed by agencies are part-time or casualised.

UNISON

UNISON is the largest trade union in the United Kingdom. It has over a million members, 72 per cent of whom are women, with an estimated 10 per cent being black (SERTUC 2000). UNISON is the result of a merger of three public sector unions, COHSE, NALGO and NUPE. UNISON members work in the public services, utilities and for private contractors providing public services. They include manual and white-collar staff working full- or part-time in local authorities, the health services, colleges and schools, the electricity, gas and water industries, transport and the voluntary sector. Many of the organisations UNISON members work in have been involved in lengthy processes of restructuring, a kind of continuous managerial revolution since the 1980s, with the advocates of managerialism trying to impose quite new types of employment relations and values on the old public sector. The introduction of cultures based on audit, targets and monitoring, with continual pressure to stay within budgets, has led to major problems of bullying, harassment and discrimination which UNISON has worked hard at both national and local level to counter. UNISON is a leader in the field of equality. The structure of the merged union, which was developed though discussion with academic advisers, enshrines principles of equality, as will be discussed in the next section.

USDAW

USDAW has about 310,000 members. 60 per cent are women and an estimated 5per cent are black members. USDAW members work in a variety of occupations and industries, which include: retail, distributive, manufacturing and service sectors. USDAW is a union with high turnover as so many of the workers it seeks to organise are in part-time or temporary employment. However, it has succeeded in increasing its membership by nearly 7 per cent since 1997. Its major remit is recruitment and selection and the organising academy is important to a union that has to recruit a significant proportion of its membership each year in order to stand still. Perhaps for this reason it had less developed equality structures than the other three unions we studied.

What is being done for BME women?

As we noted above, unions are all in very different stages of developing their race equality strategies. This was the case with our four study unions. We had deliberately chosen UNISON as the national leader in self-organisation. As mentioned previously, NATFHE had been an early promoter of equality structures. CWU was less of a pioneer, but invigorated by the Stephen Lawrence affair, it had recently commissioned a review of its equality profiles. USDAW was a much less well resourced union, whose equality structures were somewhat less well developed.

Table 6.2 provides a summary of the unions' equality provisions.

Table 6.2 Equality structures in the case study unions

	CWU	NATFHE/UCU	UNISON	USDAW
Equalities officer	YES	YES	YES	YES
Specialist race equality officer	NO	YES	YES	NO 1 year post in 2002
Equality advisory committees	YES: Race (RAC), Women, Disability, LGBT Youth Retired members	NO	NO	YES National Women's Committee National Race Committee
Black Workers' Conference	YES	YES	YES	YES
Black networks, groups	NO	YES Email lists	YES SOGs (race women, LTGB, disability, young members, retired members)	YES Equality forums (race, LTGB women, disability) black get-togethers
Reserved NEC seats	YES	YES 9 equality seats 2 for black members, I to be a woman	YES Proportionality 16 seats for low-paid women. Additional equality seats	NO
Black-member or women-only courses	YES	YES	YES	YES

Source: Interviews and union websites.

As will be seen from Table 6.2, the unions all have an array of equality structures. These differ according to the stage of development of equality provision, priorities, resources and union culture. The two public-sector unions, NATFHE and UNISON rely more on membership involvement on a self-organised basis, while those unions that organise less well paid workers rely on more formal structures, such as the national advisory committees.

Kirton and Greene (2002) analyse these kinds of provisions as examples of positive action by unions. Utilising the Jewson and Mason (1986) distinction between radical and liberal EO frameworks discussed in previous chapters, they categorise strategies as liberal that are designed to 'level the playing field' and 'enable women and black members to participate on an equal footing with white men' (2002:158): examples they give are women-only or black member-only courses and specialist women's and race equality officers. They see radical strategies as more interventionist and designed to directly and immediately build women or black members into decision-making processes: examples are reserved seats and women's or black members' committees and conferences. By such criteria the four unions all utilise a mix of liberal and radical strategies.

Whatever the differences in provision, it was and is clear that all these unions are strongly committed to the equality agenda. This can be seen on their websites where equality structures figure strongly and are easily accessed. At the time when we carried out our research, each union had a representative on the Stephen Lawrence Task Group: three general secretaries (of NATFHE, USDAW and UNISON) and a Deputy General Secretary (of CWU). Thus, not just the equality officers, whom one would expect to be heavily committed to race equality, but mainstream officials were giving attention to improving the union's contribution to the fight against institutional racism.

As we have already stated, UNISON can be seen as an exemplar for union democracy. It was born from a merger in 1993 of three public service unions, NALGO, NUPE and COHSE, which had all in different ways strong records in working for equal representation. The new union's constitution, set up with advice from industrial relations expert Mike Terry, has been described as 'the most radical in the history of British trade unionism' (Humphrey 2000:269; Terry 1996).

UNISON's approach to equality was enshrined in its constitution. The mechanism for achieving gender equality was threefold: proportionality, fair representation and self-organisation (Colgan and Ledwith 2000:246), a combination of inclusion and separateness. The union has a very complicated structure which seeks to achieve democracy and representation across a number of axes: geographical regions; occupational groupings; and diversity and difference. The NEC (National Executive Council) has 70 seats plus four additional seats for each self-organised group (SOG). SOGs for women, lesbians and gay men, black members and members with disabilities exist at national, regional and branch levels and are supported by officers at national and regional level. Election mechanisms ensure that at least 60 per cent of the executive are women, including 14 reserved seats for low-paid women. The complexity of UNISON is all the more evident with the recognition that there are 2000 branches, each of which is encouraged to have a lay equalities officer. Issues relating to black and women members feed through to the Black Members' or the Women's National Conference or via regional structures which feed into the NEC and the Annual Conference.

There is a Black Women's Caucus at UNISON which is not policy-making, but offers support, advice and an open network for black women within the union. In mid-2001, there were two BME women on the NEC. At every level of the union, when people are elected to committees or delegations, women must be elected in fair proportion to their member-ship. For example the NEC has to elect 44 women out of its 67 seats and low-paid women hold 13 seats. An equality officer focuses on NEC race policy and the membership of black members, advises and services the SOGs and was on the TUC's Race Committee in 2001. At the time of our fieldwork there were 15 people with equalities responsibilities in UNISON, although it was made clear that all organisers should also deal with equalities. In response to the Stephen Lawrence Task Group, UNISON had developed an action plan covering bargaining, organising, training and learning and the role of UNISON as an employer.

At the heart of UNISON's equality policy are the SOGs, radical organ-isations which have at times been hotly contested internally within the union (Colgan and Ledwith 2000; Humphrey 2000). The idea of self-organisation predates UNISON and Humphrey describes its origins among local activists in NALGO. These original SOGs were grassroots bodies, whereas the current ones owe their existence to the rule-book. But even though they may be criticised as 'top-down' organisations, it became clear from our interviews what a transformational effect they had on some black women's lives and how they have opened up hori-zons and opportunities. The following are comments from UNISON activists we interviewed:

> One of the big pluses for me is that UNISON does actually have a black members' SOG. I think that's one route some people have come into the union and being involved in the union is by having this SOG, and roles within the SOGs.

> I became very active by joining the black workers' group. I became active, and from that, since I started going to meetings, it followed up into um, a regional group.

The main reason I became active was because of the black member's group. I'm really into black issues, trying to promote equality within the university, so that's where my heart lies.

Humphrey, while very supportive of the SOGS, having herself been actively involved within them, raised two sets of problems with them. One is the bureaucratisation which creeps into them because of the way they are interwoven into UNISON's complex constitutional structures. The other is the danger of essentialism, as the boundaries between the groups become hardened, making it more difficult for individuals to move between them; in Humphrey's words the essentialising of identities runs the risks of 'enclosing each group in a quasi-mystical circle and segregating it off from the other groups' (2000:274). She also sees the difficulties, identified also by Colgan and Ledwith (2000), of a problematic relationship with the mainstream union structures. Here there is a potential dynamic of *double exclusion*, whereby the SOGs and their activities are marginalised and seen as trivial by mainstream activists and officers, while at the same time those not identifying with the identity categories covered by the SOGs feel themselves to be excluded and disadvantaged.

However, in our experience, the women we interviewed managed to negotiate these problems with reasonable success. Some actively chose to be in more than one group. They used their experiences in the SOGs to push themselves and their agendas into the mainstream, and attempted to subvert the bureaucratic push. Moreover, the structures themselves promote caucuses within each group, to allow for the cross-play of intersectionality, as one UNISON activist explained to us:

We all have separate times to discuss issues that affect us, black people, but there are overlapping black issues as well, as women, as disabled people, as gay and lesbian people, you know, they are similar and we actually find time to meet, we usually have a day or half a day, when all the SOGs meet together, and discuss equality issues. Because they do overlap in some areas. But black people need time for themselves, you know.

Another good example of crossing boundaries is the article in a recent issue of *Black Action*, the newsletter for black members, by Rhona, a lesbian from Jamaica who had been helped by the union to gain status as an asylum seeker and to become integrated into the black gay and lesbian community in the UK.

The CWU is similar to UNISON in having been formed out of a merger and it, too, has equality embedded into its constitution. The Equal Opportunities Department was formed at its inception; linked to it there are now six advisory committees dealing with areas of potential discrimination, which feed into a sub-committee of the National Executive Council. These are the Women's Advisory Committee, the Race Advisory Committee, the Lesbian & Gay Advisory Committee, the Disability & Special Needs Advisory Committee, the Youth Advisory Committee and the Retired Members' Advisory Committee. The Equal Opportunities Department, as well as dealing with the work of these committees and being involved in campaigning issues, gives advice to branches on equal opportunities issues and through a hotline number provides assistance to members in respect of harassment and discrimination. It also supports women's and black members' conferences. The Black Workers' Conference which the research team attended was a particularly vigorous, exciting and inclusive event, which was generating real commitment, passion and debate.

Following the Stephen Lawrence Report, the CWU had taken a bold and notable step in commissioning an independent audit to investigate the state of race equality in the union (DLA Consulting 2000). Inevitably, the report led to questioning and accusations in the union, as was evident at the Black Workers' Conference, but the report provided a good platform from which to tackle problems of racism in the union and in workplaces. CWU now has a BME women, Michele Emerson, as its National Equality Officer. There are excellent equalities pages on the CWU website and a special publication *Drum* for black members.

Also impressive is a publication entitled *Is the Communication Workers Union Representative of Its Ethnic Minorities?* This paper was produced by a Task Group sponsored by the Race Committee. It presents available statistics on BME membership within BT, the Royal Mail and other organisations, (highlighting the problems of inadequate data since the ethnic monitoring process has major gaps) and makes recommendations for future actions. Within the union itself, the report reveals that 14 per cent of CWU employees are from ethnic minorities, but they are mainly in lower grades, with only one black assistant secretary. What strikes us on reading this informative publication is the way in which CWU is able to be honestly and openly critical of its own performance, in a way that many organisations are not prepared to be.

NATFHE has also been involved in merger, with AUT, but this occurred after the fieldwork period. There was some concern among NATFHE activists that its traditional strength on equality issues might be impaired in a merger, as AUT was seen as less radical in this area. However, the prominence and interest of the equality activists was still marked at the first UCU annual conference and most of the structures for positive action have survived the merger.

When we interviewed NATFHE's equality staff, the union was busy with a major project where BME members from the FE sector were being asked to make witness statements about their experiences of racism and sexism. NATFHE had a good array of positive action strategies; there were four equality seats on the NEC, for two black representatives, one lesbian and gay representative, and one disabled representative. At least 25 per cent of the NEC had to be women. NATFHE had a range of member networks and aimed to use its website to enhance links within and between networks. It had recently produced new guidelines on handling racial grievances and a timely paper on religious discrimination.

Of interest to this project was the view among NATFHE officers interviewed that 'black women tend to go into black members' groups rather than the women's group ... they identified a felt oppression based on race not gender'. Indeed, it was felt that 'white women collude with structures which are disadvantageous to black women': because teaching is a highly feminised profession, many BME women have white line managers. In NATFHE, the prioritising of identities is brought to the fore, since unlike some other unions, members have to choose only one group to join. The collective sense of oppression identified is translated into a more closed approach to black networks in NATFHE than in UNISON or CWU. For example, unlike the CWU, only black members are allowed to attend the Black Members' Conference.

We have presented USDAW as the union with the least developed equality provision. However, it has had an equality officer since 1985. Their National Race Relations Committee came into being in 1991 and race equality work was for a time the responsibility of a Race Equality/ Education Officer. However, despite the hard work of women in these posts, support for them seemed to have been fairly limited. Some of the women members we interviewed spoke of the sexism of male union leaders. We also intuited that race had been of secondary importance, that the work got done whenever there was the time to do it. In many ways, it was suggested to us that whilst women's structures were well established, there was some 'treading water on race'. There had been positive developments in gender representation with the Executive Council (EC) now having nine women, but at the time of the interview there were no black EC members (nor had there ever been).

Since 1999, with the departure of the previous Women's Officer, some restructuring had taken place, which seemed to have some benefit since the new post holder worked through the Research Department, drew on their resources and was able to link equality work more directly with mainstream bargaining. Senior-level reporting for equality posts is seen as 'good practice', yet as this case illustrates, the infrastructure for the post may be an important factor in ensuring that equality issues do not become isolated.

At that time, the Equalities Officer acted as Secretary to the National Women's Committee and the National Race Committee. The scope of the job was wide and covered women, black, disabled and gay and lesbian members' interests. Her job was conceived of as implementing the wishes of the committees, but also to 'give them a bit of a steer'. The interrelationship between an official with expert knowledge and members with direct experience of discrimination forms part of the inclusionary process of representation between officials and members. But a problem for USDAW is that many of its members work part-time: the retail industry employs many casual and temporary workers, shift systems are complex and there is a very high turnover of employees. These are conditions in which it is very difficult to build the base of engaged activists which has developed in the other three unions. In 2000, USDAW was organising 'black get-togethers' in large cities like Manchester and London as a way of trying to build some sense of collectivism and solidarity between black members.

It was reported in the USDAW magazine *Arena* in March 2006 that the Women's and Race Committees had been replaced by a National Equalities Advisory Group, described by the Equalities Officer as 'a new beginning for everyone in USDAW who wants to make us a more inclusive and representative union'. Activities included fringe meetings at the Annual Conference, quarterly meetings and training for reps on equality issues. Parallel to the national groups would be equalities forums in each of the seven regional divisions, which would be able to plan their own activities (such as weekend schools, get-togethers and recruitment visits). It was evident that the union was working hard, but still struggling, to build up viable structures for promoting participation and representation. In part, this may reflect the nature of the retail workforce: part-timers are less likely to become actively involved in union work. Moreover, the manual-occupational class background of many retail workers may predispose them to privilege class issues ('the traditional union agenda') over newer areas such as gender and race equality. The uneven development of equalities structures across unions is thus manifested in USDAW.

Neither CWU or USDAW had reserved seats for their NEC, and we were told that the cultures of the two unions made it difficult to engage with this issue. Reserved seats were seen as at the far edge of positive action, taking things a 'step too far'. This reflects the popular espousal of meritocracy and resistance to affirmative policies and 'quotas' which we discussed in Chapter 3. It seems easier to explain the rationale for reserved seats, as a corrective and bridging measure until parity is achieved, within unions with professional cultures and where there are numbers of middle-class feminists active within the unions. Many working-class women union activists have expressed hostility towards this strategy. Jane Harrington researching USDAW women activists in the South West and South Wales found that they were unhappy with overtly feminist strategies, seeing them as 'separatist', and believing that this 'undermined their other roles as wives and mothers to sons' (Harrington 2000:109). Moreover, the issue of reserved seats is more delicate in the case of ethnicity than gender, as it was seen that the policy may not be legal under the RRA; and, moreover, as the CWU publication points out (CWU 2006), unions do not often have exact knowledge of the numbers of BME members, therefore making the principle of proportionality difficult to apply.

Conclusions

This chapter has demonstrated the considerable progress made by unions since the 'bad old days' of postwar racism, towards embracing the equality agenda and devising strategies and structures to ensure that disadvantaged groups of workers, such as BME women, are better represented within unions and by unions within their workplaces. The range and complexity of structures and initiatives offered by the unions we have studied is impressive and, as we shall see, serves an important need among black members.

Nevertheless, the problems identified by Humphrey (2000) and Colgan and Ledwith (2000) remain. Despite the attempts to cater for intersectionality, there is a tendency for the women's structures to be dominated by white women and black structures by minority ethnic men. More openness to the involvement of black women is essential if these structures are to represent the diversity of union membership; from this point of view, the merging of separate committees by USDAW might be seen as a positive move. But, as with the single equalities commission, the EHRC, there is concern that particular less vocal constituencies may become submerged within the unified structure and their problems not heard or catered for. For this reason we support the continuation of SOGs, *as long as their members deem them to be valuable and necessary.*

However, these structures alone are not sufficient; they must link in to mainstream decision-making bodies so that they have deep and lasting impact on union policies and practices at national and local level. We noticed in studying these four unions that the strength and effectiveness of equality policies often rested quite fragilely on the energy of a single proponent who had dedicated herself to the issue. The departure of such a key actor could jeopardise the continuation of vigorous action on equality. Therefore equality policy does require also *to be mainstreamed and embedded in broader union principles and priorities.*

Moreover, these policies must involve real action to confront the continuing problems of racism and sexism in the workplace which will be discussed in the coming chapters. Over and over again as we have talked to BME women the point has been made that paper policies are not enough: in the words of a NATFHE equalities officer:

> There is a need to move beyond structures and policy to actually changing things in the workplace

It is to what happens in the workplace that we turn in the next set of chapters.

7
The Women and Their Stories

This work is focused on a group of women who in many ways are extraordinary. They are employed, they are union members, are active in their union and the community and some are mothers. We do not claim that they are typical, but it is in their complex contribution to society and their communities that lies the value and interest of their stories. So far the narrative of black and minority ethnic women's workplace experiences has been told in our voices, those of two white women (British of Jewish ancestry and British-Irish). For the next part of the book, however, we want to give prominence to the voices of the women trade union activists interviewed for the *Double Disadvantage* project.

In this chapter we give some insight into the lives of the women whose stories we draw on in the next chapters. We relied on qualitative methods because we wished to understand in some depth their experiences and their evaluations of the institutions in which they worked, joined or shaped. But, first, we trace the approach that we took to the research.

The research approach

We conducted our research in three phases, between 2000 and 2002. The first phase of the research involved interviewing national and local-level officers from each of the four unions, CWU, NATFHE, UNISON and USDAW. Documentation was collected from the four unions and the TUC. The material covers a wide range of equality issues that the unions are addressing. Through these interviews and the documentary analysis, we built up a picture of union strategies and action/inaction with respect to combating sexism and racism within the union and in the organizations where unions are represented. Some of these findings were used in Chapter 6.

The second phase of the project involved semi-structured, in-depth interviews with 56 black and minority ethnic female activists from London, the Midlands, and the North West and South West regions: Our sample was identified in a number of ways: some were recommended by the case study unions; some by women who had already been interviewed (a snowballing effect) and others were approached at conferences. We also actively sought to achieve a reasonable balance in ethnicity, particularly with respect to African-Caribbean and Asian members. In fact, despite our best efforts, the sample was skewed to African-Caribbean women (the group perceived to be most active by our gatekeepers). Between 11 and 15 women were interviewed from each union. The interviews cover women's educational background; employment histories; employment experiences; history of union participation and experience of activities within the union; family background and circumstances; and the needs and priorities of the black and minority women as they themselves define them. Each interview took between one and a half hours to two hours.

All the interviews were carried out by Nupur Mukherjee, a young woman from a British-Indian background. Although the interviews were in official research terms 'semi-structured', based on a topic guide, our strategy was to allow the women as much freedom as possible to tell their own stories, even if it meant missing out some of the questions on the topic guide. Nupur proved very skilful at this and collected some remarkable stories from our participants, many of whom were very articulate and vocal. No doubt women felt it easier to open up to her because of their awareness that she would have some personal empathy with their situation, as one participant made clear:

> You see talking to you, I feel quite comfortable. I hardly know you but I know you'll understand my issues. And I couldn't talk like this if you were a white female. I couldn't talk about half the issues to you because you wouldn't understand.

The stories she elicited are very varied. Some are painful, with details of difficult life histories and accounts of appalling incidents of racism and sexism. Many are uplifting, telling of success in adversity, tremendous personal achievements within and outside their trade unions and determination to fight against racial injustice and oppression. Others are more hesitant, from women not yet quite sure of the ultimate direction and goals of their lives, or of the role of their unions in their lives. The stories are rich and lengthy. Many of these women described themselves as 'strong', 'independent' and 'forceful' and they had no difficulty in expressing and elaborating their views of life.

We also attended numerous relevant union conferences and meetings, including CWU and NATFHE Black Workers' Conferences in 2001 and 2002, regional union meetings and a number of TUC Black Workers' and Women's Conferences. The Respect Festival in Bristol allowed us to witness the way in which trade unions conducted themselves in more informal surroundings. Hence we have been able to observe the four unions in a number of settings, from regional and national level to more informal situations. Attendance by the researchers at these events helped inform an understanding of the specific issues and problems that concern women and black and other ethnic minority workers.

The third phase involved dissemination seminars with union officials and members from the four case study unions and the TUC, including many of the black women who took part in the study. This was an important phase of the study as we actively sought to test out the integrity of our findings with those who are most associated with issues of sexism and racism in unions. These were also an opportunity to exchange ideas and views and engage in discussions on key themes. This was a critical part of our study; there is little doubt that this study has benefited considerably from the feedback of the black women and men as well as their support.

The women

The most important actors in our work are the women themselves. Table 7.1 sets out the demographic details of the women we interviewed. We were fortunate in getting a reasonable age span among the women; only three women were under 30, and the largest group was under 40. The majority were married or had live-in partners, although a significant proportion was single, with a minority divorced or widowed. Throughout the following chapters, the women are the key voices. The women are identified by pseudonyms to protect their anonymity.

Over half of the women had two or more children. The impact of motherhood on careers is well recorded in the literature. Yet, as will be seen in the following chapters, many of the women manage their mothering and their work and union careers. However, it is noteworthy that just over a quarter of the women did not have children. Arguably, their careers would be less affected by the penalties associated with

Table 7.1   Demographic details of interviewees

Age	16–30	3
	31–40	26
	41–50	21
	51–60+	5
Home context	Single	19
	Married/cohabiting	26
	Divorced/widowed	10
Children	0	15
	1	12
	2	19
	3+	9
Birthplace	UK	34
	Caribbean	11
	Africa	5
	India/Pakistan	4
	USA	1
Ethnicity	African	10
	African Caribbean	32
	Asian	12
	American	1

motherhood. However, this ignores the impact of inequality regimes on their career chances.

As Table 7.1 shows, the majority of our sample were born in the United Kingdom, with just under 10 per cent being born in the Caribbean and a smaller proportion born in African, India, Pakistan and the United States. Country of birth may be important in the identification of ethnic origin but parents' country of birth may also influence self-perception. Although the women portrayed their own ethnicity in a range of ways, we use a narrow categorisation which follows common sociological terminology (see Table 7.1).

Concealed within these broad labels are the elaborations of the self-definitions with some 24 descriptors given by the women. These were often distinctive and specific and included black African, black African Caribbean, black African Nigerian, black Asian Indian, black African-British, black British-Caribbean, black British-Jamaican, black Indian, black Nigerian, black Welsh, black West Indian, black Spanish mixed and British Asian Pakistani black British. There are two points that emerge from these descriptors. Firstly, they are very precise. Women want the complexity of their ethnicity to emerge and this complexity is something which is important to them. It matters, wherever they were borne, that their family histories are acknowledged in the descriptors. So Jamaican, Nigerian and Pakistani are seen as necessary as opposed to the more generic Caribbean, African or Asian. But also women bring their nationality into the descriptor, so that 'British' is also an important part of many women's self description. This is very important because of the tendency of white people to treat visible minorities as though they are not British. This does not happen to second and third generations of white migrants. A second crucial thing that emerges is the importance of the word 'black' which recurs in most of the descriptors. The political importance of 'black' discussed in the introduction is evident in the self-defined ethnicities of the women in this study.

Union involvement and activism

All the women in our study were union members (see Table 7.2). They had varying lengths of union membership including ten women with over 20 years, and 12 with 11–20 years in their unions Thus a vast amount of employment and union experience was held by this group of women. For most, there was a continuous attachment to unions over their working lives.

It is also important to state that a distinguishing feature of our sample is that it was drawn from those who were perceived as union activists. We do, however, define 'activist' in an open way. We wanted to allow for different degrees of activism and to recognise that people may come in and out of activist roles, a point that may be more apposite to women, who tend to have different working patterns over the life cycle. Thus we sought to interview women who could be described as 'formal activists' and 'informal activists' (Fosh 1993), tht is, women who had a formal lay union role at the time of the study, those who previously held such

Table 7.2 Union membership

Union	CWU	11
	NATFHE	11
	UNISON	15
	USDAW	15
	Pilot studies	3

roles, and women who were less formally active (they attended union meetings, spoke up on issues, would stand on a picket line and so on). Nevertheless, the word 'activist' itself presented problems as, for some women, it connoted industrial militancy, political involvement or very high levels of attendance at meetings, conferences and courses. With hindsight, the term 'active participant' might have been better. In fact, our sample ranged from women executive members and longstanding shop stewards to recently recruited health and safety representatives and even women who had attended a couple of black network meetings or training courses.

Nevertheless a discussion of the term 'activism' did give great insight into the range of women in this study and to their commitment to social justice. This is explored in depth in Healy, Bradley and Mukherjee (2004a) when we argued that the term 'activist' is often used in a taken for granted way. We wished to present the case for widening the definition of activism to consider not only the credentialised steward, but other key union actors in the workplace. When asked what meanings the interviewees attributed to the term union 'activist', their replies reflected a range of meanings and a perspective over time, alongside their own specific experiences. Women's definitions of 'activism' varied. For some it was about fighting for social justice. but racism and discrimination were often to the fore in activists' self-identification. The following woman personifies the total commitment often associated with activism:

> I would define myself, first and foremost as somebody who is here to break down every barrier that constitutes discrimination, or racism, or unfairness on my colleagues or on myself. I would describe myself as somebody who fights for, and will continue to fight for equality in your day-to-day work, Monday to Friday, whatever hours you do. And if that makes me an activist then I'm an activist.
>
> (Ginette)

This total commitment to the union was also in this definition of an activist by Josie:

> Somebody that will give their all to the union basically, somebody that will try and help anybody within their branch as well as their members, and outside which I do.

Our earlier work also discusses a reluctant activism where the term is at odds with a woman's own self-definition:

> I'm probably reluctant to say yes but in the sense that if there's an issue on the board I will argue it, I will argue it to other people, in the sense that I will take a position or line on it, ... And as I said I will go out with the action and you know, suffer the consequences, so in that sense yes. But if I was arguing that I am a political activist then I would say no. You with me? It's probably because I am not consumed by it, and that's probably how I would evaluate it ... I try and get a life outside of work.
>
> (Suzanne)

A sense of the 'typical' union 'activist' as a banner-waving militant was expressed and this may put women off union engagement, a finding that also emerged in Bradley's North East study (1999). Indeed, it also transpired that the dichotomy between 'activist' and 'member' was alienating to some 'informal activists'. It may also deter women from volunteering themselves for union roles, since they see themselves as unable to fulfil the impossible ideal of 'giving their all'. The disapproval about the 'activist/member' distinction sometimes made on training courses is illustrated by Patricia:

> She (the trainer) drew a distinction between activist and members, so when she put it across to us I said I felt, that I would feel really devalued because she more or less inferred that as a member even attending the training you were not in the same league as an activist. Does that make sense? And what we were told by the tutor for this weekend, well actually (the union) has been looking at the use of this term, so you have touched in a sense on a subject that we have been looking more closely at, as to how people are perceiving these terms, and they said that we are looking towards a new term, called active members, as opposed to activist or member.

For a number of women, the way into activism was gradual, with women starting out in a relatively less overtly political role, such as health and safety representative, then moving on to become stewards and regional delegates.

Whilst the widening of formal union roles is important, greater explicit acknowledgement and encouragement of informal activists' participation is needed. This discussion led us to argue that the development of the category of 'active member' as part of union discourse may be a helpful way to enable unions to become more inclusive (Healy, Bradley and Mukherjee 2004a). This may also be a means of overcoming women's reluctance to take on tasks unless they feel they have the time and resources to 'do the job properly':

> Because there's so much going on that you need to be spot on with everything. And I'm a bit of a person if I can't do it the whole way, I don't do it at all.
>
> (Amber)

We argue that understandings of the term 'activism' are informed by perceptions of political activism and the more pragmatic evaluation of different degrees of commitment to union activity. We return to these issues in later chapters. We move now to give a flavour of the stories of a few of the extraordinary women in the study. We choose particular aspects of their lives to explore in some depth to give an idea of the character and resilience of the women through their own conversations with Nupur, the interviewer.

Ginette's story

Ginette is a particularly influential and successful woman in her union and in her local authority. She has had to make a lot of adjustments in her life to get to this level of union activism. She said that she had always wanted to become active within the union but due to family and work responsibilities, she found it very difficult in the early years. Ginette is a single mother of a grown-up son. She grew up in London, but was born in the Caribbean. Her father worked in the civil service. Her mother was an educated woman who wanted to be a school teacher, but never managed it, and ended up working as a cleaner 'until she died'. Both of them were unionised. Ginette's mother's experience reminds us of Hortense in *Small World* (see chapter three). Hortense was an educated woman but her qualifications were not recognised in Britain. Ginette is a highly determined and articulate woman who has clearly made a major contribution to her trade union and also has no doubt benefited from her union involvement. In addition she is very active in her local community and also works for an international charity. We provide insight in this short conversation of the way that

Ginette became involved in her union and challenging injustices in the workplace:

Q: When did you first join the union?

A: I joined the union 25 years ago. Because I have worked for the authority for 25 years come this December.

Q: So you joined as soon as you started working.

A: I did, because I was a part time worker, because my son was small. So you know I started part time and of course in those days you were encouraged to join because you were at a disadvantage being a part-time worker, you were further disadvantaged by being black, part-time, and a woman!

Q: Was it NALGO at the time, or was it some other union?

A: It was NALGO at the time. So, yes I have been a member for all that time.

Q: So, when did you start getting actively involved within it?

A: I have always been quite active within the union, because it was another way of showing total dismay at some of the inequality that I saw, and so it was a door that had opened, which said that I could use this as a way for knocking at other doors to let somebody know that something's not right. You know, it was good, because it was stewards there who you could talk to and who would take on board whatever that you saw that you felt that you needed to investigate.

Q: Did you feel they were approachable, the union?

A: Yes, yes. NALGO as it was called then, was, yes, it was a very strong union, yes.

Q: Did you have quite a lot of encouragement to become active?

A: Yes, yes. And active in the sense that I actually was a single mother at the time, and had a mortgage to pay, but I still went on strike which, you know, one had to believe wholeheartedly to do that. Because, you know it's the financial side of it, how am I going to do? But that was not a question that I needed to answer, because what had happened and what the call for the strike was about was again inequality and low pay, and one needed to do that.

Q: And was there a lot of support for the strike?

A: Yes, yes. We did it for better pay and better conditions, and a better environment in which to work, and we actually won all three. We won all three, so I was really glad about that.

Q: Have you personally ever had to use the union?

A: Yes, yes.

Q: Was it at the very beginning when you first joined?

A: I've used the union in that, I used to deputise for the then person-nel officer combined administrator who would pay out for petty cash and balance the books and note someone's leave when they are on holiday, and things like this and pay subsistence money and when she went on maternity leave and then subsequently left, I then applied for that job, and I was told that I didn't have enough qualifications, and it was given to somebody who had qualifications. And yet I was somebody who had been doing that for all the years that I worked in that section and I did take that up with the union. I did feel that I was discriminated against. Thereafter, I didn't really want the job and I felt that I could do better, but I needed for those people in that particular office to realise that they were doing something wrong and I was prepared to challenge it, which I did. And I think it made them sit up and take note that certain practices had to stop.

Q: Did you notice a change?

A: Yes, yes, yes. They obviously became wary of me, because I was like this little part-timer who at the time did not say much to anybody and suddenly I was challenging, because if I was good enough to deputise for her when she was on leave, or when she was sick, and actually when she got married, and was away on her honeymoon, then why wasn't I good enough to do it full time? So it was at that time, when I actually left that department and joined my present one.

Ginette's story is a good (and quite common) example of a situation where injustice is experienced and challenged. The sense of injustice was clearly instrumental in her politicisation. From this early experience as a part-timer, she understood that being able to do the job was not sufficient, and saw that the rationalisations were transparently unfair and should be challenged. Subsequently, when her child was older, she became a full-time worker, extremely active in the union but also active in her church and community.

Shahnaz's story

Shanaz was another extraordinary woman whom we interviewed. Her story is rich and complex and we have decided to draw out how she manages her public and private spheres. We show first of all how she has progressed in the public sphere (not just employment) and then demonstrate her support structures in the private sphere. Shahnaz is a qualified [...] practitioner and a senior lecturer. She is particularly aware that demands for educational specialties wax and wane and uses considerable energy to show her contribution across the board. She goes beyond this when she spells out her considerable public participation. She is the mother of two children, whose education is clearly important to her, not only their formal education, but their social and political education with respect to black consciousness:

Q: So how has the progression and movement been for yourself?

A: I've actually developed myself. I've seen opportunities, like you know if there's research in terms of evaluation going on I've got involved in that. In all the years I've been working I've contributed to every programme on campus. So I like writing. I need to make sure. And this is about being black and being counted. Not just there in body, but there in mind and intellect and as an academic...So I've always done that because it's very important to me and very important for other black people that are going to follow me...I've also got involved in lots of extra-curricular activities outside. For example, I'm a magistrate and I get time from college to do that and I'm a deputy chair for an...association worth in excess of...million[s]. Deputy Chair for that...I'm a governor of a...school. I'm an independent chair for...Complaints. So once users have a complaint, this is the highest level it can arrive and I sit on those...I'm interested in politics and I stood as a local candidate. So I do lots of things and all that helps me to keep myself alive, energised, motivated and current.

Q: It's been your initiative because you haven't actually got any support within the workplace?

A: No, no we have a supporting department which doesn't actually get in the way.

Q: But they don't actively give you these different outlets?

A: No. They don't actively say, well do this and do that, and this will get you the next job up.

Q: You want your work life to be quite challenging then, in those areas?

A: Yes I would say.

Q: It seems it's quite important then for you, as a black woman, to be recognised in different areas?

A: Oh yes definitely. Definitely. Not just for myself. I always want to be part of arenas which deliver excellence. And I would not be satisfied with anything else. And I think it sort of keeps me alive. I feel it keeps me interested and interesting as an individual. And within that, the union came.

Q: If you didn't have all these other things outside of the workplace?

A: I'd have gone. I'd have died long ago.

Q: I was gonna say it would have been very frustrating for you?

A: It is. And I always tell others how to enrich their experience, or what they can do by taking charge of their own careers. You can do whatever you like, but don't just sit still. And the union aspect is, I always sell it as another spin-off, another bow to your portfolio, another opportunity to do other things. To develop skills that your job isn't able to do. There's a whole range of careers outside, in terms of the lay careers out there. Government appointments. You can become a completely different person. So you need to introduce people how to get into these.

Q: So you've got a lot of your self-development through these different avenues?

A: Yes. My own initiative and drive.

Q: How do you manage it all with children as well and family? You know, you have your parents staying with you too.

A: I'm very lucky. I have a very supportive partner. I have very, very supportive parents. And I think we have the best arrangement ever. We're living together out of choice. Because in my family we all went away for our education. None of us stayed at home for our higher education. We all went to places far away and then came home and went to other places. So we all left home 18, 19 and never looked back. And about eight or nine years ago, the decision to set up home and to have a home that wasn't like a granny suite where my parents were facing one direction and we were facing the other, or a bungalow in the garden and we had the shed somewhere else. I wanted one family kind of set-up. And it works very well because I think my parents have a great capacity to give and take. The two families don't take each other for granted. But by my parents being at home, I know my children are coming home to their own place. They're not sitting somewhere else. To the point where I can even get people to come and – pay for them to come and drop my children off at home, so that it isn't causing any bother for my parents. And we also have an arrangement where if my mum feels like cooking, fine. If she doesn't, we'll go in and cook. And it's sort of like a happy arrangement where sometimes it's nice to have it made and other times you just go in and just rustle something together.

Or if you sit and eat. And in fact my parents will say, 'You need more time for yourself. Go out for the evening.' I mean I think we're both a bit of workaholics. I mean we keep focused. Our family's very important so our appointments and meetings and outings stop if family members or friends want to come.

Q: So you just kind of balance it?

A: I think we're chilled. We're not so organised, the unexpected comes and we're all sixes and sevens. I usually say, 'Do the best you can', you know. And that's it. I'm just very fortunate. I'm very, very supported in all that I do.

Marsha's story

We include Marsha's early story as it encapsulates the experiences of women who worked in male-dominated occupations. She is now a successful union officer, but struggled to make her way in a hostile gendered environment. Like our other extraordinary women, she had a particular interest in black issues and has been active in CWU and TUC black workers' conferences. We trace her early experiences in the following extract:

A: I actually joined British Telecom or the GPO as it was then as an apprentice.

Q: And this was just after leaving full time education was it?

A: I left at 16, but it wasn't my first job, I had done other sort of jobs, summer jobs and things like that. Wine bottling and things like that, quite interesting.

Q: That was your first full time job?

A: It was my first full-time job, as an apprentice and I was one of the first women and I didn't want to be a novelty but ended up being a novelty. But I did that, carried on doing it, and got through the grade and got to effectively what was the top engineering grade, in my job. As I said I joined in '79 so that's nearly 22 years in the same job, is quite a long time. And through the job I've got technical qualifications, you know, gradually though different courses, B.Tech stuff and various other bits and pieces. But a lot of it was incomplete, because the college I was sent to wasn't very suitable for me and the lecturers weren't very nice to me, and I was getting some serious harassment as well.

Q: And was college in conjunction with BT?

A: It was an independent college...but it wasn't a terribly good experience because of the people I was with, the 16- to 17-year-old boys and of course they are particularly immature at that age. And I being a novelty, you know, I'm the butt of all the jokes and the harassment and everything else, and a lot of experiments used to get sabotaged, my workshop work and working on the blades, things used to get sabotaged there as well, so there was lots of horrible things going on. Lots of physical injuries as a result of that time as well.

Q: How did you deal with it at the time?

A: Just coped with it myself really. There wasn't really anyone around who was going to help me out because they thought it was the usual thing that you had to put up with it, this is what you had to put up within the workplace kind of thing.

Q: Especially because you were entering a field that was male dominated.

A: That's it basically, it was very much this is a male territory and we are just allowing you in really because we have to, sort of thing.

Q: Did you really feel that you had to put up with it?

A: I did. It didn't feel right at all, and I did actually raise it with some of the lecturers, on a couple of occasions, but they did very little about it and if I wanted to complete my apprenticeship I did have to go through this you see, coz you are getting paid such low wages for apprenticeship, you want to get though it so you can start earning a decent wage when you get through that. But they weren't that interested at all…

Q: And how long was you apprenticeship for?

A: Three years and when I was actually in the workplace then I got a lot of hassle there as well.

Q: And did you feel that there was no one that you could actually turn to within the workplace, like managers and supervisors?

A: No, I went to my manager and he really didn't want to rock the boat because the team worked well together, you know, it was an efficient section Because there wasn't any official procedures and of course I didn't know the procedures that do exist. Of course I could have used the grievance procedure but then it would have been very hard to pin anything down anyway… Every morning that I woke up I didn't feel like going in at all. I thought this is horrible, you know, but it was the branch officers in my branch that actually persuaded me. They said they couldn't wave the magic wand for me and get rid of it all, but they said 'look, hang on in there and we'll do what we can'. And they were very, very supportive and they understood really what was going on.

Q: You were one of the first women who joined the union as well?

A: Well, there wasn't many because it was the Royal Mail and engineering union, which was only engineering. When we merged, we merged with the post and telecom group, which was clerical-based people, so obviously there were a lot more women then. That was in 1985 that we merged, the National Communications Union, and I was actually quite involved in the union by that stage. I was persuaded to go on union education courses and that really opened my eyes. It was really brilliant. My contact with women only started and was quite refreshing really from '85 when we had a big influx of women from the clerical section basically. And I was very surprised and refreshed to find that their problems were the same as mine even if they weren't in isolated positions. A lot of the problems that they had were very similar to mine. I couldn't believe that. I thought it's just because you are an isolated woman you're getting all this hassle, but it wasn't just that, so it was really nice not to have to explain myself because the women understood that. So we actually developed a women's support group. Which was mainly for political change but it was also to support each other as well. You know because things like harassment weren't recognised as a trade union issue at all. There was still wolf whistles at women who went up to the rostrum at conferences and things like that. An awful lot of sexism in the union schools as well. So we wanted to deal with those. Get these issues a bit more mainstreamed, so you know we did develop this women's support group which we founded ourselves. We used to meet, people from all over the country. We used to meet in London every couple of months on a Saturday and talk about the issues that we needed to pursue, how we were going to pursue them, tactics, how we were going to do that, what groups we were gonna sort of lobby, that sort of thing. That was really good, I really enjoyed that, doing that.

Marsha was very tempted to leave her job, which was well paid and which she enjoyed because the conditions she faced were so difficult and 'horrible'. Her involvement in the union was clearly a lifeline to her as was the meeting and sharing experiences with other women, something she had not been able to do in her own isolated context. Another interesting aspect of Marsha's story is the value she placed on trade union education. This was a key feature identified by many of the women in our study and also emerged in Kirton's (2006) study. Further, she exemplified the value of a women's group and what it might achieve for women in the union.

Conclusion

The stories we have highlighted in this chapter reflect some of the key early and continuing challenges women faced within their careers. The stories provide graphic insights into the nature of gendered harassment and discrimination and the negative impact this has on the safety and wellbeing of women in their working environment. The stories also show how injustice can ignite activism and lead to new union careers. They also show how determined and ambitious women can seek to have fulfilling public and private lives.

In the next four chapters we continue to draw on these stories as we explore some of the key themes that emerged from our interviews. Our key concern, here, is to present the experiences of women using their own voices and to highlight the concerns they raised with us. These moving and inspiring stories deserve a wide hearing which we feel honoured to communicate.

Here there is a paradox: African and Caribbean women, in particular, are often stereotyped as being 'mouthy' or 'aggressive', as they themselves complained to us. Yet within formal politics, their voices are quite rarely heard. It is the men from Britain's minority ethnic communities who tend to become prominent in the public sphere and get their views heard. There are a number of notable black political players: Bill Morris was General Secretary of the TGWU; Trevor Phillips was Chair of the CRE and now heads the new EHRC, as mentioned in Chapter 4 and David Lammy is a young and successful politician. Of course there are notable black women in the public realm, such as Diane Abbott MP, Gloria Mills of UNISON and the Baronesses Scotland and Amos. Arguably, they are not given the same press profile as the men. Nevertheless, the importance of black people in the public realm is crucial for white and black alike but in different ways.

We recount the importance of having black people in the public realm when we were told in a project on young BME people by a young man that his father would drag him down to look at the television whenever Bill Morris was on. His father wanted him to see examples of black success. There are still too few black people in the public eye, and even fewer black women. We are also reminded of a Radio 4 interview when Bill Morris was asked why if we needed a black workers' conference, shouldn't we also have a white workers' conference. Morris replied that we have white workers' conferences all the time. This is a really important issue. In Britain with very few exceptions, all institutions are run by white people, usually white men. Growing up in a country where all the important jobs are done by black people is quite different and more enabling than growing up in a country where all the important jobs are done by white people. When young people note that few BME people have prominent roles, it gives them the impression that they have to be truly exceptional to achieve in a white hegemony. For women, since there are even fewer women in positions of power, the paucity of black women makes the picture even more depressing. But we should also recognise the importance of the visibility of black and minority ethnic people in Britain for white people. White people, too, need to recognise that our intercultural society must reflect the way we are today, that the dominant norms associated with white are outdated and that their children can be inspired by black and white alike.

Nevertheless, it is important to acknowledge those who have succeeded and succeeded in a wide range of fields. Some of these fields are not in the public eye so efforts to publicise them are important. We have resisted the temptation to reproduce lists which name the most influential black and Asian men and women because inevitably such lists are contentious and somewhat invidious. This study provides some evidence of the achievements of women who are active trade unionists. In other fields, in politics, in industry, in small businesses, in the professions in literature, in academia and in the voluntary sector, we see similar examples of black and minority ethnic women's significant contributions to society.

Thus we want to recognise black and minority ethnic women's achievements and they are considerable. Equally, we must acknowledge that women are less likely to succeed than their male counterparts, but that on the whole black and minority ethnic women are least likely to succeed in the labour market. This is a position that urgently needs addressing by policy makers. The EOC has in 2007 made steps to advise employers what strategies they should take to improve the experience and opportunities of ethnic minority women in the workplace.

Nevertheless, in the many pages that have been written about multi-culturalism and Islamophobia in Britain, the rebellion of young Muslim men and the growing isolation of the Muslim communities, women's opinions are much less commonly solicited. In general, in the politics of ethnicity and race relations, women are less of a presence and the 'community leaders' who speak on behalf of British ethnic minorities are almost always men, with women playing a support role (and, of course, white women are quite familiar with such arrangements).

Thus it is that with some exceptions, BME women in Britain are politically rendered virtually invisible and inaudible. The first event attended for this research project was a TUC workshop, 'Making Black Women Visible'. It has always been a key concern of our research that we should contribute to making BME women's achievements in the workplace more visible. So in this chapter and subsequent chapters great weight is given to the words of our participants as they describe the issues that concern them. If they read this book, we hope they will feel we have done them justice.

8
Inclusion and Exclusion in the Workplace

This chapter continues to present material about our participants' lives, drawing on their own narrative accounts. In it we focus on the practices and structures that serve to exclude women both in their workplaces and sometimes within their trade unions. But we shall also be looking at the ways in which the unions have opened doors for women and offered them opportunities to exercise their talents in a way that allows them to gain confidence and standing within their organisations. The message here is that, despite some inadequacies, unions have a most important role in helping women confront racism and sexism at work. In particular through the SOGs and black networks they have opened up spaces for BME women to help them fulfil what Julia Sudbury (1998) has called 'other kinds of dreams'. Despite the problems with SOGs which we discussed in Chapter 6, we consider these types of organisation are absolutely crucial mechanisms of inclusion and would argue strongly for their continuation.

We start this chapter by showing how our participants have been excluded within their organisations and by discussing the barriers of racism and sexism which block them from promotion and self-development. Then we consider how unions may have helped to counter this exclusion: many women believed that the unions had empowered them and offered a springboard to career development. These women, most of whom had been representatives of their unions of one kind or another, were now using their union positions to help their BME sisters and brothers towards inclusion in their organisations.

Segregation and marginalisation in the workplace

Lorna, a young woman working in retail, gave us a detailed account of the patterns of segregation in the London store she was working in:

> As in most retail stores, the race composition is predominantly black, on the lower levels, but in terms of management it's pure whites. There's like one black manager, and even them, they are quite low down, in the store. The store manager is white and the deputy manager is white, the assistant manager is white, the whole of the personnel team, which compromises twelve people, are white.

Lorna's description, or something like it, is replicated in almost all the *Double Disadvantage* interviews, as we would expect from the statistical picture presented in Chapter 2. BME employees are crowded into certain areas in the organisation, and concentrated in the lowest tiers in organisational hierarchies. Hardly any woman spoke of having black women managers. Some mentioned that there had never, ever been a black woman manager in their organisation. A few mentioned black men in positions of authority and, in the more feminised areas such as social work or teaching, women middle managers were described as quite numerous, although at the very top men predominated. It is clear that the intersection of ethnicity and gender at work is here producing a very specific effect: that often *black women are virtually excluded from management*. We shall discuss this more fully in the next chapter.

Different kinds of problem were highlighted by women who found themselves in organisations where they were the only BME worker. These women were particularly likely to feel isolated and ignored by their workmates or subject to racist comments:

> What was coming out today is the isolation. It's so high on the agenda. People feeling lonely. They don't feel somebody's understanding what they're going through.
>
> (Bella USDAW)

For example Serena had to listen to people comparing her 'kinky hair' to that of a 'golliwog', and was asked whether as a black woman she sunbathed topless. She could do nothing about these comments which she rightly perceived as extremely offensive:

> But the thing is, right, as the only black person in that group, I felt that I wasn't in a position to open my mouth and say anything because they all think the same way. And you do feel isolated to think that … no matter how much it hurts you, what can you say?

This experience of isolation and hostility can be particularly disorienting for younger people, without the mental resilience and support structures to see them through. A UNISON member, Tamara, who had grown up in a multiethnic area, described the experience of nurse training in a rural part of Wales. As the only black trainee, she was subject to bullying and adverse comments:

> I was the only black person there are you know, I had some problems with some people. And I really hated it, I hated my training actually.

Young black and Asian women and men whom we have interviewed for other projects have been so discouraged by such experiences that some respond by seeking 'sheltered' environments, such as jobs within ethnic enclaves, or indeed some may quit the labour market altogether.

BME employees were also more likely in some occupational settings to hold more insecure posts (part-time, temporary or jobs whose permanency was threatened). For example, this seemed to be the case in FE and HE institutions: Neela, a NATFHE activist, told us that in her college the majority of the black staff were in part-time jobs, while Shahnaz explained that in her institution the inferior working conditions faced by black staff also made it hard for them to be active participants within the union:

> Lots of black people are underpaid, overworked, and not based on one campus. They're doing odds and sods all over the place. They don't have access. They don't have time … I think there are lots of black people who can really, really contribute a great deal to the union and make it seem a home for all of us. But they need nurturing, they need information, they need training, they need mentoring, they need to be networked. They need to be supported over and above the drudgery of work, because a lot of them are working to inferior terms and conditions.

Thus the potential of these women is blocked. In effect, being marginalised in the workplace also inhibits inclusion in the union.

We shall have more to say about inclusion and exclusion in the union later in the chapter, but we want to concentrate here on the problems these women have faced within the workplace. Another comment from Neela sums up the common concerns which were voiced to us:

> It's to do with discrimination, it's to do with promotion, it's to do with workloads, whether it's fair, it's to do with transparency and how thing happen in an organisation. For example, when the money is allocated, let's say for my programme, then nobody is getting it differently from you, the criteria is clear and it's adhered to, and that's the kind of thing, rather than fewer resources to my pro-gramme, or use different criteria. So those are the intricacies that are actually quite pernicious and negative for back people particularly.

The activist women, like all employees, wish to be treated fairly, with respect, with dignity, to be considered as equal to their peers. These ideas of equity, dignity and respect represent the key vocabulary for today's workplaces where old deferential values of hierarchy, allocated status and humiliation (the traditional rituals of apprenticeship and time-serving) have long been challenged, not least by women, within what we have described elsewhere as a 'climate of equality' (Bradley 1999). However, despite the near common proclamation of these values, the reality is that many of our participants reported continued levels of racism and sexism. But it should be noted that these are blanket terms: the nature of racism and sexism vary according to time, place and con-text, as we will explore in the next sections.

The bad old days: imperialist racism and patriarchal sexism

Many participants in telling their stories referred to the bad experiences of their parents as postwar migrants, acknowledging the sufferings and sacrifices that had been endured in working for a better future from which they had subsequently benefited:

> My parents and like that group, they came here, they had a family to support and maintain. Because they're economic immigrants, yeah? And they have family to maintain and all that. So they put up with an awful lot. And a lot of them didn't come on their knees, they had

things that they sold up, quite good jobs, because they were told it was better. They were invited, you see? My mum was a nurse, but she came here to better herself. She also came trained. She became a dietician, but still within a nursing field. But you still got treated like rubbish. In the end she left. and she emigrated to America where – they say America is racist, but if you've got the qualifications and the ability to do the job, they do not see the colour.

(Amber UNISON)

Serena remembered how back in 1979 when she started work, BME workers were paid a kind of 'underclass' rate, below the level of the lowest paid white employees:

They had unskilled labourers and we weren't even paid as a labourer. But yet we were keeping the company afloat. I mean, to think that all the people that worked there were black or from ethnic minorities, and we didn't even get a labourer's wage and nobody complained. But it just goes to show, you think in '79 black people were not getting the same wages within a known world company.

The racism of the 1950s and 1960s was seen as more overt and based on very clear ideologies of white superiority and supremacy (Banton 1987; Miles 1989). Racism was also much more public and people were less reluctant about expressing it openly. Linda summarised the difference:

My friends who were around at that time, we worked very hard to reach positions. A lot of my friends became sort of teachers, not many nurses, they said we don't want to be nurses. But they sort of branched off in various jobs, you know. And it wasn't, it wasn't the support from the education system, trust me. It was our hard work and our parents actually pushing us. Yeah, coz, the racism was even, well, it's bad now, but in those days I think it was more, more overt. You know, it was in your face. I think anyway. Now it's sort of more covert... You don't really think that they are being racist unless you think, hang on are they being racist? So it's not so open as it was, I don't think anyway.

The framing of social hierarchy in the postwar decades was still predicated upon what has been explored by race theorists as 'scientific racism' (Banton 1987; Anthias and Yuval-Davis 1992) of the Victorian era, which portrayed 'races' as having different genetic capacities: black 'races' were considered closer to nature and less intelligent. Sexism also was defended by quasi-scientific ideas: women were seen as 'naturally' weaker, less intelligent and less rational:

> I can still remember things in the workplace where people would say things like, well you have got a smaller brain you can't operate this kind of machine, women are really crap at operating technical machinery. It's very strange isn't it that women can operate washing machines which can be quite hi-tech and microwaves and ovens and everything else, yet when it comes to the black goods, the video and stereo etc., oh the computer, oh no you can't do that, it's too technical for you, dear, you know that sort of stuff.
>
> (Marsha CWU)

Thus hierarchies and the separation of genders and ethnic groups were habitually justified as part of a 'natural order' (Bradley 2007). As Martin Barker (1981) and others have described, this scientific racism was gradually succeeded by a 'new racism' based on ideas of cultural (and currently) religious difference. Within this way of thinking, racialised and gendered structures are portrayed as freely chosen rather than natural, but 'chalk and cheese don't mix'.

Our participants had in their younger days experienced some of these older more overt forms of racism and sexism within their family and working lives. One of the most distressing accounts of this came from Parvati, who had arrived in England from India as a young woman. She described the problems she had encountered over her child's schooling and the damage her child had faced:

> We used to live in Sussex and naturally that was the only Asian family in that area for miles. Kids were not used to seeing Asian kids. And kids were teasing her, 'You've got a chocolate face!' And she turned around and said, 'You've got ice-cream face!' You know, vanilla ice-cream, kids' stuff. She came home and told me about this and I said, 'Fine', and that was the result. Then she came back the next day and said, 'Mum, the kids were being really horrible to me and calling me all sorts of names', and I said, 'What names?' And she said, 'Some of them I couldn't even understand but what they were saying seemed quite rude.' So she was really upset and it went on for two or three days. Until one day she came home in the afternoon and she actually went straight out into the kitchen, took the biggest knife there and said, 'I'm going to take all my skin off.' I said, 'Why?'

She said, 'I've seen whenever I've received a cut of some sort, the skin that comes in underneath is very pale like my friends' skin. They won't be able to tease me after that.'

When Parvati complained to the school about her daughter's treatment the racism was transferred onto her:

She said to me, 'You bloody Asians come here and get free education for your kids and you have the nerve to come and ask me to worry about your child. She has to learn to live with the other kids. Why don't you just go back to where you've come from?' And this was the deputy head. I was just shaking. And I just didn't know how to deal with it. I didn't cry, but I was almost on the verge of it.

Parvati continued to struggle with racism, alongside sexism, in her career as a scientist, repeatedly failing to get promotions when she applied for them, although she had covered for the jobs of those being replaced:

And so I went to my Head of Department and I said, 'What am I doing wrong? If I'm good enough to do the work, why can't I get the job?' He turned around and said something – I don't know if I can remember the exact words because it was about 15, 16 years ago – he said, 'I thought you might have got the message by now that we are not gonna give you promotion here. I don't understand why you women and you Asians want to compete with us at a similar sort of level. You've got your L1. What's your problem? Your husband has got a good job. Why do you want promotion?'

Here we see an interesting example of the intersectionality of gender and racism with class: the resentment expressed by many white males about competition for top academic jobs by women and Asians was heightened as Parvati's husband was a well-paid medical consultant.

As well as racism, several women spoke of sexist exclusion in the early stages of their careers. Prejudice against married women when they have children, still an issue today, was more marked then as Nancy, a teacher, described:

Someone else was doing my job when I was on maternity and it was an awful experience actually; for eight months I had go through an awful experience where somebody else was promised my job... On the premise that she has had this child and she won't stay kind of attitude and they were promised my job by their line manager so I had eight months of, I think you would call it hell, absolute hell!

Nadia had a similar experience with a local authority:

When I went on maternity leave, obviously it was years ago, and then, there weren't many um, legislations in regards to women taking maternity leave, at the time I was the first person ever to go on maternity leave and when I came back I was made to sit in a completely different office to everybody else, which was awful. I was treated really, really badly. It was like a punishment that I had taken this time off...I never took the full entitlement. I came back to work when my daughter was three months because I felt guilty.

Women from the CWU were the most likely to experience overt sex discrimination, however, as they were working in a male-dominated area. It was clear that in the past, women's presence in 'men's jobs' was resented and attempts made to keep them out. Marsha described her struggles to qualify as a telephone engineer:

It wasn't a terribly good experience because of the people I was with, the 16–17-year-old boys. And of course they are particularly immature at that age. And I being a novelty, you know I'm the butt of all the jokes and the harassment and everything else, and a lot of experiments used to get sabotaged, my workshop work and working on the blades, things used to get sabotaged there as well, so there was lots of horrible things going on...One time I had to take a test in electrical principles, which is a lot of writing, lots of equations. I still have got the scars now, someone slammed my fingers in the locker and of course all my fingers were bleeding and they had to be bandaged up, right? So the next day my hand is bandaged up like this and I said to the lecturer, 'you know look I can't take my test , can I take it another time', and he said 'no you can't'. 'Well', I said, 'can I have some extra time, you know 'coz it's hard for me to hold the pen?' 'No'. I didn't get any concession whatsoever from him at all, so I thought okay. I passed it, I managed just to pass that one. But that was not a very pleasant time at all, during the apprenticeship. In one workplace I got really sort of group harassment, I used to spend my lunch times in the women's toilets and stuff like that and tea breaks. You know, it was my only refuge because nobody else went in there of course, because there were no other women. They used to nick my tools and do stupid things like that. Posters used to go up, awful posters.

Interestingly in this case Marsha found that male bonding outweighed ethnic solidarity. One of her colleagues was a black man who joined in with the harassment, but was himself harassed on racial grounds:

I had a word with him once and I said, 'you know what it's like, why are you giving me all this hassle?' He says, 'well if I don't join in then they'll have a go at me.'

It is heartening to report that this kind of treatment, though it made individual women extremely miserable, led in the end to resistance, in the form of collective action and the first steps of spontaneous self-organisation. Many of the UNISON activists remembered the birth of the black workers' and women's groups within NALGO described by Humphrey (2000). Ginette told us the story:

I and a group of other workers formed the black workers' group and created those opportunities. We tackled the housing service about institutionalised racism way back in 1986…We held a day called 'A Day on Race' where every black worker within the housing service had to leave whatever work they were doing and attend at the civic centre. A lot of the policy that they now use is based on what came out on that day. For instance, it then became policy in this authority that no interviews could take place without someone from the black and minority ethnic community and a female person on there regardless of colour or creed and that is still the practice today. And out of the black workers came Section 11 Equality Officers posts and they were based in every area office; and that's the direct result of the black workers' group.

The not-so-good new days: an array of racisms

As Linda's comment quoted above indicated, racism today tends to take a different form. Norms of the much derided 'political correctness' have contributed to a climate in which people are wary of expressing racist or sexist opinions openly. This has been reinforced by recent increases in legislation. There is also a vocal anti-racist public and many young people are strongly supportive of the values of multiculturalism. Not that racism has disappeared; it has just been driven underground. But the most common manifestations are what we have referred to in other writings as 'everyday racism' (Bradley, Healy et al. 2007): remarks, actions and behaviours which, in a small way but persistently, emphasise difference from the majority: for example, phrases such as 'you people', 'you lot' or 'that's one of yours' which immediately posit the BME person as part of 'the other', or repeated failures to invite the black employee to be part of a group going out to lunch.

This type of racism can be compared to subtler forms of sexism, in which language is used to imply that women are secondary to men:

> It doesn't have to be blatant sexism, for yourself as a woman to feel that you have been undermined because of your gender. You know even language, the use of language, like being called Mister all the time, Chairman, you know, all these things. When you raise these issues people think you are being, oh god, what's she saying, can't say chairman anymore, and I try and explain to people that it's not just that word, it's a whole package of stuff that just undermines women in the workplace. You end up feeling invisible by the use of language. It excludes or includes, doesn't it? Language is a very powerful tool in that.
>
> (Marsha CWU)

Sexism also continues to be used to trivialise women as 'little people' whose minds are full of things incompatible with the serious business of the workplace. Vicki, a Royal Mail engineer, described male comments during an equality course:

> 'Oh yeah, well women, when they're sorting letters, they start doing their finger nails.' And you're just like, come on, like! You've probably seen someone do it once, but the way that people were going on it was like women were still put in a category of being, we wear make up, we spend all our time doing it, we do it while we're driving, we do it while we're working, you know? And one guy even said to the point where women do their toe nails when they're like doing the letters!

The absurdity of some of these comments would be laughable if the consequences were not so serious. This almost running commentary about the nature of 'you people' (Bradley, Healy et al. 2007) may seem a small thing, but in its persistence and prevalence is extremely undermining. It may be conscious or unconscious, and its subtlety makes it difficult to complain about. Women we have interviewed for this project and others often impute it to white people's ignorance. Muslim women complained to us that they were pestered with 'why do you do that' type questions about wearing headscarves, or fasting during Ramadan. Similarly, Verity experienced ignorance about Caribbean life:

> When I met a white person they just assumed that I was either from Africa or Jamaica. Now people are more educated, so there should be no ignorance, and in the schools people should be taught about all the different countries. In the Caribbean there's several islands, there's not just one island, Jamaica. You know, things like that. I mean, my manager asked me if, she asked me if the Caribbean was run by one prime minister! I thought, I can't believe that you could be so ignorant.

This kind of cultural ignorance can also be a problem within the union as demonstrated in the following comment from Serena which also raises the key issue of the English drinking culture. Many women told us this makes it difficult for them to socialise with white colleagues; it is hard to join in pub-based forms of social networking. The prohibition of alcohol within Islam makes this a particularly worrying issue for Muslim women, yet if they don't join in with this culture they may be viewed as boring and stand-offish. This is true both in workplaces and in union circles as Serena's account shows:

> There's no kind of um...even thoughts for cultural things. I mean black people don't really sit in pubs. Even whilst I was going on the coach going down, I said I didn't drink and somebody else, one of the other reps, said to me, 'Well how do you enjoy yourself?' And I thought, if he knew anything about anybody's culture...we're more sort of going round having a good meal, but our social life surrounds food! [Laughs] You know what I mean? It's not going to the pub, having a packet of crisps and a beer. That's not our way. So they didn't think. Even a union that's all for equal ops, they had no thought.

However, not all racism is covert. Nadia gave us a lengthy account of the problems she had to tackle as a union rep when a positive action scheme was introduced in her college security department. In this story, overt racism from the portering staff is allied with everyday racism from managers who assume that 'the public' is all white:

> Within the security department it was, until about two years ago, predominantly pure white culture, it was just white men, and we

spoke with the branch secretary to the HR, and said that it does not reflect the college as a whole, and that they should have some black security guards. So we took some positive action and they bought in 30 black security guards, which has just caused so much conflict now ... A lot of these guys are middle-aged, they are about 45 to 60 years old. And they have been here for years and then all of a sudden they have got all these black guys working with them. You know, they say things like, 'they can't speak, and I can't understand them, they smell'. And the black guys are complaining that they have to do all the chores such as patrolling, while all the white guards are just sitting in there, letting people in ... The management are saying to me, 'Nadia, how would you feel if you came into this building and somebody is there trying to direct you, and you can't understand a word that they are saying?' And I said to her, 'To be quite honest, if I was an African person come to the front door, and a black person was directing, I would feel really good.' They are not looking, all they can see is that there are white people coming in, they cannot see the college as a whole ... People are refusing to work with them, won't open doors because they don't want to work with them, you know, it's just blatant. They don't even realise that they are being racist. I mean, there's this one guy, and I get on really well with him, always have for years, there's tension between us now. He didn't realise I was a union rep and he would say, 'Oh, Nadia, I can't understand it, they bring all their funny food', and I was just looking at him, thinking, well I'm black and you are telling me these things, and he is just bizarre, you know. He doesn't see.

This also illustrates nicely the way racist stereotyping is subjectivised. Her colleague doesn't perceive Nadia's shared ethnicity with the portering staff because he thinks of her as a friend. Stereotyping occurs when such individualised personal responses are overridden by prejudiced thinking. The prevalence of stereotyping is one of the major issues raised by our participants. Again, the 'you people' scenario is employed to attribute characteristics to a whole group of people:

It has always been deemed that, if you are black, you cannot manage ... people say it is because of our temperament, it's because of the way we are, you know, it's that, you know, you people, you're all very highly strung.

(Ginette UNISON)

One common stereotype about which many complained is the idea of Caribbean and African women as aggressive:

> I think you are anyway as a black person, you are stereotyped straight away. You've definitely got a chip on your shoulder and you are definitely aggressive simply because you are black.
>
> (Jane CWU)

> White people perceive black women to be aggressive, I would say I'm assertive, but white people would say that I'm aggressive. I don't know, I think, I suppose this is one thing common amongst most black women is that um, that I don't wrap things up in cotton wool when I am telling you something, I try not to be rude, but I say it like I hear it or see it.
>
> (Nadia UNISON)

> In black people, assertiveness is aggression, and in white, aggression is assertiveness.
>
> (Amber UNISON)

By contrast, Asian women tend to be stereotyped as submissive and docile and people respond with shock if they behave differently. Thus Parvati was told that her problems were due to her strength as a woman, perceived as doubly threatening, as it was another case of inappropriate female 'aggression', but also challenged popular views of Asian women:

> Strength is the biggest weakness for men because they can't deal with that strength. And I said, 'Why should I be subservient?' Yes, they couldn't cope with that. They feel that, oh Asian women are supposed to be mild, subdued, subservient.

There is also a continuation of the old imperialist views of racial inferiority which stereotypes black people as intellectually weaker than white and therefore suited for 'lower-level' jobs:

> That's the way they make blacks feel. They make us feel like as if we don't have brains, even if you do cleaning, they say you are not doing it properly ... This is the way they treat us ... They have written us off before they even know us. In many case, most of these manager, they are white, they have got basic qualifications, they started treating graduates like a pack of idiots.
>
> (Jessica USDAW)

Again, a complex interaction of masculinity, racial stereotyping and class resentment may be at play here as in the account given by Lorna, who was working as a cashier while doing a degree:

> My previous manager said to me, 'Oh, you are just one of those people who think they go to university and know it all', and I goes 'no I'm not, you don't know the first thing about me, I mean don't project your insecurities on me, What is the highest level of education you got up to?' He goes 'I've got a couple of O Levels.' I goes, 'There you go, straight way coz I go to university you see me as a threat; before you start to put your insecurities on me you should take time to find out about me and what sort of a person I really am.' So I do think that the fact that I have got a degree, studying for a masters, that I'm quite stable, I've got my own house, got a car, things they haven't got. My manager lives at home with his parents, you know.

Practices of racism: condoning discrimination and victimisation

We have already noted that BME women do not necessarily take things passively and, as figures from the Tribunal Service discussed in Chapter 4 show, many do attempt to raise complaints about racial harassment within the workplace. But a common complaint was that managers failed to take effective action in such cases. We view this failure to act as being in itself a form of racist behaviour: letting racists (or sexists) get away with it is effectively condoning discrimination:

> The human resources manager basically said to me that, oh that they would watch him in the future and if he did it again then they would deal with him and blah, blah, blah, and basically rubbish, you know what I mean?
>
> (Cassie USDAW)

> A couple of weeks ago, for example, a member of staff called me an 'effing black bitch'. Um, and I lost my rag because I had been report-ing this member of staff to the manager for like seven months and he didn't do anything about it. For seven months I have been getting abuse from this particular member of staff, and I went through all the procedures and he wouldn't do anything about it.
>
> (Lorna USDAW)

This failure to act is particularly prevalent where racism comes from customers or clients:

> There was one occasion where a patient refused me to look after her and she was being awkward towards me. When I said to my ward manager, I'm not going to deal with that patient she's being difficult, she went and spoke to that patient and told me not to go near her and that was it!...And, there was another occasion when a patient shouted racist abuse at me, and um, the next time I went into work they said that I had to move wards.
>
> (Tamara UNISON)

Many nurses have told us that Tamara's experience is common within the NHS. Here the victim of racial harassment is being treated as if she was the problem.

Another form of racism and sexism which the participants reported was victimisation of people who protested about discrimination or who, as union representatives, defended others who experienced it. Thus Nadia felt that her employer was responding to her activism by pushing her to take redundancy, being eager to be rid of her:

> Because I am too vocal, um, too militant, yeah. So they would give me the money to go, it's just a matter of time, everyone I negotiate with wants me to leave. So I'm just waiting for them to tell me how much they'll be offering, and they are just dragging their feet, but in principle I have been told that it's going to happen.

Neela believed that her union activism had adversely affected her career opportunities:

> I don't think I have gone up as far as I would have liked to and expected to. In a way some of it was positive development and some of it was negative and a lot of it had to do around issues of equal opportunities. So if I found myself being very vocal, at one point. Um, so at some stages it prevented promotion.

Shockingly, Nuala found that once she had become am USDAW rep the management started bringing accusations of theft and drinking at work against her in order to facilitate her dismissal:

> I've been having peace within myself until I was made union rep. I was facing a lot of problems. Even as of now, too, I'm still facing war

at the moment. . They say they suspect me in a condition with alcohol. I say, 'What alcohol?' And I know there is no case there and the hearing is Friday. So it is very hard.

Mary's experience was similar and she also complained that her union branch had not helped her to fight against victimisation, despite the amount of equalities work she had carried out for them:

Social services do not think that it's compatible to be a manager and a union branch officer, or shop steward. So I've had a lot of what I call kind of harassment and bullying and threats and trumped up charges and all sorts, over the last couple of years particularly. The union have been aware of it and I've been feeding it to them, and I haven't seen any kind of outcome. Certainly the fact that I haven't had a job for a year and a half, and that it's obviously vindictive.

Inclusion and the trade union

Although Mary was not the only one who made this kind of complaint about the failure of her union branch to protect her, across our sample the women's experience of becoming involved in the union was very positive. In fact, by and large, we can say that the union acted as a mechanism of inclusion for BME women where employers might be dragging their feet in terms of EO implementation. This mechanism worked in a number of ways. First, it was a way of bringing together BME women through black networks, conferences and so forth, so that women were able to share their experiences and not feel that they were alone in their difficulties. Second, it provided them with knowledge and information which they were able to use to improve their position. Third, it offered them status in the workplace with their colleagues whom they represented, expanding their social networks in their own workplaces and outside them. Fourth, it opened up new opportunities for activities such as educational courses or legal work in grievances or tribunals. Finally, for some women, as we shall see in a later chapter, it opened up alternative careers in which their frustrated ambitions and talents could be properly engaged.

When we asked the women if they felt empowered by their experience, the answer was overwhelmingly positive as these comments from two UNISON members show:

I feel empowered and I can actually talk more on behalf of my black colleagues because I attend more meetings and I will go up to the front and say what I have to say. But it has taken years to actually feel that I'm knowledgeable enough to you know.

(Linda)

I am now acting convenor and people have said, 'how are you doing?', and I have said, 'it is empowering'. It is empowering as a black woman to sit in meetings with people who are on pay scales that are off the scale, you know, maybe £80,000 a year. I have been doing this job now for 12 years and I am sitting with people who are directors and assistant directors and I know that I have got the upper hand, and it is empowering.

(Ginette)

Despite stereotypings of black women as 'naturally' aggressive, a number spoke of shyness and lack of confidence arising from the circumstances of the prior lives:

I was lacking in confidence, very much so. I was an army wife. I used to stay at home and look after the children. Being involved in the union has really changed my life. It's given me so much more confidence. I'm sure I was confident when I was younger, and then marriage and sort of having children and not having any adults to talk to most of the time, sort of wears you down a bit.

(Shelly)

Definitely more confident in myself, yeah. Because when I first joined I was shy. I went to meetings and I would sit there. And you'd know what you want to say, but because there was like 99 men and you're the only one woman there, you just thought well they're not gonna listen. I must give credit to the Branch Secretary. He noticed it and he said, 'Oh don't worry, I've been there', and he was really and truly supportive. And this is when he started me on training and he said, 'You need training on this and that and the other.' And I went and yeah, I must say when I go to meetings now, you'll be hearing my voice.

(Gita CWU)

Gita's comment underlines the importance of training, which was seen by many participants as the crucial factor in their self-development. White women, too, have told us of how they find it difficult to speak unless they really know what they are talking about. BME women, as EOC research has shown (EOC 2007c), are particularly avid for learning and have snapped up courses on offer from both their own unions and the TUC. The comment of Rita, a retail worker, illustrates this well:

> I'd had my training as a safety rep and I thought, 'Oh, this is good!' And you start learning a lot of things and going different places. And you're meeting other people and you're hearing from them. Because when I first started doing it I'm thinking what have I let myself in for? I had this girl the other day, she said to me, 'Oh, you're like a book of knowledge!' It's taken me years to know what I know now. As they say, 'Knowledge is power', isn't it? So the more knowledge you've got, the more power you have to sort of challenge anything that's going.

The stories of the activists also show how much these processes of inclusion are a two-way thing. The BME women gain confidence, skills and contacts, and eventually power, which enables them to resist personal oppression:

> The thing about the union and everybody helping each other and it being very – well, supposedly – inclusive. I think that sort of brought me on to the point now where I've got to the stage in my life now where I won't take any rubbish. I won't take any crap at all from anybody.
>
> (Shelly CWU)

But they use that power positively on behalf of the union. They are prepared to put long hours of time into union work, help others with their problems and actively recruit others into the union. This is definitely a 'win-win' situation. Unions have much to gain by making black women active:

> They did something for me and that gave me sort of a sense of yes they are doing something, so let's see what there is and how far we can go to help the others as well. Not just myself, but others you know? And since then I've been with the union and doing all sorts. You know, helping people with health and safety, taking grievance cases and so on. And each time you achieve something, you win that case, you get that sort of uplifting and you think it's worth doing it. And I try to sort of recruit a lot of ethnic minorities.
>
> (Gita CWU)

Now I have realised that, any job you are in, try and join the union, especially blacks. You've got to join the union, otherwise you will be moving from one job to another, and you will be receiving the same treatment and you wouldn't even have the mouth to talk. So union can be your mouthpiece. They can be there for you. They can be your support and for that you can keep your job longer. It's an organisation which is, I wouldn't like to say it's compulsory, it's up to you, but I think it's necessary, they are a necessary instrument that you need to have as blacks.

(Jessica USDAW)

Such women, in sum, make incredibly committed union members who can help in the process of 'union renewal'.

Struggles within the union: men, power and exclusion

Unfortunately, not everyone within the unions seems to have grasped this truth. Although many women had gained so much from unions, the picture was not all positive. Some women had had negative experiences and found that their particular branch personnel were acting in an exclusionary way towards them. This can be attributed back to the long tradition of male control within unions:

The union is white, male dominated, it's a man's domain, being a union person, it was always a man's world. And you are talking about people in the car places like Dagenham, it would be a man, it would never be a woman. Do you see what I'm saying? That's tradition.

(Ginette)

This tradition made it hard for women to climb to high posts within the union, and also implied a certain style of behaviour which women as individuals found hard to cope with:

And our General Secretary at the time was very old school. You know, sort of a bit of a boxer.

Within the trade union, the higher you go, the more schoolboy it is.. There's not really a female, being black or white, up in the top ranks. They're all men. So it's hard. It's a struggle for women. It's because they've got that old schoolboy rule.

Women perceived the existence of the double bind and the double standard here: to be seen as an effective officer you need to appear tough; but for a woman to appear tough is against the rules of femininity:

> Men, who say that I'm being aggressive because I'm standing up for myself so that's not being assertive, that's being aggressive, when they are standing up and making bold speeches and everything else, oh aren't they good, they are good public speakers and all that. They are not being aggressive even if they are going like that (pounds table) and shouting and pointing the finger and everything else. Um, they are not seen as aggressive, so there's double standards in operation. And I think again in the trade union movement um, the powerful speakers and the thumpy table negotiators are always seen as the best.

As some men fight to defend what they see as their territory, they may quite actively block women's paths within the union. We were told of opposition to black networks being set up, of information about training and events being withheld, and of some women experiencing considerable resistance when they stood for office or if they succeeded in getting onto committees.

> There is a double bind, and there's still that kind of old boys' network, um, and they just keep information to themselves and they still do that. I'm the only woman as one of the officers to go to management meetings with them, so they still do have little prior meetings themselves and I feel excluded from it, and they tell me about it occasionally. They have meetings that I am not included in, with the branch officer.

We have already highlighted the importance of the Macpherson Report as a spur to change within unions and the TUC Stephen Lawrence Task Group was designed to tackle the kinds of blockages discussed above. As mentioned in Chapter 6, all four case study unions had Task Group members. But while top officials had espoused the Task Group's ideals, this had not always filtered down to branch level. We asked all our participants whether they felt the Macpherson report had changed things for them and the answers were very varied. Many felt the report had been an important turning point in race relations. Thus one paid official stated that it had entirely changed employers' approaches: 'now we are pushing at an open door.' However, some women stressed the failure of their branches to implement the report's recommendations, either because of lack of understanding or because they were inherently opposed to it:

> We've got a joint statement on institutional discrimination, institutional racism, effectively as a result of the Stephen Lawrence Inquiry, but even that I think they failed to understand what it actually means. They think it's individual racists that make the organisation institutionally racist, but they really don't understand the concept.
>
> (Marsha)

> UNISON have just told them, 'There's the report. File it and implement it', which a lot of them haven't. Because a lot of them are against it – you'd be surprised how many trade unions are against self-organised groups. You know, branch officers and secretaries, they're terrible. But it's a game really, and you know it's just you need to know how to play the game to get what you want!
>
> (Alexa)

Nevertheless, as Alexa's comment indicates, shrewd strategising using the report can be utilised by women to make progress and the positive effects have been experienced by other women, such as Shelly who had become a TUC tutor as a result:

> As a spin-off from the Stephen Lawrence Inquiry, obviously everybody's looking at themselves – how the unions are. And the TUC couldn't remove themselves from it. They had to look at themselves as well. And they obviously looked at their tutors and thought, 'Oh, we haven't got many black tutors. We've got very, very few black women teachers.' So they contacted all the affiliated unions and said, 'Have you got any black members that would be interested in being tutors in TUC?' So it was like a fast-track course. So I went through that route.

Changing the union: networks, training and intersectionality

Women like Shelly are slowly getting themselves into a position where they can influence union practices to become more receptive to black women. Although we heard examples of struggles to get change accepted, it would be a great mistake to underestimate the power and determination of such women to effect change. Their experience of racism and sexism within the union often appeared to strengthen their will to resist.

Some of the changes they see as necessary would benefit all women of any backgrounds, especially in male-dominated unions. Some of the problems long identified by women activists remain unaddressed:

> Black people, for instance, they want to join a union, but the union hasn't actually prepared or done their homework when working with ethnic minority members. First of all childcare facilities. If you're gonna have meetings, say, once a month, they would definitely need childcare. Somewhere to take their children to, because most of the meetings are in the evenings after work, like 6 o'clock.
>
> (Gita CWU)

But in terms of the specific needs of BME women, a very strong theme emerged that setting up of some kind of black networking or liaising structure was a necessary first step for improving their participation. This was the way many of our interviewees found their way from passive to active union membership (Bradley 1999). Nadia's account illustrates this:

> The reason why I became really quite active within UNISON is because a guy called Jacob, he actually sent round an e-mail about a black workers' group, to start a black workers' group; ... so I was intrigued by this, so I went along to the meeting just to see why we need to have a black workers' group, and when I attended the meeting with Jacob, there was myself, another woman called Alice and another women who left, so it was just four of us. Oh, yes there was an Asian guy who actually explained the reason why there are black workers' groups and the mechanisms, and that was it. That was it for me. I was in there.
>
> (Nadia)

We argue, then, that despite the problems with SOGs discussed in Chapter 6, they are a crucial and effective mechanism of inclusion. Although there remains the problem of white women dominating the agenda within the women's structures and black men dominating within the race equality structures, some BME women are able to bridge the structural divide and to develop their own personal awareness of intersectionality:

> I have done a course with the black and minority black workers and I did a course with a gay and lesbian group, and I think that

there are similar things that we all should be doing as well as with the women's group. Um, because you know, as a woman there's so many things one has in common and colour does not even come in to it.

(Ginette UNISON)

You have to deal with the sexism as well as the racism.. Because um, if you just deal with the racism, it's not going to stop black women getting harassed because of their gender. Sometimes obviously it's difficult to tell if a white person is harassing a black women, is it because she is black or is it because she is a woman? I think that if it's a white man harassing a black woman, I would say firstly it's because she's a woman and secondly because of her race.

(Marsha CWU)

Serena commented that although her own concerns had been for visible minorities (black workers and women), her union involvement had taught her about the problems also experienced by gays and lesbians: 'it's opening up your mind'.

Conclusion

In this chapter we have highlighted the persistence of sexism and racism which perpetuate the exclusion of women in the workforce. BME women continue to be channelled into certain types of jobs and to be denied promotion chances, an issue which will be more fully explored in the next chapter. Although many organisations are working to develop more effective inclusionary practices as part of their equality and diversity programmes (Bradley, Healy et al. 2007), at the time of our interviews these did not seem to have made a great impact on the working relationships of our participants.

In contrast, the trade unions were providing many of these women with opportunities which made them feel more included both within the union itself and subsequently within their organisations. Unions offered them space and resources which enabled them to channel their resistance to racism and sexism. While trade unions themselves can be exclusionary, especially at the branch level where white, male lay officers may be quite resistant to central EO initiatives, these women were using their black support networks and the training they had received to fight their way into union structures. While black members' and women's SOGS may be seen by some people to be divisive and to encourage separatism, we consider them to be extremely effective mechanisms of inclusion, providing women with the necessary resources to develop careers both inside and outside the union, as we will discuss in the next two chapters.

9
Career and Career Development

Introduction

In Chapter 3, we introduced the concept of the 'career' and defined it as the 'the dialectical relationship between self and circumstance' (1985). This relationship encapsulates perfectly the careers of the women in our study. To capture the richness and complexity of their careers is a challenge. We have charted already their experiences of exclusion in Chapter 8, and in Chapter 10 we shall explore their union careers.

The women in our study undertook a wide range of work: they were nurses, clerical workers, personal assistants, administrators, team leaders, social workers, IT officers, teachers and tutors, engineers, sales assistants, training officers, kitchen designers, receptionists, cashiers. In other words, they covered a wide span of work and worked at different levels of responsibility. Some were in jobs characterised as gendered either because they were done mainly by women, but also in fewer cases by men. They were also in jobs where men and women were in roughly equal numbers. Some worked with mainly white staff, others with black staff. Some dealt with the public, black and white, for others their work was to focus on particular ethnic minority communities. They worked in the public sector, the private sector and the voluntary sector. Their length of employment ranged from one year to 30 years. Thus, in examining their experiences, we shall be capturing a wide range of career stories that will give us important insights into black and minority ethnic women's experiences.

This is not a conventional chapter on career development since we do not only focus on the hierarchical career. This is partly because of the experience that the women in our study have of blocked careers, as outlined in Chapter 8, but also because the women were special because of their union involvement. This latter point has an important effect on the choices which they wish to make and the way their careers unfold. Whilst the next chapter examines how their union careers unfold, here we provide insight into their employment careers.

Further insights on career emerge from Hughes (1956) who saw careers as both objective (the way a career looks to others) and subjective (the individual's view of his or her career experiences). Sikes, Measor and Woods' view that the adult career is the outcome of a dialectical relationship between self and circumstances (1985). Thus we do not use the 'career concept' as limited to a vertical career, but instead embrace the horizontal, temporal, individual, collective, gendered, ethnicised and dynamic aspects of career (Bradley, Healy and Mukherjee 2004). Drawing on our earlier work (Bradley, Measor and Woods 2004), we argue that the dynamic nature of career may be characterised as 'career development'. From the work of, for example, Arnold (1997), Becker (1952), Dex (1984), Evetts (1989), Sikes, Measor and Woods (1985), it is evident that popular associations of the term 'career' with promotion and material rewards will provide only partial insight. For Arnold the term 'career development' may be seen as the 'particular way that an individual's career unfolds' (1997:18) arguing that 'development' may have positive, unwelcome and neutral overtones (ibid.:19). We argue in our 2004 paper that career developments, or unfolding work profiles, are shaped by the opportunities and constraints provided by the particular structural context as mediated by the particular actor and the available degrees of agency, and involve vertical, horizontal, temporal and spatial movement including career curtailment. Yet 'career development' in the literature is firmly placed in the unitary mode of management or as part of the individual's own responsibility and free choice. Whereas in reality, as Chapter 3 argued, choice is severely constrained and this constraint is gendered. Crompton with Le Feuvre (1996) conclude their study of women in banking and in pharmacy by stating that 'many of the opportunities available to women in respect of paid employment are in practice open only to those who are prepared to behave as surrogate men'. Indeed, much research suggests that women who cannot, or do not wish to, adopt masculine practices, behaviours and values will be hampered if they seek senior promotions to senior posts (Marshall 1995; Wacjman 1998).

Our study reveals that, similarly, black and Asian women if they wish to succeed, must behave as if they were not only men, but white men at that. It is the case that the individual has responsibility for their careers, but this is inevitably within a constrained context, within what we referred to earlier as 'variable degrees of freedom' (Mouzelis 1989:630). The circumstances for black women in any employment context therefore are shaped by the gendered and ethnicised relationships and structures they encounter. Their particular circumstances will also be fashioned by the employers' enabling or constraining role in career development, which may of course be mediated by trade union involvement (Bradley, Healy and Mukherjee 2004). Thus to understand the careers of the women in this study, we need to understand the contexts in which they work.

The context of work

The work contexts were in many ways quite different. The women in our study worked in colleges, universities, hospitals, local government offices, telecommunication offices, in the community, in shops, in postal sorting to name but a few. The previous chapter has outlined their experience of racism and sexism at work. This is a critical aspect that will shape the way that careers unfold. Drawing on Acker (2006), the visible aspect of inequalities will also shape this context. In many of the organisations where the women worked, the hierarchies were dominated by men. Where women held senior roles, they tended to be white women, although these tended to be fewer in number.

In the health services, women reported:

> only one black manager, the people in the canteen are black or Filipino. Clinic clerks are black and Asian. Sisters are all white...the cleaners are going to be black.

In retail, the picture was similar:

> it's predominantly black on the lower levels, but in terms of management it's pure white...the store manager is white, the assistant manager is white, the whole of the personnel team which comprises 12 people is white.

Taking the example of her college context, Miranda described the visible inequalities:

> even though you've got a high percentage of black staff at classroom level and below and within the domestic staff as you move up through the administration level and through the management level they get fewer and fewer, the percentage reduce dramatically as you go up, as you go through...it's predominantly male in

management, managers are predominantly male, I don't know, that's probably just perception without counting, without doing the statistics.

Thus the work context was seen as dominated by white managers, thereby showing the very visible shape of inequality. This example is particularly important since Miranda worked in a college where there were predominantly black students. Governments talk of raising the aspirations of young people. There are obviously different dimensions to understanding why some young people have high aspirations and others do not. But the evidence of visible inequalities before their eyes may often be stark, and contribute to reducing aspirations in different ways. Julie expressed it very positively in the context of black teachers as role models for young people:

There are a lot of black people and ethnic minority here, and seeing a black woman as a teacher, you know, you are a role model to them. And I think that has a lot to do with their learning. And also you cannot separate culture from learning, you know, and that's an advantage.

However, we noted that where there were black and minority ethnic managers, they tended to be women. This was not unproblematic in the context of colleges where the majority of students were black:

from my own observation, I find that if there is any black and ethnic minority in positions of management, they are women, the majority is women. If there is ten, seven are women. That says quite a lot for the students, because there's I would say a large number of male students around so role models aren't there.

The above quotation from Candy suggests that there needs to be a greater gender balance for role models to have some impact. Widespread concern about the underachievement of black boys underpins this view.

Notwithstanding the comments above, Miranda also suggested that being black offered more opportunities under particular conditions:

I'm sure there is [scope for development here), um if you think about it and sort of put yourself forward and network so to speak and demonstrate that you are interested in sort of moving forward, if you put the effort in, I'm sure you can, there is scope here especially as a black woman, black person, I think there is more, I feel there is more scope here, there are limitations, don't get me wrong and there are problems here like anywhere else but there's, it's a greater opportunity here than I've seen in other colleges, where the minority of, the black staff, i.e., people who are not European, non-European they tend to have a less, reduced opportunity, here there are greater, because of the location in London, the location of the college.

This quotation is complex. Miranda states that 'there are less reduced opportunities'. Thus by implication, opportunities are more, but still not equal.

Relationships with other staff also shape the work context. Again, Chapter 8 has dealt with this in respect of racism and sexism. But we see a different picture when we set the work context in a multi-cultural environment. Here the cultural and linguistic skills of black and minority ethnic staff may be much in demand. Again drawing on Julie:

And we give a lot of support to the white staff on issues like that, because we have students from Nigeria, Ghana, Syria and Caribbean, I mean all, I mean even the subcontinent from the Asian countries and all over. And there's a lot, you know, I think education and culture are interwoven. Do you understand what I'm saying? And then we're there, as a support for the department, and I think our colleagues find us invaluable, find our contribution invaluable to the department, and they do say that openly.

Informal appreciation is an important aspect of career development. Knowing that your contribution is valued by peers may shape future relationships and indeed underpin opportunities for vertical development. However, in our study for the EOC, we noted that such linguistic and cultural skills may be taken for granted (Bradley, Healy, Forson and Kaur 2007). Undervaluing of skills can shape interactions and cause resentment. Linguistic skills were often mentioned in this context. Where someone spoke a second or third language and where this was not part of their job requirements, it seemed that this was perceived as a 'taken for granted' free resource available on demand. The individual either accepts extra responsibilities flowing from their cultural skills, or resists. Without resistance, their skills will continue to be undervalued through their compliance in the process. The following example provides a good illustration of this ethnicised undervaluation.

> I am Bangladeshi and you know, I can speak Bengali and, obviously at parent conferences, there is a lot of parents don't understand English well so they need people to translate...I am, happy I've got that skill, I can speak two languages, but it does feel a bit like you know, please don't put me in that situation because I've got my own workload to deal with.

In Chapter 3, drawing on Collinson, Knights and Collinson (1990), we noted how segregation is produced and reproduced through vicious circles of segregation. Critical to this is the role of gatekeepers and it is evident that human resource managers play a central role in the gate-keeping process. In our study, as quoted above, it was found that the personnel teams tended to be all white. This lack of ethnic visibility among gatekeepers does not inspire confidence among groups who are underrepresented in key positions. Further, human resource managers may, too, be the guardians of gendered and ethnicised rationalisations that lead to the exclusion of black women. Thus we find gender segregation remained strong, but it was overlaid with ethnicity, with white women more likely to dent the segregation practices than black women.

Moving on up

Careers may be linear, with individuals following a logical step-by-step approach with clear direction. But often careers are incremental, accidental and circumstantial. The following is a classic example of the less traditional way many people may enter the teaching profession.

> I started as a volunteer, teaching and then became, started to become as a part-time, visiting lecturer and then I went in for teacher training, on the teaching training qualifications which came along and got finally did the degree and I then I became full-time just about, soon after, before or after doing the degree, I can't remember now it was several years ago.

Thus Miranda's route was shaped by voluntary as well as paid employment experiences. This example also provides evidence of commitment to the work itself. It sounds easy when written down in a paragraph as we have done, but the time to obtain the training and degree qualifications would be immense, particularly while working. Thus moving on up in a career may be about developing and building professional skills and moving to more rewarding work.

The nature of the work that the women do, as well as their personal home life, will influence the degree of choice that women have. Some work has intrinsic qualities that may act as a deterrent to hierarchical development. Teaching is one such occupation. In an earlier study on schoolteachers, we showed that teaches had an intrinsic commitment to the work itself (Healy 1999a). However, this study provides further insight into the nature of this commitment and how our understanding may be also be rooted in the intersection of gender and race. Candy's story illustrates these complexities well:

> I've had opportunities to go higher, in terms of being course coordinators, manager, whatever but I choose not to do that, because I feel that, if you do you tend to sort of lose touch with the grass-roots, and the grass-roots for me is the students and I feel like I am a role model in that capacity, I have to be hands on, you know, I have to be there that they can relate to me when they're at their most vulnerable. Because, I teach basic, very basic students, and they're vulnerable and I feel that being the kind of person that I am, you know I am a people's person and I, I want to be there at that stage, that I can give them the support and the confidence to sort of become stronger and face things out there, I am not saying that I will be able to do it, but at least they can look at me and say well yeah you know I can relate to this person, and I feel that if I move too far up the ladder, I am going lose touch with that, and that, that's not what I want to do, so.

Thus for Candy, the intrinsic value of her work is closely tied up with helping her students challenge the inequalities they may face. Further, for her, being a role model to her students is more important than hierarchical career development which would take her away from her 'grass-roots'.

Kara from Unison also shared a similar commitment to her work and the value that it gives to minority groups. Kara worked for a voluntary counselling organisation for individuals, primarily from the minority ethnic communities, who misuse drugs and/or alcohol. She had a huge commitment to her work:

> Really enjoy it, that's why I'm still here. It's very challenging, however, I believe in it. I believe there's a huge need, and yeah, I enjoy it and er, yeah, very committed to the cause.

Commitment to voluntary work often has a price and this can be gendered and ethnicised, as the conversation with Kara exposed:

> Q: Do you feel that there's a lot of opportunity for you to develop personally as well?
>
> A: Yeah, I do. Yeah, I think I could grab what I want and run off, definitely, and get a much better salary and much better working conditions. However, I'm not that career-minded, actually. Like I said, I'm Bristol born and bred. I've always lived somewhere around this vicinity, and that's my client group at the moment, and that's where I feel I should be. So yes, I think there are some opportunities, but it's not something that I'm sort of holding my breath and thinking yeah, that's it, I'm gonna be up there in the next few years.
>
> Q: How about room for progression and things?
>
> A: I think finance is, in the voluntary sector, finance is always such a big issue. It is such a big, big issue. I mean, I think I'm on pittance. I'm being paid pittance, and I see like there's another organisation…who are on our doorstep…Now they're basically our white counterparts. They're the white organisation. They've been around a lot longer than us, I have to say that, but their posts, you know, every one that's advertised, are probably 22 to 24. Here, I'm on 18, so you know, and I mean, and I manage the project, so it just makes you think, well. But, as I said, career minded I'm not. I do want, I feel like I need more money, and I'm making lots of noise about it now, but um, it's not a case of I would pack up and leave just because of that.
>
> Q: So how do you see your future, in terms of your work?
>
> A: Right, in terms of my work I would like to continue to do my best, um, to work closely with this team, you know, to carry on, you know, working towards our mission statement.

Women in this study also critically appraised what being a manager would involve and how the management role would affect their health.

Tanya had wide and long experience and was asked if she would like further promotion:

> I just don't fancy it, I don't fancy the added stress, the added pressure, I've got two children at home and I wouldn't want to go home and take it out on them or have no time for them, if I knew it wasn't stressful and demanding, I suppose I would have gone for it ages ago, but I've seen some managers stressed, they go off with stress, because I could have sort of like been a sales advisor or go up to be an account manager but when you see the after-effects of some of them, you just go no, I think I'll stay where I am, yeah think I'll stay where I am. I actually, I don't actually see anything here, that I would say yeah I'd go for, so I either stay here and see what's happening.
>
> (CWU)

Thus the context of work is critical in understanding whether promotion is perceived as desirable. It is outside the scope of this study, but inevitably the work undertaken by its existing incumbents is relevant. If the work is designed around a long working-hours culture that suits those without other responsibilities (mostly men), then these jobs will be undesirable for those who have more complex commitments. Thus, women may not wish to act like 'surrogate men' (Crompton and Le Feuvre 1996).

In the case of other women, they feel that despite their strong work ethic (see Chapter 3), they will have difficulty in 'getting on'. Many reported that they were passed over at work. Many of the women in our study had qualifications that were significantly higher than the qualifications required for their current work. Particularly in retail, we found many women from Africa with undergraduate and postgraduate degrees working as store assistants:

> As a black woman, it's difficult to get anywhere... They want you to remain on the till for ever.

It seemed that the rationalisations around black women worked to negate the value of their qualifications. Women told us that they perceived a widespread belief among white managers that black people did not have the abilities for higher positions. Ginette provides a good example of the way that rationalisations are made to individuals to explain their lack of success:

> It has always been deemed that, if you are black, you cannot manage, it's a bit like saying that you cannot supervise, you know, because it's just the assumption that we are not able to do it. I have heard many reasons, people say it is because of our temperament, it's because of the way we are, you know, it's that, you know, you people, you're all very highly strung.

> (Ginette UNISON)

This quotation is very important. It illustrates a stereotype of black people, which is ascribed to all black people regardless of ability. Utilising this stereotype, the ludicrous consequence is that the same temperament is assumed to be shared by all black people. But on another day, a different stereotype may be ascribed to all black people, for example that all black people are laid back and therefore will not work unless pushed. Despite their contradictory nature, such stereotypes may be wheeled out by the same people seeking to justify unfair actions. The paradox is that that those who subscribe to contradictory rationalisations may not recognise the contradictions. Instead, such rationalisations abound. 'You people' (as stated to Ginette) or 'these people', are terms often used to negatively describe all members of particular ethnic groups; they continue to be used and form part of the vicious circles of segregation for the women in our study.

Thus our study revealed many examples of blocked opportunities, with black women confined to the lower levels of the hierarchies in whichever kind of organisation they worked. This applies as much in the college environment as it does in the shop or the office. Perhaps unsurprisingly, we noted the consequence of these demotivating experiences upon the women themselves. They reported feeling especially bitter about being confined to low-paid, low-grade jobs, given that so many of them had been sufficiently committed to their careers to acquire greater 'human capital' in the shape of qualifications and training, but did not get the recognition that this commitment deserved. It is crucial to remember that individuals may often be reluctant to seek promotion if they feel that their managers are not supportive. The above examples can deter all but the most determined from making promotion applications. When they do, they often face further contradictions.

Women's experiences of seeking promotion are particularly enlightening. The myopic nature of managers making promotion decisions is often startling and may act to the detriment of black women. Jane complained that:

> It was always the case, well you're not doing this, or you're not doing sufficient to qualify for that, but never actually say well what you need to do to qualify for it.
>
> (CWU)

Jane's example suggests that the manager needs to provide Jane with particular working experiences. Instead, the onus is put on her and she does not know how to tackle what is perceived as her lack of qualification because she cannot get clear advice. Negative assessments not accompanied by advice to improve are commonplace. The following example captures the experience of those at the mercy of negative rationalisations:

> I had five internal interviews, always someone else was promoted above me. One of the first reasons was because I did not smile enough at interview, the second reason was given that I didn't sell myself enough ... Then, they said you don't have the right personality, then they said, you weren't ready for it yet. So every time, there was an excuse.

This 'shifting sands' associated with promotion decisions has been evident in other studies on ethnicity, for example, our work on the health services (Healy and Oikelome 2006). The lack of transparency around the above woman's experiences is glaring. Yet decision makers continue to play these rationalisation games. In this case, it would appear that there was clear discrimination at work.

Yet in other circumstances, it may be that a woman is not ready for promotion. If this is the case, careful and helpful advice should be given on how that person might prepare themselves for the next promotion round. However, whilst this is important, it does presuppose that this advice will stand the test of time. In higher education, lecturers may be told one year to concentrate on their research, the next to focus on the student experience, and the next to focus on administration. The wider parameters around which many organisations make promotion decisions are open to abuse and therefore may be subject to claims of discrimination.

We also found concern about people being promoted beyond their current competencies. The rationale behind this may be a cynical attempt to meet ethnic monitoring targets and to ensure black representation in a department. In such cases, those promoted or recruited may not be given the appropriate preparation and training to undertake the job in an effective manner, yet they will be expected to perform at an adequate standard. However, what an adequate standard is may remain obscure. This practice can lead to tragic consequences for the individual involved. Linda explained what happens in these circumstances:

> Although that black person may not be doing too well, and is not the right person for the job, they may put them in positions, so to me that's racist because you're setting up people to fail, and that happens quite a bit in the department. That's when you get all the disciplinaries.

> (UNISON)

Being set up to fail is a major concern. It impacts negatively on the individual concerned and may well destroy their career prospects and their confidence. It will also confirm any racist rationalisations that will associate all black people with the failure of this one person.

Context is central in providing opportunities. Yet the context might equally constrain. In the following case, the organisation where Rosanne worked has gone through constant reorganisation. Rosanne went into her organisation as a full-time clerical officer and was told at the beginning that:

> Come in as a clerical officer fulltime and the idea was the company's growing and if you stick with us then in a short amount of time you will be promoted and things will be wonderful and it's an opportunity for you.

> Q: Right and how has it gone?
> A: Regression really, I've been demoted and departments have closed down, I've been drifting around, I drifted around for about four years, the main department I was in closed and we just weren't placed anywhere and I was like hold there's a lot of us in the same situation. Some people left, I stuck with it and ended up working up in the Customer Service Department for, they said six weeks initially, its been about three years now and now, you are part of our department you are here, you are staying here and staying put, but it took a long time to get settled in

because there's uncertainty, I could be moved anywhere do any-thing...yeah it is quite tough.

Rosanne had worked for the organisation for over ten years. In other words, she had invested considerable time in working there and yet had experienced constant change but no development:

> It's just, this I need to move on really from here, there is nothing for me here...apart from staying, sticking with what I am doing and get-ting paid the same wage. Things aren't looking good...they're get-ting larger and the job's diminished and the control of your day is less, less and less because you're all, you're like battery hens really sitting there and churning out the same work and doing the same thing, there is no variety anymore, there's no scope to move to other departments anymore, its all very closed. It's a whole lot of changes, they are very subtle changes but I've noticed them over the years and having worked in most of the departments over the 12 years, I can see the changes as well, so err but I just know that my face doesn't fit, especially being in the union. I am not going to get anyway, I worked before, before I sort of got involved I realised that anyway and just confirms it the things I've been doing.
>
> (CWU)

It was evident that conditions of her work had significantly deterio-rated. Further, that her own role in the union had damaged her career prospects. We shall return to this issue in Chapter 10. Rosanne recog-nised that she should move on but was aware of her time investment in the organisation and hoped that there would be some pay off for her. She stayed because of:

> hope of redundancy to tell you the truth, there was rumours and all the uncertainty, I was convinced that I would be able to go and with putting in sort of eight, nine, ten years at a time, I thought well I might as well stay and see what I can get.

Most career decisions are made in the context of uncertainty of knowl-edge. This is an important example and shows how the structural con-ditions can lead to contraction of opportunity and force the individual to make career decisions in conditions of uncertainty.

Whilst the above example provides an example of a situation where structures shape and disproportionately constrain the choices available to the person to develop in an organisation, the following example provides insight into the horizontal dimension of the career which is not a career terminus, but allows personal development. Candy was an example of a highly motivated woman prepared to stretch the boundaries:

> And then I did an exchange to Trinidad for a year, that was my second ever bestest job. I insisted, coz by then I was a nursery school teacher and I actually wanted to go and work in the nursery sector in Trinidad and it's voluntary, and it's community-based, so I ended spending half a day when you were in school and one day a week it was office-based, you know. So I had three, four days when I had afternoons free so it was just such a fantastic opportunity to just learn about Trinidad, and visit and travel and see the country, as well as find out about the education and schooling system. It was a lovely opportunity.

Adapting work to circumstances

One of the striking features of some of the women's experiences was the way that they adapted their working patterns once they became mothers. This often involved a change of occupation. Candy's experience was not unusual in that many women shift to education after having children:

> I've been working, I've had various jobs; I did nursing at a very early age then I went off to have my children and I didn't work while they were at school except for getting active in their school life, i.e., parent governor, nursery helper, book librarian you know, things like that until they came to secondary school. I got a job in the secondary school, they all went to the same secondary school and I got a job there working in, just helping out at the dinner times and then I became a parent governor there for a couple of years so that was my work while they were at school. And then I came into adult education when my youngest was about three, I started as a crèche worker then I got the opportunity to get trained and as a literacy tutor and I've been working for [London borough] for about 18 years in that position.

Candy showed how involvement with the school lives of her children led to a reshaping of her career. It also well demonstrates how through voluntary work she built a set of skills and knowledge about the educational field. Thus her role as mother was central to this. But importantly, this experience led to her getting formal acknowledgement of skills by training in the field of literacy.

Thus, being a mother and the associated experiences may actually provide opportunities and open up new worlds for career development. In an earlier paper, we showed how women who return to work may aspire to be teachers following their experience of being in and sometimes contributing to school life as mothers (Healy and Kraithman 1991). Candy's experience illustrates this well.

For other women, they may redirect their careers following child-rearing. Miranda's story is relevant here. It was Miranda's mothering role that shaped the direction of her career:

> I knew nursing wasn't a profession where you would um, nursing and childcare doesn't mix effectively. The hours of nursing, the hours of nursing and childcare, full-time nursing and childcare do not mix, basically yeah if you want to have children, and I have seen others, the way other nurses have suffered and the juggling, and I decided that that wasn't going to be practical so basically from the very outset, I decided to give up nursing.

Here Miranda graphically illustrates that some workplaces are unfriendly for those with family responsibilities. It is of course significant that nursing is a female-dominated profession and yet did not offer Miranda's peers the flexibility they would need to undertake a full-time nursing role.

Future career strategies

We asked women about their future career strategies. Some, like Asha, sought to plateau their careers. They sought to combine work and family and reconcile these by continuing in their current role:

> Well, it's rather funny because it's rather like living, spending your time living. At present I'm looking for a house to buy. So this kind of fits nicely into my life. Which I see as being devoted to the family and you know, I'm in this field, I don't really have to struggle hard to be, you know, to come up to grips with this because I am already in it. I know what I'm doing, I'm going to a refresher course, so I'm on the level, I don't have to devote a lot of extra time. So I can devote to, like,

looking for a house, and coaching my kid up for his entrance into a good school when he is 13. So things like that. So once I settle all that then maybe I'll do some extra research in biology or botany or something like that. But I have to stick on to this.

Asha did not rule out further development in the foreseeable future, but as a knowledgeable actor about her own conditions, she sought to balance the finite resource of time available to her.

Suzanne was at a later stage. Her children were older and she was seeking to plan ahead in terms of career development. Her story is interesting in that she received a boost of motivation following attendance at a conference for black and ethnic minority workers. Such conferences are valuable in that they enable people to meet, to hear other stories and to listen to those who have been successful and who act as role models:

I went to a conference on the 11th October, in Birmingham, which was a conference to do with equality for black and ethnic minorities in further education. And I found the conference very positive and it actually gave me the feeling of empowerment. I can see my future as progressing and developing and looking towards a management area. So I've actually asked for a form, an application form from the Learning and Skills Council, and I'm in the process of putting an application in for them. And I'm hoping I can get a sponsorship, ... having spent, having had about 23 years experience in, more or less, valid teaching, I feel, I've got a wealth of experience, skills and potential to move on. But the right time hadn't come, but I think I'm beginning to see myself moving towards a position now in that direction, because my children are much older, because they needed a lot of support when they were younger. But the first being 16, 12 – they're still young, but in the next couple of years, I feel I just need to move on and use all the skills that I have, you know, into different directions. I wouldn't give up teaching because it's something I love, and people have always told me that I'm a natural teacher, and so I've had a lot of [laughs] praises. Praise and things are very positive that I've had from colleagues, from my line-manager. The line manager's even said, 'I don't think you should leave teaching at all because it would be a big loss to education. You should be in education, but if you want to try and progress, you know, let's look at your career and the future. It should be something that you should at least give a priority to.' So I love teaching and will always be a teacher.

Importantly, she also received support from her line manager and, as we have stated above, this also can be a critical motivator.

Conclusions

This chapter has confirmed our understanding of the complexity of career. It is evident that the women in our study faced particular challenges, some of which reflected the demands on them as women and others because of their ethnicity. Thus the importance of being aware of the intersection of gender and ethnicity is underlined in our approach to career.

However, our picture of careers is, so far, partial. It is to the next chapter that we must turn to get a fuller picture. This requires an understanding of the relationship between careers and the trade union, or as we shall call them, alternative careers.

10
Shaping Careers from a Trade Union Perspective

In Chapter 9 we considered women's subjective and objective organisational careers. In this chapter we consider how subjective and objective factors lead to union careers. A unionised context shapes the circumstances in which a union may enable or constrain career development. The trade union role has been more associated with the defence of jobs and their equitable allocation than with the promotion of individual careers. Evetts (1992:16) pointed to the influence of macro-level actors such as representatives of employers and governments, trade unions and professional associations in the interactions and negotiations of career structures. Yet at the level of the organisation, the literature tends to treat career as an individualistic process (e.g., Arnold 1997; Donnelly 1992), thus neglecting the value of collective insights. Exceptions to this include Waddington and Whitston's (1996) study of union joining and bargaining preferences, which showed that white-collar staff place great emphasis on union involvement in setting the parameters within which careers may be pursued. Similarly, Healy (1999) demonstrated that unionised teachers recognised the union role in career development.

Our study is about women and this chapter is about women's involvement in trade unions. Women's involvement in trade unions is an issue of contemporary concern with the decline in the heartland of unionism, while women's recruitment has become an urgent matter linked to union survival and revival (Kirton and Healy 1999). This is problematised by studies suggesting that women have a lesser belief in trade unions than do men (Sinclair 1995, 1996), that unions are an often alienating environment for women (Cockburn 1982; Colgan and Ledwith 1996; Kirton and Healy 1999) and that women activists may often be balancing work, union and home demands (Cunnison 1987;

Ledwith, Colgan et al. 1990; Wertheimer and Nelson 1975; Bradley, Healy and Mukherjee 2002, 2005).

The multiple strands that shape union involvement lead activists to consider union careers as alternatives or in parallel to their conventional careers and personal lives (Kirton 2007). It is this aspect that we focus on in this chapter. Crucially, we argue that subjective histories are influential in women's involvement, and indeed their degree of involvement, in trade unions. But as we shall see in this study, different areas of life interact so that progress or setbacks in one area have repercussions for other aspects of a person's life (Watson 1988). Thus both subjective and objective factors will intersect in shaping women's routes to trade union activism and to the (often unintended) building of a union career. The nature of union careers are complex; they may follow a conventional bureaucratic route, but for many women, their union careers may be characterised as alternative or parallel careers (Bradley, Healy and Mukherjee 2004; Kirton 2007) to their main paid work activity. In these careers, women may commit the energy and resources that others may reserve for their paid work careers. To explore women's union careers we consider their prior orientations to collectivism through their routes to union involvement and activism. For this part of the chapter, we draw on our earlier work which focused in particular on concepts of individualism and collectivism (Healy, Bradley and Mukherjee 2004a). We then turn to women's experience of union involvement and the way that women cope with the extra work shift which union careers involve; in doing so we particularly draw on our previous publications (Bradley, Healy and Mukherjee 2004, 2005).

Routes into collectivism and union activism

The women in our study demonstrated three main routes into union activism what we characterise as the traditional route, the radical route and the social justice route. We recognise that these may overlap and interrelate. We deal with each of these in turn.

The traditional route: families, communities and socialisation

A major way in which collectivism has been fostered in the past is through the tradition of solidaristic values and organisation, being passed from generation to generation. It is often characterised by the 'them' and 'us' rhetoric which has long been associated with certain types of working-class milieu. Many qualitative studies of trade union members have shown continued evidence of such values developed and reproduced in families (Bradley 1999; Ledwith, Colgan et al. 1990). This was evident in our study in many of the CWU interviews:

> Well my father was in the post-office and he was always a union man and I'd always...I'd always admired the union – suffragettes, the whole works – I'd always respected them.
>
> (Serena CWU)

Postal work is highly unionised and collectivist principles remain strong in this industry in contrast to many. Indeed, the postal strikes of 2007 stood as rare events in the early part of the twenty-first century. The Post Office was split in 1974 into British Telecom and the Royal Mail, but collectivist values survived in the technologically more dynamic BT, as the following interview also demonstrated:

> My dad worked for BT and he gave me a bit of advice. And he did say to me that when you start working for BT, one of the most important things you need to do is join a union. That is number one. And I can remember sort of questioning and saying, 'Why?' not really having ... I mean I'd worked, but I'd done part-time jobs and had no understanding about trade unions. My dad's always been, he's worked from the minute he stepped off the boat and came to England, he's had a job. He worked for the railways first of all, so he was a member of the railway union...And he'd always been a labour supporter and he'd always been a member of a trade union.
>
> (Mel CWU)

In such solidaristic contexts, joining a union is a 'normal' practice for employees, learned as part of an unspoken political socialisation:

> When I say parents... it's like it was just the done thing. You started a job and you joined a union...It was the same thing as my parents always voted Labour, so until you actually grow up and have got a mind of your own, sort of thing, you voted Labour.
>
> (Vikki CWU)

> Yeah, I've always been a union member. In the DSS I was a union member there...But I wouldn't consider working somewhere without being in a union.
>
> (Mona CWU)

One of the interesting points that emerge from this study is the way that collectivist values are transferred across national boundaries. Indeed, studies that focus on the English working class may very much reflect an Anglocentric perspective. Our study draws out the important link between African values and collectivism. Thus these values reflect a moral imperative to get involved in trade unions:

> Because of my African upbringing, you're always fighting for your corner. You're brought up not to be selfish. You fight for everybody else's standards.
>
> (Bella USDAW)

A political influence was clear in Leila's experience of growing up in an Indian state which is 'communist leaning'. This had led to a high level of union consciousness:

> So people do know a lot about unions. So you do your work, and all around you there are unions demanding things for their workers...When I was growing up I was a union member, university union councillor, and um I was at the college union as well. So yes, I was aware of the union from a very small age.

Leila's parents were socialised by university unions in India, which provided values and awareness of professional workers' unionisation in a socialist context.

It is clear that many of our interviewees were continuing to maintain this tradition within their own families, and indeed in the broader community by encouraging friends and relatives to join unions. The importance of family in shaping union orientation was evident in the accounts, for example:

> Well, it's just been, it's been a mutual thing. Once I joined the union they all joined the union, yeah, it's crazy.
>
> (Lorna USDAW)

These accounts show that traditional solidaristic collective motives for union participation are still important for some of this group of women. At the same time, it is clear that class is not necessarily the only driver in solidaristic approaches. Despite advocates to the contrary, a link between differentiation and increased individualisation of society (Purcell and Ahlstrand 1994; Zoll 1995), differentiation of the labour force does not mean the end of the intergenerational transfer of collective values.

The radical route: political activism, feminism and black consciousness

We noted elsewhere that women from middle-class backgrounds and particularly those with higher education experience presented another route into collectivism through their involvement in the anti-racist and socialist struggles of the 1960s onwards (Healy, Bradley and Mukherjee 2004a). This had been their form of political socialisation and Candy provides a good example:

> I mean I was fighting for black identity when I was 15, 16 in the sixties when my mother was afraid of me going out and saying I'm black and I'm proud you know and actually sort of making it known by my sense of dress and by my activities that I was black...I used to go on demonstrations and things like that you know I was very active, I was, they would call me a militant at the time.

Suzanne presented a reflexive view on her political orientation. She recognised the importance of black feminism interacting with her own upbringing in the shaping of her political ideas:

> I came out of a black woman's politics of the 70s and 80s, the black consciousness that was around at the time, and it advocated social justice and better life chances. It's interesting because I sometimes wonder if, in terms of my own upbringing, if it would have come to the fore anyway. I don't think so, I think circumstances kind of come together to do that.

Support for trade unions was consistent with the ideological values that formed her political outlook. Suzanne went on to explain that for her, union membership was not optional. Indeed, she recognised that the union may need to be changed, but not being part of it was out of the question. Her political values meant:

> You had to belong to a trade union. In the sense of both in terms of your own kind of security, in terms of work, and in terms of your own political education. So I have always felt it was, it was necessary, it wasn't always optional, you know, the union. You have great disputes with their line and with their position. But I have never, I

have never felt that I could not be in a union, or I wouldn't join a union, even if I decided I would change union.

Rather than being alternatives to trade unionism, social movements (whether the women's movement, black consciousness or left-wing political parties) appear to foster collectivist values and feed into contemporary trade unionism, although this is likely to involve a challenge to the longstanding union agenda. This is evidenced in other studies of black activists (McKenzie 2003; Virdee and Grint 1994) and socialist activists (Calveley and Healy 2003).

The social justice route

In Kelly's (1998) work on mobilisation, he shows how a sense of injustice is part of the mobilising process. Thus the women in our study recognised that as employees they were vulnerable to unjust actions against which they would be powerless to defend themselves. Therefore they turned to the union as illustrated by Meryl:

> I've never been without the union, never, because you never know. If they want to discipline me and I don't know how a disciplinary works, then obviously I'll be told by a representative. I wouldn't believe the person that's actually gonna discipline me. I'll believe the representative more because obviously that person's not on my side are they? But the union rep who's representing me is on my side and they're biased, sort of thing. You know what I mean? Even when you're wrong, they're still on your side.

Jane's story also illustrates this. She had experienced bullying and felt that the union was a necessary defence for her:

> I had one manager and I just thought, this is getting too much. And I think I felt I was forced to join a union simply because of it, because I was…mentally bullied I think would be the right word, for sort of years. And I was just getting to the stage where I thought, well I can't deal with this anymore. I can't cope with this anymore. I need help if only to give me advice as to what you should or shouldn't be doing. So that's how I got involved.

For the women in our study, this sense of injustice was often aroused by discrimination they had experienced or observed because of race. Thus their union careers were ignited because of their commitment to race equality or, in some cases like Amina, equal opportunities generally:

> What made me want to join was equal opportunity. That was the post actually I went for and I didn't get it and I was so upset because I am really passionate about equal opps, I am really, really passionate. I mean I don't read about it or anything, but I just see things going wrong that I know that shouldn't and I just want to put my foot in it and make it right.

This commitment to trade unionism arose from both injustice in the workplace but also had arisen from the experience of growing up and living in ethnic communities. The importance of community is explored in greater depth in Chapter 11. Thus, many interviewees suggested that though unionism wasn't part of their family background, commitment to minority rights and community activism very much was. Injustice/ justice is perhaps the key concept which arises from this experience of ethnicity and community activism. This can become an absolutely crucial motivator both for voluntary work in the communities and for trade union activism. Indeed, women who espouse these values tend to interpret unions as being vehicles for the struggle for justice:

> But at the end of the day they are still fighting for everyone's rights so I just feel, I love fighting for people's rights anyway, I fight for everyone's, I fight for my family's.
>
> (Amina)

> I consider myself an activist because the job that I'm doing, I'm doing full-time union work. I think that if I had moved to outer Mongolia or something like that and decided to run a guest house or something like that I'd still have to get involved in, in issues of injustice because I feel it and I can't get away from it. You know, there's injustices and there are bad things in this world that need changing, and I want to be part of changing the world and making it a better place.
>
> (Marsha)

Balancing union, work and home

As argued in earlier work on work life balance (Bradley, Healy and Mukherjee 2005), if women are to develop union careers, the demands on their time will be considerable. Apart from the time required within the workplace to deal with problems and negotiations, union activists will be expected to take part in training courses and summer schools, attend conferences and rallies, sit on various committees at local, regional and national level. How did women manage to cope with a third set of duties and responsibilities when many were already shouldering the 'double burden' of employment and household management?

It was clear from the previous chapter that one of the constraints on developing the paid work career was the commitment of family responsibilities. One the of curious aspects of our study was the way that women may simultaneous reject hierarchical development because of time poverty, but take on roles in the community and in the union.

The story and comments of Tania may stand as a typical case among our respondents. Tania is in her thirties, a single parent with two children, one aged 14 and a little one aged three. She is a Londoner and works as an office manager. When asked why, with her long experience of her organisation, she had not gone for higher management, her reply highlighted family commitments and an unwillingness to be drawn into the long hours' culture. Yet despite her resistance to the long hours' culture, Tania works for her local residents' association and is becoming active in her union, holding a branch post. She was typically enthusiastic about her union work, telling us that she wanted to 'delve deeper into her role', that it was 'exciting to be part of it'. How, then, did she manage the balance?

> Err, balance home and work, when I take my foot out here and go through the gate, I don't think about work, I go home, I go pick up the little one (from nursery), big one normally at home, and it's sort out dinner, then Clara will be in her room, Janie will be in the corridor playing with her friends, I'll be sorting out dinner, and whatever, six o'clock we sit down to eat and then I chill, I chill out.

It is clear here that the network of female family support, characteristic of Caribbean culture, comes to her aid. Her elder daughter Clara helps out with chores and when she has to go away for conferences and training, her sister or her mother look after the children: 'yeah and it's like a miniature holiday because I haven't got them [laughs] so I get a child-free day'.

It is instructive that Tania has put work for two voluntary agencies, the union and the residents' association, before any kind of personal work-based ambition. This was typical of our respondents, relating, as we have shown, partly to their ambitions being blocked in their jobs, but also, as in Tania's case, because of their greater commitment to equal opportunities and supporting their own ethnic communities. However, like Tania, all must weigh up options. In Bradley, Healy and Mukherjee (2005) we distinguished three overlapping patterns of response. For some people, caring responsibilities clearly dominated and limited the amount of time they were prepared to give to their voluntary activities; a second group, whom we might call 'second chancers', tended to discharge their caring duties till children were grown up enough to be independent and then take up union activism, often with extraordinary levels of commitment. Finally, there was a small group of 'exceptional women' who seemed to be able to juggle an amazing array of activities without flagging.

Shahnaz was one of the most extraordinary women we interviewed. As well as being a leading union activist, she had an array of other activities, including being a magistrate, a Labour Party activist and local candidate, and a housing association officer. She also had two children, and stated that she would not be able to manage without a very supportive husband. She put down her incredible level of energy to ambition to be the best at what she does:

> It's hard. I think we work a lot harder than our mothers did. Because they knew exactly what they were doing and we're trying to be super-women. And I suppose I still have this thirst, this hunger. I just want to get to the highest point until I decide I've burned out and I just want to sort of crash and chill out completely.

Shahnaz was relatively young, but Gita and Shelley who were older with grown-up children seemed to have escaped from 'burnout'. Gita had a major union post and did voluntary work for the homeless as well as looking after grandchildren. She reflected on the mental strains of her life:

> It's very hard, very difficult indeed ... because you're thinking of ... say for instance in the union you've got a case, you're dealing with that. Then come Friday you have to leave it. Monday, you've gone to your other job, you're carrying all the work with you. You're taking the union work with you, back to the other office ..., So you're always thinking.

But, when asked how she copes, her reply was indicative: 'I don't know how I do it really. But if you *really want* to you can.'

Shelley was also extremely active in the union with ambitions to rise to the very top. She described herself as a traditional wife whose life had been changed and invigorated by her union involvement. Two of her children were grown, but the third was three years old. How did she cope?

Oh! Juggle! To be honest I couldn't do it unless my husband was as supportive as he is.

Nonetheless she was forced to turn down the chance of becoming a tutor in race awareness because it would involve residential work and long absences from home which she considered incompatible with having a young child.

Experience in the union

From the above discussion, it is clear that women's union careers are to an extent shaped by prior solidaristic values, but it also illustrates that these do not always arise from 'traditional' class and occupational affiliations. Nor should we assume fixity of values. Collectivism may emerge from the workplace experience or a prior collectivist orientation may be affected by this experience. Union involvement creates significant networks both within the union and within the organisation including management. This can provide a more enabling environment which may facilitate (or in some circumstances impede, see Calveley and Healy 2003) career development. The following quotation provides an indication of the resources that flow from this involvement:

The funny thing is when you join a union, you get to know more people in an organisation quite quickly... You get to know management and non-management people by actually being in the union. Also you get to know exactly what you can or cannot be asked to do at work, and find out what's happening in the workplace.

(CWU)

Getting involved in unions offered women a range of power resources, such as access to information and data, contacts, the potential use of collective power and access to positions (see Bradley 1999:31–7 for a theoretical development of gendered power resources).

The subjective aspects of union involvement emerged strongly from the women in our study and took different forms. The following conversation with Meryl who was relatively new to activism is an example of the unexpected benefits of getting more involved in the union:

> Q: Yeah. How have things changed for you since you've become a rep?
>
> A: I feel more…what's the word? I can't think of the word to use. I feel more able to do things. I feel like I've got more of a backing behind me.
>
> Q: Empowered?
>
> A: Yeah. I feel like – not that no one can't be rude to me and all that, but I just feel that they know where to draw the line. They can't treat me like the way maybe they used to treat me before.
>
> Q: Right. So do you see a difference?
>
> A: I do. I do, because sometimes the managers crack a little joke on me. Like, 'Oh, we've got to be careful with that union rep!' You know, it's just a joke, I say, 'Oh shut up, you stupid idiot!' But I get on with most of the managers and we can have a joke and have a laugh. It's just the way it is. But I think things have changed a little bit.
>
> Q: And are you enjoying the position?
>
> A: Yeah, I'd say so because you can go off to meetings and you can go away for training. You go on health and safety courses. It opens your eyes to a lot of things, especially where health and safety is. I knew health and safety was important but I didn't realise how important it is. I've met people that are actually in charge of health and safety and go to meetings, and that's helped me a lot to know how important you are as a rep. What you can do to back people up.

Meryl had not anticipated that with union involvement might come a new form of respect and fulfilment. Union training courses are a route to empowerment as exemplified by Kirton and Healy (2004). This is typified strongly in the case of Marta who explicitly weighed up the fulfilment gained from her paid work and her union activities in the following words:

> I don't think the social work was actually fulfilling. I think what I do now in terms of being a convenor – representing members, empowering members, looking at different types of procedures and having an input in the changes within the authority – I think that's rewarding for me. I feel as though I'm achieving something for those people that are around me.

Nevertheless, the women in our study were not uncritical union members. On the contrary, union deficiencies in dealing with sexist or racist behaviour may have prompted their greater activism and committed them more and more to their union careers. In Healy, Bradley and Mukherjee (2004b) we showed how the experience of union involvement led the women in our study to adopt strategies to challenge what were, in effect, their experiences of a splintered form of collectivism, whereby traditional solidaristic behaviour excluded women and black people. Their action took a number of forms from initiating separate structures, such as black networks or self-organised groups, to mounting challenges to gendered and racist behaviour. Importantly, the women's commitment to collectivist values provided a spur to improve their union experience when it was found exclusionary rather than simply to quit the union (although this was also an option adopted as we shall see below).

Equality networks

Networks are often seen as important enablers to career development although Ehrenreich (2006) demonstrates the negative side of networking. However, equality networks offer the potential for enablement since the network members share an interest and commitment to equality in the organisation, and in the case of this chapter, the union. The union career may therefore be influenced by union initiatives to engage and involve underrepresented groups. Our research revealed many initiatives being developed today, which recognise the different constituencies in unions and reflect a community-oriented approach to unionism. Note, for example, the annual Respect Festival and other local initiatives such as community and family oriented 'fun days' organised by some unions.

Coping with sexism in the workplace was a recurrent theme. Marsha, whose experience of working in a male dominated workplace was discussed in Chapter 8, built a women's support group:

> So we actually developed um, a women's support group. Which was mainly for political change but it was also to support each other as well. You know because things like harassment wasn't recognised as a trade union issue at all. There was still wolf whistles at women who went up to the rostrum at conferences and things like that.

As we saw in Chapter 8, the establishment of self-organising groups was a catalyst for many to get involved. Nadia had been a union member for 20 years, but it was getting involved in a black workers' group that provided a trigger for greater activism:

> He was voted the black members' officer, and I was voted as the convener or something, and then I went out there on a campaign (laughs), I got everybody, every black person I knew in college and told them to tell friends and all that, so we had our first meeting and, it became quite big. The group when we started off, it was just us four...we had a lot of conflict between us, because...he wanted to do it in a different way and I wanted to do it in a different way, so his way didn't work first and then my way worked, and then loads of people came but um, so it was quite big at first, but then there was a lot of internal conflict.

The mobilising potential of black groups is considerable. Self-organising groups will experience a complex mix of social interactions which may impede action based on common value orientations. Self-organising groups based on gender and ethnicity will theoretically cut through vertical and horizontal divisions in organisations. However, in practice, class, gender and ethnicised relations will intersect. The research revealed that white women tended to dominate women's groups and black men tended to dominate black groups. Similarly, McBride (2001) found that middle-class women dominated UNISON's women's groups.

This array of groups is an important part of contemporary union activity. Whilst we have concentrated on a group placed at the intersection of gender and ethnicity, there are other groups outside our scope that merit study, for example, young workers, lesbians and gays, people with disabilities or groups characterised by the nature and terms of their employment. The involvement of this diverse membership in union activism is central to contemporary mobilisation. This is evident from the account of the SOGs. Most of the women in our study were encouraged to get further involved in the union by the existence of black and ethnic minority networks. The importance of these cannot be overstated in the context of a perception that women and black people's voices are not heard. Such events were described as 'inspiring' and 'eye opening', for example:

> Just imagine you're in the room and it was about 26 to 28 people, all black and Asian. You know and it was so intense because it was the first time that...they had ever had so many ethnic people.

Bradley, Healy and Mukherjee (2002) argue that union activism offered other resources apart from a desire to help minority 'brothers and sisters'. It presented women, who in many ways felt blocked and excluded in the workplace, with a new arena for their talents to flourish and a focus for self-development:

> I feel like I've grown. I've really grown. It's amazing... I've really challenged myself as well. I have done certain things that I wouldn't have done before and I'm like, people are coming up to me and I'm like reeling it out on the top of my tongue and I'm like standing back and thinking to myself, did I just say all that? You feel good within yourself.
>
> (Josie UNISON)

Courses, conferences and black gatherings were often a way into more general union activism, and many women stated that racial issues were their main interest. Lois described how she was empowered by attendance at a NATFHE Black Workers' Conference:

> I found the conference very positive and it actually gave me the feeling of empowerment. I can see my future as progressing and developing towards management.

Black networks allow a reflexivity of thinking and a sense of being able to challenge and overcome constraints. This is particularly important in the light of the effect of a resilient institutionalised racism and the necessity that the effects of this do not go unchallenged:

> It's because of the system. People feel... even if I've got all these qualifications, I still won't be able to get a good job... it's something people have accepted as, you know, a way of life. That I cannot change anything because I'm black. I cannot change anything because I'm Asian, or you know, so I just have to sit back and watch. It doesn't matter what happens, I've got to accept it. But what I've learnt from the conference that I went to in Birmingham is that you don't have to accept that. You have to really push yourself forward and let them know what you are capable of doing, make them know you've got the qualities and you're also equal with your white counterpart. Do you understand what I'm saying? And that is something that I've picked up from that, a positive thing, you know.

In many ways, Lois is articulating the transformative potential of such networks. She now knows that she can play a part in challenging constraining structures and enable a change. Union networks have made women more knowledgeable about how to manage their own careers and protect those of others.

The career indeterminacy of union women

Many of the women in our study would not have anticipated that their lives would be shaped not only by a paid work career but also a union career. As we have set out above, this occurred in different ways. The way that career aspirations are shaped is complex, but the role that unions play tends to be neglected in the recent literature (exception include (Bradley, Healy and Mukherjee 2004, 2005; Kirton 2007; Watson 1988). Yet new avenues opened up for the women in our study as a result of union involvement. Indeed, the indeterminate nature of careers is particularly well illustrated by bringing unions into the discussion.

> I needed a change of career, and I always feel that this has landed in my lap because I wasn't searching for it.

How the union involvement intersects with career development is well illustrated by Bella when asked what her aspirations were in terms of work:

> I've always made it clear that I don't want to be a team leader or a manager, because the company I work for, they work stupid hours. I'm sorry but life is for living. I don't want to come to work at 6 o'clock in the morning and still be there at 6 o'clock at night. You've got a family. You've got a life. And I couldn't do it and be able to do the union, do the politics, be a school governor. I just couldn't do any of those things. So yeah, it's a price you have to pay.

Bella's career aspirations to work for a union were shaped by a desire to challenge injustice rather than sacrifice her time to a vertical career in a large retail store. Ironically, unions are acknowledged as time-greedy organisations (Franzway 2001) and therefore the time demand might be as great as in the retail organisation. The difference is in the perceived intrinsic value of the work.

Concern with social justice may go hand in hand with the comparison between their experience of working in a particular organisation and a possible career in a union. In Bradley, Healy and Mukherjee (2004) we showed how woman who had been seconded to her union for a time, when asked if the union might be an alternative career, responded in the following way:

> Yeah. I mean, yeah it would be good if I could stay within the (union) and continue it because there are so many problems within (my organisation), and the mind set of people working there.

There is little doubt that working for the union may well provide a better quality of life compared to some fields of work. This is in no way to suggest that the work will be easier and less demanding; on the contrary. However, it is considered more worthwhile. A number of our interviewees who were working up the ladder of lay activism expressed a desire to become paid officers.

For others, the union experience has given them skills and knowledge that enable them to widen their horizon and develop their aspirations, as Lois explained:

> I mean, my hope for a better future is to continue with my work. Be positive, be good in my job, develop my skills further and also a hope of a career development, as I was saying, maybe think of going into management. Probably not in this organisation, maybe somewhere else, I can't say because nobody knows what's going to happen even in the next year or two years or three years. But I've got all these skills that I've developed over years, and I just need to make my move.

Widening horizons was not just about promotion and career change; it was also about a sense of empowerment about what could be achieved in their own careers and those of others. The powerlessness that may be caused by a racist culture was challenged by their experience of union involvement. Marsha expresses the difference that many of the woman in our study made to their own and others' working careers and quality of life:

> I know I have made a difference to people. I have stopped people losing their job you know. I have stopped people getting into all sorts of difficulties. You think, I haven't done anything really, all I've done is listen, but you know you have made a difference.

Rejecting the union career

We have shown that a collectivist spirit, acquired through a number of life experiences, was strong among the black women activists. We should also stress the complexity of people's attitudes and motivations whereby solidarism, instrumentalism, plus an ethical commitment to justice, combine within many women's narrative accounts. However, the conditions that encouraged the women into the trade union and their subsequent desire to become active is not universal. Younger workers have a different history. They have not lived through the highly political 1960s and 1970s; instead, they grew up in the 1980s and 1990s when Thatcherite individualism was at its height. We are not claiming that there are no threats to unions from a culture increasingly marked by individualism and by an adoption by many, especially younger workers, of an entrepreneurial self (Casey 1995; Du Gay 1996; Grey 1994) linked to more linear career success and promotion. Casey and others see this as inimical to union membership. There was concern among the women respondents about the lack of young minority and white activists:

> My biggest worry at the moment is there are no young people – be it black or white – there are no young people coming through, becoming active in the union. In my union, I'd say the average age of the branch officer and activists is about 50, which is not good. And there's nobody new coming in. So I think my priority – and I don't know how I'm gonna do it – is to try and encourage more youngsters to get involved.
> (Shelly)

Many reasons were offered to us as to why young, and some older, black and Asian women, were reluctant to be involved in unions, but the issue of fear cropped up a number of times. There was great awareness of the inherent conflict between management and unions. Further, management implicitly operated within what Fox (1966) has characterised as a unitary framework and therefore joining a trade union and getting involved might be seen as an act of disloyalty. Whilst we have shown above how union involvement can help build a conventional career, it can also damage a conventional paid career. The following interview points to the way that union activism can act against promotion success:

> And people are still wary about becoming actively involved in the union because of the fear of ... their job is maybe at threat especially

if they would like to apply for management posts maybe, so they don't want to be seen as disruptive.

(Miranda)

Whereas Rosanne pointed to the way that people kept their membership secret in case it could be used against them in the future:

> Yeah that is the fear, I mean I'm not saying that everyone wants promotion or something but just to get on with their job. I think they feel there is something, would be a mark against them if it's known that they are members. Some people don't care or it doesn't matter or they'll deal with it, but most of the people don't want managers to know or their colleagues or team leaders to know because you never know who gets promoted in the future and they'll remember it.

Lorna was warned about both management punishments for union membership and also about the limitations of union power:

> My friends, (discouraged me)…not for any sinister reasons, just because they thought I would get into more trouble, I would get sacked, they were concerned that you would join the union, and that they can't protect you all the time.

As the quotations suggest, those workers who have developed a strong sense of identity linked to career may be reluctant to engage with unions not from any anti-union values, but because it may put their job in jeopardy, damage their promotion prospects and inhibit their self-development. And there are other negatives, too, that may accrue from activism. Raising ethnic minority issues in the workplace is difficult and challenging and may fall on deaf ears. Having the courage to be the one to stand up and be counted is not easy, as the following quotations indicate:

> There are issues about how far the people are prepared to raise those issues. That's the danger, I think the danger is if you are one, or very few of you, that you get labelled as the person who'll always raise issues.

(Neela)

> I don't care where you come from, as long as you are black, because together we can fight this. You can't fight it on your own, but unfortunately the majority of us don't see it that way. They want to be an individual.

(Jessica)

Nevertheless, unions and their members need people who are prepared to stand up and challenge injustice in the workplace. The importance of responsiveness to members' needs and the effects when they are not met is evident from the following woman's experience. Neither her management nor her union were prepared to tackle a form of racist sexism:

> It (the union) didn't do me any good, but it did give me the urge to join it, to get involved in it when I had a problem. That was the good thing about it but I've been disappointed ever since.
>
> (Joanne)

Her experience was all the more disappointing since, as a feminist woman, she believed that she had the personal resource to challenge sexism. Yet when she turned to the union, they did not respond. By becoming a shop steward, she learnt to defend others against injustice. However, others may not be so determined and persevering:

> As long as the union ignores issues of race, more and more black members are going to pull out of it, 'cause they are in it because they want to be part of the collective community, but they will leave if the community is not working for you.
>
> (Lorna)

It is clear that trade unions need union members to think in terms of paid and unpaid union careers. Yet to do this, unions need to address their (white) male-dominated culture. Unions also need to note that equality policies are more likely to be influential where those who are most likely to be affected by such policies are active agents in their introduction and implementation. Women are more likely to be interested in equality initiatives than are men (Healy 1997, 1999a) and where there are female or black trade union officials, equality bargaining will make the greatest progress (Ball 1990; Heery and Kelly 1988).

Conclusions

There was little doubt that the women in our study experienced complex forms of discrimination in their careers resulting from the cross cutting impact of gender and ethnicity (see Chapters 8, 9 and 11). Racism and sexism led to a sense of exclusion in their everyday lives as well as from the resources that may enable them to progress through the hierarchy of organisations. As our study shows, black and minority ethnic women may be more likely to have difficulty accessing power resources in all its complex forms (see Bradley 1999) to break the vicious circles of segregation (Collinson, Knights and Collinson 1990). Indeed, our study demonstrated how the experience of discrimination can lead to disaffection and ultimately career curtailment. However, as this chapter shows, this disaffection may also lead to union involvement.

By examining the ethnicised and gendered order in organisations, we are able to show the impact on conventional paid careers and the link with union careers. Our study indicates a resilience of gendered and racist practices, which, despite much rhetoric, organisations are failing to address. Nevertheless, as we argue elsewhere (Bradley, Healy and Mukherjee 2004), by examining the effects of union involvement and the impact of black networks, we were able to show how such involvement may provide the resources to empower and challenge racist and gendered practices. Union involvement and black networks provide personal and knowledge power resources that have enabled the women activists in our study to represent and defend the careers of union members. It also enabled them to reflect on their own situations and provide alternative strategies of action. The skills and knowledge gained in union roles, in some cases, provided the resources to enable the women to apply for development within their own or other organisations. Others sought to become full-time employees of their unions. What was interesting, therefore, was the way that union involvement provided opportunities for alternative careers in the trade union movement, opening a new set of options for women, many of whom were in the later stages of a working life.

The unfolding nature of careers (Arnold 1997) certainly emerged from our study, which also demonstrates the importance of the indeterminate and non-linear nature of careers. By focusing on the dialectical relationship between self and circumstance (Sikes, Measor and Woods 1985), we are able to show the negative effects of racism and sexism in women's working lives, but also how women are active agents who seek to control and transform these negative circumstances. The women in our study were particularly strong and utilised the strength of black union networks and union resources. Such trade union resources are not available to all black and minority ethnic women but, for those who access them, they provide openings to alternative careers and the chance to fight for better opportunities for other women.

11
Unions, Communities and Families in Women's Lives

In the last three chapters we have studied the experiences of minority ethnic women in workplaces and unions, with a particular focus on careers as a central focus of their activities. In this chapter, however, we move to a broader focus, showing how the women's working lives intersect with their community and family roles and concerns, and also with their broader political interests.

Studies of women's employment have long made the point that women's work experiences cannot be fully understood in isolation from their domestic lives and commitments (for example, Bradley 1999; Pollert 1981; Westwood 1984). Miriam Glucksmann (1995) has developed the theory of the 'total social organisation of labour' to explain how the relations of production and reproduction (and indeed consumption) are deeply intertwined, meaning that women and men enter the labour market on significantly different terms. Research carried out on young women and men in Bristol in 2000–2 (Fenton, Bradley et al. 2002) confirms that this remains true even for a more liberated generation of women who are supposed to have escaped from the inevitability of a domestic regime (Walby 1997); young women aged 20–35 who had children were considerably more constrained than young men with children, and many had put their careers 'on hold' while children were young. This also meant that more women than men in the survey worked part-time and that women earned less than men. Feminist sociology has thus revealed that work relations within family and employment relations cannot be fully understood in isolation from each other.

In studying trade unions and industrial relations, however, researchers often stick within a more traditional model of analysis which is more firmly concentrated on the workplace, only really considering family lives and responsibilities as a 'barrier' to woman's participation (Cunnison and Stageman 1993; Fosh and Heery 1990). While this remains true to some extent, our research revealed a much more complex picture of how union activism was involved with women's family and community values. In their useful study of unions in Canada, Briskin and McDermott (1993) showed how unions can become much more effective if they work with community groups. British unions, too, are beginning to realise the value of such alliances. The ILO sums up the thrust of community unionism and links it explicitly to equality and to the organisation of women workers:

> Community unionism is critical for expanding the union member-ship base, building solidarity across communities and diversities and keeping the gender equality agenda alive. Importantly, union efforts to reach out to atypical workers and those in the informal sector, the majority of whom are women, commonly are community-based, rather than centred on the workplace.
>
> (ILO 2003)

While for individual women managing the 'triple burden' of employ-ment, domestic work and union activism may sometimes be a headache, the collective impact of the linkages between these aspects of life opens up the possibility of more constructive work on equality, as we shall show in this chapter. To illustrate this we start the chapter with the story of Bella, an activist from USDAW whose remarkable career has encompassed a range of commitments bringing together her union and other political interests.

Bella's story

Bella could not be said to be totally typical of our participants: she is a particularly extraordinary women. But her story only displays an extreme version of elements which were common in other women's experiences.

Bella came to England from Africa as a young mother. She soon found herself rather isolated on a housing estate in Northern England. But this did not discourage her: she immediately sought ways to connect to the local community:

> I've always believed that you have to go out and say, 'I'm here. I want to be part of what's going on.' And my daughter was young. I thought,

what can you do. So I went to what they call 'mums and toddlers', where parents met up. And through me doing this I met people. Then I started saying, 'What can I do? There's other ways I can meet people.' I started doing Avon, Avon lady. I started knocking on the doors. I wanted to get involved in the community, so I started doing Avon. Then I got a bar job, which is one of the best jobs you can have because you meet people. People look down on it, but it's a very sociable job. So that was my first job.

It was not uncommon for women to tell us that they got into community work through their children, perhaps working as volunteers in schools or nurseries or getting involved in local campaigns for resources and facilities. Thus Bella explained how her first political interests arose from her involvement with her children's primary school:

The government then brought in what they call parent-governors and the PTA as well. I didn't believe I should take my children to school and just leave them. I felt it was a partnership between the school and myself. So I went into the parent-teacher association and through there, the parent-governorship came out. And people said, 'Oh you must go Bella. You must put yourself forward.' I'm thinking they wouldn't vote for me. It's full of white parents. Why would they vote for me? So I put my name forward as a parent-governor and I got elected by all these parents.

Bella explained that the experience and understanding she gained from being a school governor led her to want to do more, so she joined the Labour Party. This eventually led to a four-year spell as a local councillor. More recently she was involved in a regional 'partnership for power', which had included a visit to Tony Blair in Downing Street to discuss Labour Party policies and have an input to them, an event she described as 'exciting'!

Bella made it very clear that her political activism and her union involvement were closely linked:

I realised that the Labour Party and the union are entwined in a way. I know sometimes people would like to think they are not, but they're joined at the hip as far as I'm concerned. I joined the union because I was in retail. And more or less spontaneous within a few months of each other, I joined the Labour Party in April and I joined the union.

Her achievements for USDAW were remarkable given that the store she worked for did not recognise a union. Nonetheless, she recruited individual members from her fellow workers and eventually, with USDAW's help, a branch of the union was established, and, as it was a small branch, she found herself running it: 'It ends up you're the shop-steward, health and safety, secretary, and all!' Currently Branch Secretary, she hoped eventually to work as a paid official for a union.

In the meantime, like many other activists we interviewed, she continued to play a wide range of roles in her local community. She was a member of the local REC, had applied to be a magistrate, organised all the functions and parties in her workplace and was a fundraiser for charities such as Children in Need.

Children figure prominently in Bella's view of the world and what needs to be done:

> I could stop being a school governor. My children have gone. They've grown up. But why should I? There's other children that need my help. And all these years of experience, why should I just abandon it just because my children are not there. Other children need my help. I'm carrying on being a school governor. I used to be on two. I've just, about a year ago, come out of one. Because I've done a lot for that school. I've got a lot of money for them. And when I was in council, I helped to set up an athletics initiative. It started off with primary school boys and extended to secondary school. Which means that the children are trained or have some sort of sporting activities.

This concern was certainly typical of our participants, particularly the African-Caribbean women who were disturbed about their children's futures and especially about the public perception of young Caribbean men. A key motivation for many in their political involvement was to build a better world for the children of the future. And, like Bella herself, many saw themselves as role models for younger people:

> Yeah, role models in a way There's a lovely young lady, Victoria. She thinks I'm [laughs], she thinks I'm whatever, because she sees what I do. She worries me sometimes – anything I do, it's like gospel to her. Well, Bella will find out. Bella this, Bella that. And then suddenly this individual, that's a very shy person, she's doing an NVQ. She's

got a little boy. Six months ago it was just, 'Oh I don't think I'll bother.' Now it's, 'What can I do?' You can't stop her now. She wants to do this and do that.

Bella imputed her own incredible activism to her upbringing and the values it inculcated:

I'm involved in a lot of things because I'm a doer. There's something about me and representing the underdog... And I suppose because of that and the African upbringing, you're always fighting for your corner. You're brought up not to be selfish. You fight for everybody else's standards. You're a charity, basically, to everybody and fight for everybody... I just want things to be better than they are.

Like many of the women we met, Bella awed us by her energy and exuberance. All her successes and achievements had not, however, stopped her from being a friendly and approachable woman:

First and foremost I'm Bella, who goes in a night-club, as you saw last night, I just dance. I don't even need a drink. I just dance... I have a good time. I enjoy myself. Life is for living and I think that's what people are missing sometimes.

Working for the community

Bella's story exemplifies the way that women we interviewed talked about community. The term is often viewed rather negatively by sociologists because of its looseness: some even question whether such a thing as community has any meaningful existence (Anthias and Yuval-Davis 1992; Brint 2001). Communities can be viewed as imaginary bases of identification, in the sense that Benedict Anderson analysed nations as 'imagined communities' of belonging (Anderson 1983). However, it is clear to us that the idea of community has a real resonance to laypeople. The sense in which it was used by our participants fluctuated between two meanings identified by sociologists: first, being part of a group seen as having shared characteristics and conditions, in this case the ethnic community/communities, and, second, a particular geographical location (which may cut across ethnicities).

The notion of community unionism, now commonly accepted by both academics and activists has a similar broadness to it, in describing the variety of ways in which unions can work within communities (in both senses mentioned above) and collaborate with a range of community organisations. Tattersall defines community unionism in this broad sense:

> The strategy of community unionism includes working to build power at the scale of a place, a union working with community organisa-tions, and unions working on issues of community identity (such as with immigrants, women) or on broader community issues (such as public education or peace). Within this, union-community coalitions refer to one kind of community unionism-coalitions between unions and community organisations.
>
> (2006:4)

Unions may become involved in these kind of moves either defensively as a way to combat falling membership and recruit new members, or more radically as a way to politicise the union's work. This latter kind of initiative is often encouraged by younger, left of centre members who would like to see unions more positively embracing a socialist approach, rather than a 'responsible' (i.e., apolitical and moderate) union stance.

Whichever sort of motivation, however, the point to make here is that the BME women activists could play a key role in facilitating such alliances, given their levels of voluntary participation in community campaigns and organisations. Our participants reported being school governors, magistrates, Labour Party councillors, AIDs workers, members of REC committees, sports organisers, mentors and Industrial Tribunal members. They were members of women's groups, black women's groups, the anti-racism movement in football, the Cuba Solidarity Campaign, play schemes and tenants' groups. They told us about voluntary work with mother and baby groups, elderly people, day care centres and Victim Support. They were involved in teaching on supplementary schooling schemes, lay tutoring on TUC courses and in local colleges, and a range of local fund-raising initiatives. In sum, these women were taking an extraordinarily dynamic role as community activists and activators.

Some of these roles were taken as part of a broader political package in which union membership was one strand. But, conversely, voluntary work within the community was also a way in which women acquired skills, interests and experience which helped them into the labour market and subsequent union involvement, as they switched from voluntary to paid work. For example, Joanne described how some of her earlier activities led her into counselling:

> I was with Women's Aid. I did an AIDS centre as well, for a year. That was just making teas and so they came in and they could sit there and relax, that sort of thing, while they waited to get counselling. They had proper counsellors there. And that was part of my counselling – I did a counselling course over in Tottenham and it was a three-year one. And you had to go to different places as an observer, sort of thing, a bit of research. So then I did that and I worked for a feminist organisation. I'm on the committee for the Women's Refuge in (her current locality).

Similarly, Mary moved from voluntary work to train as a social worker:

> From around 14 I was involved as a volunteer in the local tenants' association play schemes and things like that. By the time I was 16, um, in the early '80s when there was all the uprisings I set up a black project looking at young black people around police, education and employment. I then got full-time employment from them, from 18 to 21, as a senior outreach and development worker. So I was kind of studying and doing that; I did my degree and social work qualification whilst working.

Illustrating the complexity of such crossovers and linkages, Marta, another social worker, told us that she felt her current union work was more valuable, helped more to change lives and was more personally fulfilling than the profession for which she had trained, as we mentioned in Chapter 10.

Conversely, some women who had gained knowledge and training as union activists subsequently moved to utilise their skills in the wider community, such as Nadia:

> I'm a qualified counsellor now, so I have two jobs. I work here full-time and then I also work part-time doing telephone counselling. That's quite good actually, because it's an assistance programme and I also do employment advice, as well, legal advice as well as telephone counselling or one to one counselling, so my aim when I leave here is to is to become self-employed as a counsellor. I am also a case worker elsewhere for race discrimination.

Thus interest in equality and diversity issues spilled across from the union to the community as in the case of Neela, a NATFHE activist:

> So this is part of the reason why I do a lot of voluntary work, 'coz a lot of my equal opportunities issues I can do that as part of my union programme, but in terms of policy I do it as a part of my voluntary work outside this organisation, elsewhere. Because that's an area that interests me, so I'll do it. I belong to the local REC and I will do it as part of that.

The crucial thing about these accounts is that they emphasise the sense of solidarity, belonging and rootedness that community membership brings to women *however that community is defined*. For example, for Nancy the key thing about her involvement was the multiethnic nature of the localities where she lived and worked:

> In these community-based programme I felt that with my experience and their experience and bringing that together, that was to me, that was the harmony, and I was learning myself and still am learning how things are done differently and things which are the same and how people can group it together and mix together and work really well together and cultural influences. You know, everyone was sharing in the formation together which was really nice. That was a real strong community of different cultures working together and, and being a community, being neighbours, being friends it was wonderful. I talk to friends of mine and they look at me quite strangely thinking well, they never had that. It is so rare, and I think the reason for it is, the people that were there they all travelled, people came in from Ireland, people came in from Jamaica, from the West Indies, so people were new coming into an area.

Contested communities

Nancy's comment that her experience of a harmonious multicultural community setting was 'rare', may chime with the views of sceptics about interethnic engagement. We certainly would not wish to paint an overly rosy picture. Some of our interviews revealed tensions between ethnic groups; for example, between Asians and Black Caribbeans, between Africans and Caribbeans, and between Jamaicans and Caribbeans from other islands. Mixed-heritage families might find themselves in difficult situations between such rivalries, as Asha, an Indian married to a Nigerian had found:

> Although we are a black family and we are viewed as a black family by the ethnic majority and by other ethnic minorities, we are probably not viewed as part of the Nigerian community.

These conflicts might break out in the workplace (e.g., if one group was perceived to be getting all the supervisory posts), or in the community over resources. Community associations often represent a particular ethnic group and then find themselves in competition for limited funding from the local council or other sources. They may then be involved in intricate local politics and power struggles as described by Neela in relation to her experience as a community development worker:

> I was doing this mainly for African Caribbean communities, this was under the old ILEA, but within the structures they found it very difficult to find money for Caribbean communities, but they would find it for Bangladeshi communities, any linguistic minorities. And it was to do with the power base of the African Caribbean community in this borough, because they would want the resource and they would want the control of it, whereas at that stage, this is going back about ten years, the Bangladeshi community was seen as meek, we could give them a little bit of crumbs here and there and it was fine, they would not demand too much.

There is, therefore, an unfortunate level of contestation as to who belongs to the community and who is deserving of support and help within it. As Lorna asked rhetorically, regretting the refusal of some ethnic groups to identify as 'black', 'Who are our community leaders? What is our community? Especially if we are all separated, you know.' The interethnic tensions, both between the minorities and with the majority, have become increasing clear in the post-9/11 context. An additional source of tension, perhaps less remarked on, arises from the intersection between class and ethnicity, which was a major issue for Sunita at the NATFHE union conference she had attended:

> They were talking about the black communities, you know the working-class black communities, and academic staff and lecturers and it was as if you couldn't be both. It's the idea that if you live in a more affluent area or you consider yourself to be middle class you are selling out to

your community. You could be an academic or you could be a member of a black community, that there were these two different communities and it was about making those choices…So that if legislation enables black individuals and black communities to progress and become professionals but by the same the token if you do that you are selling out.

In contrast, she believed that it should be possible to make alliances among black people across class barriers. Perhaps it is here that the more inclusive policies of unions may be able to help establish a new kind of model for sections of the community to coexist harmoniously.

Family influences and values

The community has another important role in these women's lives, in assisting in their endeavours to balance out their work and family needs. Among our interviewees, over half were in their forties and fifties so that their children were now grown up, freeing them to develop their activities outside the household . But around three-quarters of them (41 out of 56) had children. The largest group were married or cohabiting (27) with 19 being single and ten separated, divorced or widowed. A number spoke of the way family friends and neighbours had helped with childcare, enabling them to work:

> If I needed to work in the evenings, or I needed to go to an evening class or whatever, I always had someone to turn to for support, so in that way I have been very fortunate.
>
> (Miranda NATFHE)

Nancy's account of her community involvement reveals how specifically helpful work in the community can be to women with small children. She was involved in teaching women within community settings:

> It was all part time. I knew from September to July there were different courses that I was involved in. For instance, I worked with a group of women from Kings' Cross and um, it was a clothes-making course that we did and then in return they taught me Asian Cooking and how to wrap a sari, it was absolutely wonderful. And I worked with the homeless family group. Yes, family workshops as well, especially during the summer periods when school was off you could take your children with you, you could take your child, so I took my daughter with me. So my daughter was always with me, a lot of the

time. Because there was a crèche facility there, so that she could get involved. So it wasn't like putting my child away somewhere, I had her with me, you know.

When we talked to Bangladeshi and Pakistani women's groups in Bristol, as part of a later project, they emphasised that jobs in their community organisations especially appealed to women because they could bring their children along. Within these Muslim families, there is still a tendency for husbands to require their wives to shoulder domestic burdens unaided and, for example, to make sure they are at home when family members return from school or work, thus restricting their options for paid employment.

Elsewhere (Bradley, Healy and Mukherjee 2005) we have argued that while BME women do often have heavier burdens of child care and domestic work than white women, their characteristic family structures and women's neighbourhood networks may be more supportive than those of the majority nucleated family-type in terms of providing help with looking after children; however, this hardly means they have an easy time! Many women we interviewed were single parents; and as the analysis above suggests, it was hard for us to understand how they could manage to bear such immense 'triple burdens' of not only paid work and domestic work, but also voluntary and union work How did they balance it all?

> I don't know! [Laughs] I'm just extremely organised. But most important, people forget that you need the support at home. I've got a very, very good, supportive husband. He helps tremendously because apart from anything, he thinks I'm crazy. When I talk about it, it sounds a lot, but when I'm doing it, it doesn't seem so hard because they're all in a slot, and I have a big board ... in the kitchen on the kitchen wall. Everything is plastered on there. Highlighted and then keyed, so I can organise some of them.
>
> (Shahnaz NATFHE)

Women had developed excellent skills of organising, juggling and channelling their energies to carry out these arrays of tasks. In doing so, the boundaries between home, jobs and union work became very permeable. Carol, for example, talked of how she took what she had learned in her union training back to her own children:

> And because I've got children, I take that information and I'm saying, 'No, you're not doing that right. This is how you've got to present

yourself. This is how you've got to present your paperwork.' So I'm sort of a backup teacher to help them do their information.

Many told of how they had also encouraged family members and friends to join the relevant union in their job. They were, in effect, becoming advocates for unionism:

> And my son, I encourage to join the union. Because he works in an engineering firm in Aldershot, but it was non-unionised. But he still wanted to join a union, so I put him in contact with somebody from the GMB locally and so he joined. And my daughter's working part-time in a shop, so I'm going to encourage her to join USDAW.
>
> (Shelly, CWU)

In a way that harks back to the unionism of the nineteenth century, some women saw their unions as closely linked into their communities and families, not as the impersonal bureaucratic organisations into which they too often have mutated. Serena reminisced fondly about the old days in the CWU:

> Our union was part of everything we did. So it wasn't like you were trying to be awkward as part of a union, it was part and parcel of what you did. Even when we went to strike and everything, everybody was still there. We went to work every day just to stand outside and picket, but we were together on that. And it was I think it was a situation before privatisation – it was like you had a situation where there was like husband, wife and all the sons working for the company. So whatever cuts were getting done, it was affecting the whole family because it was a family thing. Because in those days you used to get letters in your pay-slips saying there was so many jobs going or apprenticeships, do you know anybody that wants a job? So you could have generations of family working within the company. It was like even though it didn't affect you personally, you knew somebody else that it affected...So when we went on that three-day strike, it was like everybody was there together.

The women often had imaginative ideas about how to regenerate this kind of sociability in their unions. For example, Serena's two comments below envisage unions becoming more 'family-friendly' spaces:

> Now we have our union meetings in the pub, which I suspect a lot of people...you know what I mean? Why not have like straight after work,

a little social that we can invite your kids to? ... There's like an adventure playground in our area. I said why don't we just get 100 tickets, we've got the funds. We'll offer it to people, just to bring people in to show them that we do think about families. Because everything's surrounded by the pub. We go to the pub and that's that. People aren't gonna do that. If they're gonna leave work to come straight to the union, prepare something, they can have something to eat. You could bring your kids. They'd get more members if they did that.

And I went out there to Ireland, and it is totally different to us because Ireland is more family orientated. So all the women come with their children and the whole works.

Children and the future

The comment that the unions could recruit more members by allowing the inclusion of children is important, because children were central not just to the daily lives but to the ethos of these women. Thus Nancy's reflection on what her parents had suffered to produce her emphasised her concerns for the future of the next generation and the impacts on the community:

> You think of race relations and um, how my parents and their generation came into this country and what they had to deal with and the acceptance or the non-acceptance and the experience that they had to deal with and then we look at us, my age group and our generation and the kind of things that we have to deal with. And then I look at my children, and I think, my goodness it's getting worse you know, because if we are saying that we are living in a diverse cultural society with this whole aspect of racism and what is happening in our communities with the violence and the new gun culture. How are our children going to survive within this particular society that we live in? You think of things like where you live and if you want to move where do you move to? Is it safe? What support mechanisms are there to support our children, to um, educate on all fields so that we can live in harmony with each other? We have broken up the whole aspect of community, broken up families because people can't afford to live within their family environment and community environment.

While a few women were despondent and pessimistic about the future, many were determinedly optimistic about the potential for change, such as Lois, who had been fired up by her visit to her NATFHE union conference:

> But what I learnt from the conference is that, no, you can change the
> system. You have to work at it. If we all sit back, then we're just
> allowing it to slip through our fingers, and it just goes on from one
> generation to the other. Because the children are there watching.
> Our children are watching. We are their role models. I mean, we
> don't all have to be footballers. I mean, we don't all have to be athletes
> and musicians. There are academics as well, black academics. So we
> need to promote people in that position. You know, the role models,
> people who have positive contribution to the society in terms of the
> black community. And that has a lot to do with the children's
> education and development, and how they see themselves.

As Nancy's and Lois's comments show, these women, almost universally,
like Tony Blair, believed in 'education, education, education' as the key:

> Education is the key to everything. If we can get more black people
> interested in the education bit, then we can sort of move in other
> directions. I'm getting tired, I want to do something else (laughs),
> but I feel I don't want to let my brothers and sisters down. I know
> that I have knowledge now, I want to share it with them, I want to get
> more people in before I take a back seat, because I want to move to
> other things. I'm interested in training.
>
> (Linda UNISON)

> I feel that unions need to go into the schools. I think they need to go
> into the schools, not only as unions but self-organised groups. They
> need to get in there, or colleges as well.
>
> (Beth UNISON)

> I see myself as a role model, erm, in many ways, in terms of bringing
> up three children single-handed in Hackney, erm that's an achieve-
> ment. Being black, being a woman in this position, I see myself as a
> role model in that way and that I relate to the students.
>
> (Candy NATFHE)

It is instructive that Anita, an USDAW activist, when asked about her future,
expressed twin ambitions, for her children and for herself in the union:

> That my kids will be good citizens, and that one day they will appre-
> ciate and speak up for the black community and they will always be

proud of who they are. And to become an area organiser and hopefully have the strength that my area organiser gave to me, that I can give other members

Changing the union

To fulfil such hopes, unions need to develop and grow in specific ways. As we have mentioned, a number of British unions, such as UNISON, USDAW and ISTC, have begun to explore the potentials of community unionism and community-union alliances. However, unions also need to continue to work on becoming more inclusive, and in particular to recognise and build upon the energies and talents of their black female activists. If they fail to do this, they are shooting themselves in the feet! For not only will they be missing out on the assistance this group of hard-working and committed members can offer as individuals, they will be overlooking a resource which could contribute to processes of union renewal (Fairbrother 2000; Fosh 1993). As we hope this chapter has shown, such women embody a type of collectivism, which has been lost by many of their white colleagues.

> The idea of a union is, I think, very important and the fact that as workers we can get together, because that's where your strength will lie, as a group. If you come together as a group, as opposed to working as individuals, each individual trying to solve their own little problem, if you come together as a group and then to sort of sit, at least negotiate for improvement in your terms and conditions.
>
> (Miranda NATFHE)

Their rootedness in community has helped them stand against the general current of individualism which has been seen as such a threat to union organisation.

Some of the women spoke explicitly of wishing to see unions expand their community and political activities:

> I'd like to see UNISON taking more of a part within the – I know it does have a little voice within government, but I don't know exactly how much and how much it could actually help it grow.
>
> (Laurel)

Black workers for the Greater London region has um, organised and will be carrying out a seminar on Lupus, which affects black people and I think people from the Mediterranean. And so that's a one day seminar, and people from the branch here have been invited to go and stewards have been invited to go, and just ordinary people have been, as many as they can, have been invited to go along. And the next seminar that black workers in the London region has organised, which I will be doing and participating in delivering, is mental health for black people from the age of 18 to 25. So I link in with what they are doing and make sure that the black workers in the branch are aware of these courses because it's things that we deal with in our day to day work.

(Ginette)

One or two contrasted their own interests and insights with the more limited perspective and materialism of the more 'traditional' union members:

I think a lot of the older people think the union is there just to fight for wages and to fight if you get sacked or anything like that. They don't think of it as a learning process. That they can use the union to go on courses and to educate themselves and to forward themselves in promotion and everything like that.

(Carole)

The women are pointing the way to a new sort of unionism, with a broader agenda and which is able to draw on the talents and concerns of its different member constituencies. By contrast, over and over again women complained of the racism and sexism of male paid officers and stewards, and a macho culture no longer appropriate for contemporary union growth. Indeed, that culture continues to deter many potential member. As Marsha put it:

You need to overcome the maleness of the trade union movement anyway, the image or the myths that are being portrayed about, you know, they are going to blow a whistle and every one will go out you know, and I'm alright Jack-type thing, and Peter Sellers, and these stroppy blokes who bang the table. We are trying to change that image, so people like me are, I'm not saying that I'm a role model or anything like that, but if people see me not dressed up in a suit, something different. A woman, who looks like an ordinary working woman, you know they can relate to that.

Conclusion

This chapter has highlighted the tremendous achievements of this group of black female union activists across a range of community and political spheres. We have seen how work, community and union activities spill over into each other and inform them. This community-embedded nature of BME women's approach has been noted by other researchers; for example by Sudbury, who cites the 'transformation of the local community' as one of the core achievements of black women's voluntary organisations:

> Although black women's organisations are not limited to the local sphere, much of their activism has attempted to transform local dynamics. By asserting their right to organise autonomously, black women have changed the political environment ... establishing black women as a force to be reckoned with in black communities and as 'players' in the local political economy.
>
> (1998:236)

While the backwoodsman behaviour of some male power-holders has been frustrating, there is a sense in the women's stories of progress and of hope for the future. At last some of the unions are beginning to grasp what they have to gain from utilising the enthusiasms and skills of their BME women members. The notion of community-union alliances is a crucial development promising to harness the energies of different stakeholder activists in common causes. Although the axis of difference and disadvantage is that of race not class, the passion for justice that inspired the trade union pioneers is replicated in the ideals that motivate these 'inspiring activists' (Healy, Bradley and Mukherjee 2004a), as exemplified in this comment from Ginette:

> I'm obligated to people like my parents, who are both dead, to fight on for justice, for the right that black people should have the same kind of equal treatment and equality of service in every aspect of life. I personally believe that Martin Luther King was right when he said that he wanted his children to be judged on the content of their

character not the colour of their skin, and that is what motivates me, people like him who've passed on his beliefs and did not live long enough to see some results in the struggle that I continue to do. I am only a tiny drop in the ocean, but I still think that I can make a difference.

12
Conclusions

Gender and ethnic employment gaps

In its valedictory report before being merged into the new Equality and Human Rights Commission (EHRC), which was entitled *The Gender Agenda: The unfinished revolution,* the EOC highlighted the following economic gulfs between women and men:

- The **'pensions gap'** will take 45 years to equalise: retired women's income is currently 40 per cent less than men's.
- The **'part-time pay gap'** will take 25 years to close and the 'full-time pay gap' 20 years. Women working part-time earn 38 per cent less per hour than men working full-time. Full-time female employees earn 17 per cent less per hour than men.
- The **'flexible working gap'** is unlikely ever to change unless further action is taken. Even though half of working men say they would like to work more flexibly, currently women are much more likely than men (63 per cent more likely) to work flexibly.
- At home, the **'chores gap'** – the difference in the amount of time women and men spend doing housework per day – will likewise also never close, with women still spending 78 per cent more time than men doing housework.
- The **'power gap'** for women in Parliament will take almost 200 years to close and it will take up to 65 years to have a more equitable balance of women at the top of FTSE 100 companies.

We could add another gap, the **'graduate pay gap'**. Other research in 2007, by the Higher Education Statistics Authority (HESA) , showed that three years after graduating the median salary for women was £1000 less than for men (Curtis 2007). This is important as it focuses on the young generation of well-qualified women, and shows how this is not just a problem of time lag, but an ongoing structural phenomenon.

This analysis gives a disheartening picture of the slow rate of progress towards real gender equality in the United Kingdom. Those of us who have lived right through this 'unfinished revolution' can certainly see improvements in many aspects of women's lives (increased labour market participation, educational success, greater sexual freedom, a wider range of job prospects, better rights in respect of marriage and divorce). Yet there is a long way to go. We have seen how, in the sphere of employment, patriarchal attitudes and behaviour persist, with male-dominated work cultures still making it hard to get to the top; while the 'chores gap' is still a key factor preventing women competing with men on equal terms (Glucksmann 1995). It is hard to resist Sarah Delamont's assertion in her recent survey of gender relations in Britain (2001) that not only have men not changed very much, women, too, have not changed greatly, certainly not as much as is so often claimed in the media.

In the above EOC report 'woman' is used as a generic term. If the figures were available, the gap for BME women on these measures would certainly be greater, as the analysis in Chapter 2 has demonstrated. The exception is that some groups of BME women are more likely to work full-time and therefore on average earn more than white women (as discussed in Chapter 2). This should enable some BME women to compete more effectively in the labour market. The 'ethnicity gap' or the 'BME' gap is influenced instead by the complex interrelationship of the inequality regimes faced by BME women.

Chapter 2 pointed to the basis of inequality gaps and showed that overall BME women faced greater labour market disadvantages in comparison to white women. Because of the complexity of different ethnic groups' experience within the broad category of BME, concluding comparative points are difficult to make. Yet BME women are confined to a more limited range of jobs. Around one in ten women from the black African group and one in seven women from the 'other Asian' group were working as nurses in 2004, compared with around one in 30 white British women. Indian, Pakistani and black African women were around four times more likely than white British women to be working as packers, bottlers, canners and fillers. Pakistani and Indian women were respectively around six times and four times more likely than white British women to be working as sewing machinists (Office for National Statistics 2004). We pointed to the hierarchical complexity of the inequality regimes with respect to the shape and degree of inequalities in Chapter 2.

White women were more likely to be managers and senior officials than minority women who, on the other hand, were more likely to be members of professions. This chapter also showed that Chinese and Indian women were more likely than their white counterparts to be senior officials or managers, whereas Indian, Pakistani, Bangladeshi and black African women were all more or as likely to be members of professions as white women. The struggle for black Caribbean women seemed greater.

To complement the 'gaps' identified by the EOC and to understand the complexity of inequalities faced by BME women, we identify a number of *gendered ethnic employment gaps* in this final chapter as they provide focus to the difficulties experienced by BME women. We note the **employment difficulties gap**. Over half of Pakistani women (56 per cent) and black Caribbean women (54 per cent) aged 16–34 said they often found it difficult getting a job. Almost half of Bangladeshi women (49 per cent) said they often or sometimes struggled to find work. Only just over a third (34 per cent) of white British women said that finding work was sometimes a problem (TUC 2006).

The **skill achievement gap** is very important given the high investment of BME women in education and training. Of the same young women who struggled to find employment opportunities, while just over one in 20 of the white British women (6 per cent) said they had ended up taking a job below their skill levels, almost a quarter (22 per cent) of Pakistani women had accepted jobs for which they were over qualified (TUC 2006).

The **presumptions gap** is evident in the differential way that women are treated as a result of their ethnicity. Employer attitudes and presumptions about ethnic minority women are also causing problems when prospective job candidates are called for interview. Whilst only 14 per cent of white British women had been asked about plans to get married or have children, the figure rises to a fifth (21 per cent) of Bangladeshi women, and around a quarter for black Caribbean (24 per cent) and Pakistani women (26 per cent) (TUC 2006).

In many ways, these gaps reflect the consequences of the vicious circles of segregation in the recruitment process that we discussed in Chapter 3. Recruitment decisions ostensibly based on notions of 'merit' may have at their heart a white bias. Indeed, critical writers question the concept of merit. Iris Marion Young, for example, challenges the assumption that merit is a neutral concept, that it is possible to make judgments on an individual's competence according to impartial measures of such competence (1990). Indeed, for Young, for the merit principle to apply it must be possible to identify, measure, compare and rank individual performance of job-related tasks using criteria that are normatively and culturally neutral. In reality, for most jobs, this is not possible and most criteria of evaluation used in our society, including educational credentials and standardised testing, have normative and cultural content. Thus we would argue that working solely with the liberal approach to equality tends to lead to the appraising of all individuals (regardless of ethnic background) according to a white gendered, normative and cultural bias.

The role of the key actors in equality and diversity

Chapters 4 to 6 considered the major actors' part in relation to the promotion of equality in the labour market. The state has played a central role in determining what in law is acceptable and what is not. Yet, while we have had some 40 years of equality legislation scripted predominantly in the liberal paradigm (see Chapter 3), inequalities have persisted and in some cases taken on new shapes. The New Labour government has recently strengthened the law as a result of the outcome of the Stephen Lawrence Inquiry (Macpherson 1999) and as a result of European Directives. This recent commitment by the New Labour regime to improving legislation and rights for women and ethnic minorities is welcome, but so far has been limited in its effectiveness. The future role of the new EHRC will be critical; the final reports from the CRE and DDA highlighted the persistence of inequalities and disadvantage in the same way as the EOC report. It remains to be seen whether the merger of the three equality bodies will produce a more powerful and better funded agency and whether its leaders will steer the EHRC to take a strong campaigning role. It is hoped that early fears that gender may have a lesser priority are unfounded.

Recent legislative duties have been confined to the public sector. One of the deficiencies of the state's approach to legislation is its refusal to make gender and race equality duties binding upon the private sector. Thus many employers continue to evade their duties under the original legislation as Chapter 5 showed. It is the case that some larger and more progressive employers develop equality strategies and structures that are often based on the business case for diversity. However, we have argued in Chapter 5 that the framework and rhetoric of 'diversity management' imported from America to replace older equality approaches is potentially damaging in its focus on individuals rather than disadvantaged groups and in its emphasis on the business case.

This leaves an important role for trade unions in promoting more radical forms of the equality agenda. Despite their often appalling past records in dealing with women and BME members, most unions have now acknowledged the value of the diversity of the workforces they represent and, in face of the importance of recruiting women and BME workers to maintain union density, have developed some important initiatives on equality. The impact and legacy of the TUC Stephen Lawrence Task Group (SLTG) has had an important policy impact on the individual unions' approach to racism. The TUC website is full of valuable resources for union members to use to challenge racist behaviour. As we saw in Chapter 6, unions have also introduced structural changes with the aim of involving more women in union decision-making. However, there is still some way to go in tackling racism and sexism in unions' own ranks, as our interviews with active union members demonstrated. Male branch officers are seen as a particular problem and can use their power to block the progress of BME women within the union. There are important parallels here with the negative role often played by line managers.

In her study of black women's organisations, Julia Sudbury speaks of four types of 'visions of transformation' that the women she interviewed developed in their struggle to 'assert their agency' (1998:235). These were: personal exploration and consciousness-raising to develop confidence for action; the realignment of family life to escape stigmatisation and oppression; action within the community, as discussed in Chapter 11; and finally, moving out from the local to the global, to oppose the exploitation and suppression of women's rights in post-colonial contexts. In our discussions with our participants, we saw evidence of agency in all these areas; and we believe that trade unions, with their traditions of campaigning and collectivism, can be an alternative locus for BME women to pursue their visions of transformation.

An intersectional analysis of BME women's disadvantage

In Chapter 3 we raised some theoretical issues, to which we now wish to return. We have tried throughout this book to highlight the importance of an intersectional analysis to an understanding of minority ethnic women's work experiences. In our chapters reporting our findings, we drew attention to some specific examples of intersectionality. Our interview material, discussed in Chapters 8 to 11 pointed to some of the issues which lie behind the statistical picture presented in Chapter 2. Women made it clear that they commonly experienced racism and sexism; the precise ways in which racism and sexism interacted varied, with women in male-dominated areas complaining more of sexism than others. Overall, women agreed that sexism and racism combined to create specific patterns of discrimination for BME women. Here we want to draw out a few more general conclusions with respect to an intersectional analysis.

Intersections: gender, racism and ethnicity

The women in our study were drawn from five different ethnic groups: black Caribbean, African, Indian, Pakistani, black American and mixed heritage. However, given the small numbers involved, we differentiate them as black and Asian in order to make some comments on the differences amongst them.

All the women faced racial discrimination, but its specific form and impact varied. The intersection of gender and black ethnicity is marked by stereotyping; Caribbean and African women stated that they are perceived as aggressive and difficult, which leads to their exclusion from management jobs and helps perpetuate the patterns of segregation described in Chapter 2. Colonial prejudices also appear to be involved in the undervaluation of their qualifications. This is most nakedly shown in the refusal to credit university qualifications gained overseas, which afflicts African women in particular. But the HESA research mentioned above showed only 67 per cent of UK black graduates (female and male) were employed three years after graduating, as compared to 75 per cent of Asians and 74 per cent of whites (Curtis 2007).

However, what emerged from our research was that the problem for black women (as opposed to black men) was not so much *getting in* to the labour market as *getting on* within it. Black women's labour market experience is therefore characterised by segmentation, both horizontal and vertical, and by blocked careers and failure to get promotion; these were major issues that concerned our Caribbean and African respondents.

The situation of the smaller number of Asian women we interviewed has some similarities: they too complained of failure to get promoted and those with overseas qualifications also experienced the same undervaluing and disregarding of their qualifications. However, the most striking feature about this group was their relative absence from the study. We struggled to identify any Asian women activists to interview. We only managed to interview one Pakistani and no Bangladeshi women. This may partly be due to fear (it was suggested to us that Asian women preferred not to risk being seen as 'troublemakers' by becoming active within the union), but of course it also reflects the low economic activity rates for these two groups. Thus for Pakistanis and Bangladeshis, there is a major problem of *getting in* as well as *getting on*. In this case the intersection of ethnicity and gender results in labour market exclusion.

We have studied this problem more fully in our recent work for the EOC (Bradley, Healy, Forson and Kaul 2007) which revealed the difficulties Pakistani and Bangladeshi women have in finding employment, especially those born abroad. Census data for 2001 analysed by Sue Yeandle (2007) reveal that 48 per cent of UK born Bangladeshi women aged 25–44 were economically active as opposed to only 19 per cent of non-UK born. The figures for Pakistani women were 47 and 24 per cent respectively. There are clearly some problems of limited English skills and lack of confidence which affect those born overseas, but the danger is that lack of English may be used as a rationalisation. The reality is that of those actually in employment, Pakistani, Bangladeshi (and black Caribbean) women are more likely than white women to be graduates. Yet as we stated above, despite qualifications, they are also more likely to be unemployed (EOC 2007c). There also very strong indications in our EOC research of gendered anti-Muslim prejudice, which manifests itself particularly in response to Islamic dress codes. Women choosing to wear the headscarf or veil find it particularly hard to get jobs. Thus religion, ethnicity and gender combine to create a pattern of marginalisation and exclusion, forcing women back into the home or into work in the ethnic economy.

There is evidence, as some of our interviewees told us, that some Muslim husbands may put restrictions on their wives' labour market involvement if it is seen to interfere with household duties. This is one reason why education is a popular choice for British Muslim women, as it allows women to confine their working time to school hours. However, we want to emphasise strongly that we are not here offering an explanation purely in terms of cultural attitudes. The material conditions of life in British Muslim families, marked by poverty, ensure that domestic work and childcare are heavy burdens for Pakistani and Bangladeshi married women with children. Their husbands tend to eschew housework; but so of course do many white husbands/partners as noted by the EOC (the 'chores gap'). Above all, we want to avoid an explanation in terms of the 'passivity' of Asian women or their greater orientation to domesticity. They do put a high priority on their families, but so do all groups of women whom we have researched. Despite this, however, they do want to secure employment and, in particular, to find good jobs. Yeandle (2007) reports that over 37,000 Pakistani women and 12,000 Bangladeshi women of working age are unemployed or economically active but say that they would like paid work.

Gender, ethnicity and class

The other important intersection we need to explore is that of gender and ethnicity with class. Class can still be seen as the most important source of material inequality in contemporary Britain (Bradley 1996). Class and the social and cultural capital associated with it has a crucial impact on educational success (Fenton and Dermott 2006); children from upper- and middle-class backgrounds go to well-resourced private schools or the most sought-after state schools; they go on to take degrees at elite universities, which help them secure the most desirable and best-paid graduate jobs.

In effect, class can, at least to some extent, compensate for ethnic or gender penalties. In the Bristol young adults' study, a few young middle-class women who went into professions such as law, medicine or business consultancy were able to match white males' salaries (Fenton, Bradley et al. 2002). This can be seen in the position of the Indian women in the *Double Disadvantage* study. They were concentrated in professional jobs (social work and teaching) and were more likely to reach supervisory or middle-management levels. The one Indian woman who was currently employed in retail, Neera, was also in the final year of a marketing degree. These women were from highly educated, middle-class families. Their husbands, like Parvati's, were likely to be in well-paid professional work, thus opening up a broader array of choices for them about work-life balance, obtaining qualifications and so forth. This mirrors the position of Indian women nationally as shown in Chapter 2. Indian women can use their class assets (Savage, Barlow et al. 1992) to achieve something close to economic integration with the white majority. Of course, we should caution against generalising about the class position of Indian women, since they are a heterogeneous group with many working in manufacturing and packing as stated above. The point is that Indian women are more likely to have a class advantage than most other BME groups. By contrast, many Caribbean, Pakistani and Bangladeshi families are more likely to be working class and live in deprived inner-city areas, with the older family members having filled manual jobs or migrated from agricultural backgrounds. Thus class disadvantage compounds their ethnic disadvantage.

The indeterminacy of career

We have emphasised how seriously many BME women regard their work lives. In Chapter 3 we asked a number of questions with respect to the degree to which black women choose their careers. We saw very clear evidence in Chapters 9 and 10 of the way that the women's careers were shaped by the dialectical relationship between self and their circumstances. Part of this relationship will be shaped by the historical context of the 'circumstances' and by the woman herself. Chapter 9 demonstrated the shifting sands that the women faced in seeking to develop their careers. The boundaries for future career development were constantly changing and were rarely clear. Time and time again women reported that their gender and ethnicity were factors that led to blocked careers. Contradictory stereotypes were used to rationalise their lack of progress. Chapter 9 also demonstrated that not all women wanted hierarchical career development. Some rejected the possibility of promotion because they favoured greater work-life balance. However, a gendered understanding of career allows us to recognise that this does *not* mean that women will rule out development in the future, although employers may interpret it that way (another example of a 'partial truth'). Further, when they are ready to accelerate their career, they may have missed the narrow 'age window' when promotion is available. For women, age is an important factor in career development. The years when they are more likely to interrupt their careers or remain on a career plateau are the years when men are making strides in their careers. When they return they may be forced to pay the price of lack of advancement for such a break or plateau, that is, for deviating from the male norm in career.

Importantly our focus on careers also draws out the nature of an intrinsic or moral commitment to work activities, where women will undertake work that allows them to make a contribution to their communities. Implied in much of the racist and sexist discourse is that women are not committed to work. We have provided evidence of black Caribbean women's strong attachment to the labour market, yet 'getting on' remains difficult for them. Nevertheless, our study showed the extraordinary degree of commitment to work in the public sphere by many of the women in this study. Whether it was to political life, their churches and, of particular relevance to this study, their trade union, the women demonstrated extraordinary energy and commitment. Thus they built alternative union careers or in some cases what Kirton (2006) identifies as parallel careers.

Without doubt, our work crushes the notion of career as a purely hierarchical concept. Instead, for us, our use of the career concept recognises that it spans both objective and subjective aspects of social life allowing it to show the links between macro- and micro-phenomena and the relation between institutional and interpretative aspects of activity (Layder 1993). Rather than the linear career, we show how careers, and gendered careers in particularly, are characterised by indeterminacy. The rich picture we have painted of black women's careers shows the impact of institutional constraints and how women actively seek to reshape, build and challenge such constraints in making their subjective careers. Thus whilst they may not consciously 'choose' their careers, they are active architects seizing opportunities and working within and pushing back the constraints they face.

Inequality regimes

Throughout this book, the concept of inequality regimes (Acker 2006a) has informed our understandings, explicitly or implicitly, of the findings of our research project. Indeed, intersectionality, as considered above, is central to inequality regimes. Therefore in this section, we would simply like to argue that the concept of inequality regimes provides a valuable and comprehensive approach to making sense of inequalities in organisations. Crucial to the concept of inequality regimes, as we see it, is that the different components intersect and interrelate. If an organisation (of whatever kind) cannot (or will not) understand the *bases of inequality* (the first component) as they apply to that organisation, they will be unable to address them. If an organisation does not take the trouble to understand the *shape and degree of inequality* (the second component), then the time spent 'doing the documents' (Ahmed 2007) will be of marginal value. Each organisation is part of the wider society, so inevitably it will be shaped by the gendered, ethnicised and class order dominant in that society. However, these socially constructed orders will take different forms in different organisations and they should not be seen as deterministic.

Acker's third component (the *organising processes that produce inequality*) focuses in on the minutiae of organisational life that shape and reproduce inequalities. The vicious circles of segregation in recruitment and selection identified by Collinson et al. (1990) demonstrate how sex segregation is reproduced in the recruitment and selection process and that the analysis of inequality regimes delves into the organisation's systems, procedures and everyday life to observe the production of inequalities. The women in our study provided important examples of their experience of how such organising processes around human resource management practices (as opposed to policies) shaped and reproduced inequalities. As we have seen, these were played out with respect to promotion blocks and in the negative experience of workplace interactions. We observe that inequality regimes may work in different ways and at different organisational levels. These organising processes resulted in the major causes of complaint being low pay, limited opportunities, failure to recognise overseas qualifications, stereotyping and, above all, difficulties in getting promoted. It was, then, blocks to their careers which led many women to devote themselves to work within the union, which for some led to alternative careers as union activists and representatives. A number had aspirations to develop those careers further by becoming paid officers, although here some encountered problems in the shape of white males who, they believed, were actively blocking their progress.

Exploring how the *legitimacy of inequalities* in an organisation is validated draws our attention to the way inequalities may be viewed differently at different points in the hierarchy. Stories in our research indicate that many managers and trade unionists do not view inequality as an issue of legitimacy. Nevertheless, we have important examples where women were advised and guided by those (management and trade unions) who did not condone practices of inequalities.

Acker's fifth component is the *visibility of inequalities* in organisations. This emerged in many of the women's stories. There were graphic stories of sharp horizontal segregation and the consequence of this for women working in male dominated areas. Time and time again we heard stories of the persistent vertical segregation with black women more likely to be at the bottom of the hierarchies. We are mindful of Acker's (2006a) view that visibility varies with the position of the beholder: that men tend not to see their gender privilege and white men and women tend not to see their race privilege, ruling-class members tend not to see their class privilege. Women and BME men and women are more likely to note segregation within the workforce. They are also more likely to note visible minorities as role models. Indeed, almost without intending to do so, women in our study became role models for others. We would argue that role models are important for black women in a society dominated by white men. The lack of role models for young BME women may socially construct a limit to their ambitions of what might be perceived as possible.

Finally, Acker introduces the sixth component, *control and compliance*. Wherever there is compliance within organisations, there will be resistance. Trade unions seek to assuage the worst effects of capitalism which have a differential and uneven impact with respect to gender, ethnicity and class. Resisting inequality regimes therefore falls to trade unions, the main institutionalised form of resistance. In reality, as this book shows, those who are likely to take up the mantle of challenging racism and sexism in organisation are women or black trade union members. In other words, those most likely to be most affected are those most likely to put up the strongest resistance.

The women in our research exemplify such resistance; they did not sit quietly in the face of discrimination; in very different ways they resisted being made 'victims' of racism: by taking grievances or appeals, by working for equality within the union, by seeking new employment opportunities where their abilities would be appreciated, by anti-racist campaigning in the community. As we emphasised in Chapter 11, the women were motivated not just by individual ambitions, but by a strong commitment to social justice and a desire to build a better world for their communities, and most especially for their children.

However, we should also recognise that our study revealed other women who succumbed to gendered and racist control and chose the path of least resistance, the path of compliance. This is hardly surprising. It is not easy being the one person who constantly feels that they have to stand up and challenge management and colleagues for their behaviour, to be the person constantly told that they don't have a sense of humour, to be the person who is accused of being oversensitive, and to be the person who is constantly risking their job or their opportunities for promotion. Thus the women in our study did not take an easy route.

Moving forward or standing still?

This book has been written at a time when immigration is again to the fore of the public debates. We are seeing massive exploitation of migrant workers as cheap labour, and at the same time there are calls for curbs on immigration. Indeed, the curbs already introduced favour European migration at the expense of migration from outside Europe. The effect of this is that white migrants are given preference over black. Yet, as we have seen, black migrants and their descendents have played a huge role in the British economy and kept many sectors (such as the health service) afloat.

Whilst we recognise the importance of the law in providing a framework to challenge inequalities, it is also the case that compliance is necessary for change to take place. Recent revelations that government departments were failing to comply with statutory duties (Travis 2007) demonstrate the importance of closing the implementation gap between policy and practice. It further raises the question of sanctions for non-compliance.

Nevertheless, we do see evidence of change. There is a general concern about the pay gap shared by the two main political parties. However, we would argue that attention needs to be paid to the proper valuing of work done mainly by women in order to close the pay gap. The trade unions have sought to change their character so that they have made important structural changes and are now campaigning for equality representatives.

We have many examples of individual successes and role models as shown in Chapter 7. Indeed, the women in this study are important role models in their own milieu. We see important educational improvements which the EOC which will enhance work prospects. It is pleasing to hear of women taking initiatives to create different options for success: it was reported in 2007 that one in five new Asian businesses are being set up by women (Ward 2007). One of the most heartening aspects of society is that the aspirations of the young are high. Society needs to do all possible to enable them to meet those aspirations. Ladders, not blocks, are needed to remove the constraints outlined in this book and enable young black and Asian women the freedom to shape their careers without discrimination

Thus the imperative must be to move forward in the equalities project. Standing still is not an option for society nor for black and minority ethnic women and their children.

Bibliography

Acker, J. (2006a). 'Inequality regimes: Gender, class, and race in organizations'. *Gender and Society, 20*(4), 441–64.

Acker, J. (2006b). *Class Questions: Feminist answers.* Lanham, MD: Rowman & Littlefield.

Ahmad, F., Modood, T. and Lissenberg, S. (2003). *South Asian Women and Employment in Britain: The interaction of gender and ethnicity.* London: PSI.

Ahmed, S. (2007). '"You end up doing the document rather than doing the doing": Diversity, race equality and the politics of documentation'. *Ethnic and Racial Studies, 30*(4), 590–609.

Anderson, B. (1983). *Imagined Communities: Reflections on the origin and spread of nationalism.* London: Verso.

Anderson, B. (2000). *Doing the Dirty Work: The global politics of domestic labour.* London: Zed.

Anthias, F. and Yuval-Davis, N. (1992). *Racialised Boundaries.* London: Routledge.

Archer, M. (1995). *Realist Social Theory: The morphogenetic approach.* Cambridge: Cambridge University Press.

Arnold, J. (1997). *Managing Careers into the 21st Century.* London: Paul Chapman Publishing.

Aston, J., Hill, D. and Tackey, N. (2006). 'The experience of claimants in race discrimination Employment Tribunals'. DTI Employment Research Series No 55.

Atkinson, J. (1984). 'Manpower strategies for flexible organisations'. *Personnel Management, 16*, 28–31.

Atkinson, J. (1986). 'Flexibility planning for an uncertain future'. *Manpower Policy and Practice*, Summer 26.

Atkinson, J. and Meager, N. (1986). *Changing Work Patterns: How companies achieve flexibility to meet new needs.* London: National Economic Development Office.

Bagilhole, B. and Byrne, P. (2000). 'From hard to soft law and from equality to reconciliation in the United Kingdom'. In L. Hantrais (ed.), *Gendered Policies in Europe.* Basingstoke: Palgrave Macmillan.

Ball, C. (1990). *Trade Unions and Equal Opportunities Employers.* London: Manufacturing, Science and Finance Union.

Banton, M. (1989). *Racial Theories.* Cambridge: Cambridge University Press.

Barker, M. (1981). *The New Racism.* London: Junction Books.

Barrett, M. (1980). *Women's Oppression Today.* London: Verso.

Becker, G. S. (1985). 'Human capital, effort, and the sexual division of labour'. *Journal of labor Economics, 3*(2), 533–8.

Becker, H. (1952). 'The career of the Chicago public school teachers'. In R. G. Burgess (ed.), *Howard Becker on Education* (reprinted in 1995 ed.). Milton Keynes: Open University.

Bhattacharya, G., Gabriel, J., and Small, S. (2002). *Race and Power: Global racism in the twenty-first century.* London and New York: Routledge.

Bhavnani, R. (2006). *Ahead of the Game: The changing aspirations of young ethnic minority women*. Manchester: EOC.

Bielby, D. D., and Bielby, W. T. (1988). 'She works hard for the money: Household responsibilities and the allocation of work effort'. *American Journal of Sociology, 93*(5), 1031–59.

Blackaby, D., Leslie, D., Murphy, P. and O'Leary, N. (1998). 'The ethnic wage gap and employment differentials in the 1990s: Evidence for Britain'. *Economics Letters, 59*, 97–103.

Blackwell, L. and Guinea-Martin, D. (2005). 'Occupational segregation by sex and ethnicity in England and Wales, 1991–2001'. *Labour Market Trends*. London: ONS.

Borchorst, A. and Siim, B. (1987). 'Women and the advanced welfare state: A new kind of patriarchal power?' In A. S. Sassoon (ed.), *Women and the State*. London: Hutchinson, 128–51.

Boston, L. (1987). *Women Workers and the Trade Unions*. London: Lawrence & Wishart.

Botcherby, S. and Hurrell, K. (2004). *Women and Men in Britain: Ethnic minority women and men*. Manchester: EOC.

Bradley, H. (1989). *Men's Work, Women's Work: A sociological history of the sexual division of labour*. Cambridge: Polity Press.

Bradley, H. (1996). *Fractured Identities*. Cambridge: Polity.

Bradley, H. (1999). *Gender and Power in the Workplace: Analysing the impact of economic change*. Basingstoke: Macmillan Press – now Palgrave Macmillan.

Bradley, H. (2006). 'Whose flexibility?' In E.Skorstad and H. Ramsdal (eds), *Facets of Flexibilityi*. Proceedings from an international workshop on flexibility, Ostfold University College, Norway.

Bradley, H. (2007). *Gender*. Cambridge: Polity.

Bradley, H., Healy, G. and Kaul, P. (2007). *Ethnic Minority Women and Workplace Cultures: What does and does not work*. Manchester: EOC.

Bradley, H., Healy, G., and Forson, C. (2007). 'Inequality regimes', paper to *Gender Work and Organization*. Keele University.

Bradley, H., Healy, G., and Mukherjee, N. (2002). *Double Disadvantage: Ethnic minority women in trade unions*. London: Unison.

Bradley, H., Healy, G., and Mukherjee, N. (2004). 'Union influence on career development – bringing in gender and ethnicity'. *Career Development International 9*(1), 74–88.

Bradley, H., Healy, G., and Mukherjee, N. (2005). 'Multiple burdens: Probems of work-life balance for ethnic minority trade union activist women'. In D. Houston (ed.), *Work-Life Balance in the 21st Century*. Basingstoke: Palgrave Macmillan.

Bradley, H., Erickson, M., Stephenson, S. and Williams, S. (2000). *Myths at Work*. Cambridge: Polity.

Bradley, H., Healy, G., Forson, C., and Kaur, P. (2007). *Workplace Cultures and Ethnic Minority Women*. Manchester: EOC.

Braybon, G. (1987). *Out of the Cage*. London: Pandora.

Brint, S. (2001). 'Gemeinschaft revisited: A critique and reconstruction of the community concept'. *Sociological Theory, 19*(1), 1–23.

Briskin, L. and Macdermott, P. (eds) (1993). *Women Challenging Unions*. Toronto: University of Toronto Press.

Brook, S. (2004 October). 'Labour market data for local areas by ethnicity'. *Labour Market Trends*. London: ONS, 404–16.

Brown, A., Erskine, A., and Littlejohn , D. (2006). 'Review of judgments in race discrimination employment tribunal cases'. DTI Employment Research Series 64.

Brown, C. (1984). *Black and White Britain*. London: Heinemann.

Brown, C. (1992). ' "Same difference": The persistence of racial disadvantage in the British employment market'. In P. Braham, A. Rattansi and R.Skellington (eds), *Racism and Anti-Racism: Inequalities, opportunities and policies*. London: Sage.

Bruegel, I. (1989). 'Sex and race in the labour market'. *Feminist Review, 32*, 49–68.

Bureau of Labor (2005, 2006). *Statistics*. Washington, DC: Bureau of Labor.

Calveley, M., and Healy, G. (2003). 'Political activism and workplace industrial relations in a UK "failing" school'. *British Journal of Industrial Relations, 41*(1), 97–113.

Carvel, J. (2007). 'Higher fertility, immigration and longer lives fuelling Britain's population rise'. The *Guardian*, 24 October.

Casey, C. 1995. *Work, Self and Society*. London: Routledge.

Castles, S. and Miller, M. (1998). *The Age of Migration: International population movements in the modern world*, 2nd edition. Basingstoke: Macmillan – now Palgrave Macmillan.

Chambers, G. and Horton, C. (1990). *Promoting Sex Equality: The role of Industrial Tribunals*. London: PSI.

Cheung, Y. and Heath, A. (1993). 'Ethnic origins and class destinations'. *Oxford Review of Education, 19*(2), 151–6.

Cockburn, C. (1982). *Brothers: Male dominance and technical change*. London: Pluto Press.

Cockburn, C. (1991). *In the Way of Women: Men's resistance to sex equality in organizations*. Basingstoke: Macmillan.

Colgan, F., and Ledwith, S. 1996. 'Sisters organising – Women and their trade unions'. In F. Colgan and S. Ledwith (eds), *Women in Organisations – Challenging Gender Politics*. Basingstoke: Macmillan.

Colgan, F. and Ledwith, S. (2000). 'Diversity, identities and strategies of women trade union activists'. *Gender, Work and Organisation, 7*(4), 242–57.

Collins, H. (1992). *The Equal Opportunities Handbook – A guide to law and best practice in Europe*. Oxford: Blackwell.

Collins, H. (1995). *Equality in the Workplace – An equal opportunities handbook for trainers*. Oxford: Blackwell.

Collins, P. H. (2004). 'Learning from the outsider within: The sociological significance of black feminist thought'. In S. Harding (ed.), *The Feminist Standpoint Theory Reader – Intellectual and political controversies*. New York and London: Routledge, 103–26.

Collinson, D., Knights, D., and Collinson, M. (1990). *Managing to Discriminate*. London: Routledge.

Connell, R. W. (1987). *Gender and Power*. Cambridge: Polity.

Connor, H., Tyers, C., Modood, T. and Hillage, J. (2004). *Why the Difference? A closer look at higher education minority ethnic students and graduates* (Research Report 552). London: Department of Education and Skills.

Coote, A. and Campbell, B. (1982). *Sweet Freedom*. London: Picador.

CRE (2006a). Factfile 1 'Employment and Ethnicity'. London: CRE.

CRE (2006b). Statistics: Labour market http:/www.cre.gov.uk/research/statistics

Creegan, C., Colgan, F., Charlesworth, R., and Robinson, G. (2003). 'Race equality policies at work: Employee perceptions of the "implementation Gap" in a UK Local Authority'. *Work Employment Society, 17*(4), 617–40.

Crompton, R. (1997). *Women and Work in Modern Britain.* Oxford: Oxford University Press.

Crompton, R., and Le Feuvre, N. (1996 August). 'Paid employment and the changing system of gender relations: A cross national comparison'. *Sociology, 30*(3), 427–45.

Cunnison, S. (1987). 'Women's three working lives and trade union participation'. In P. Allat, T. Keil, A. Bryman and B. Bytheway, B. (eds), *Women and Life Cycle.* Basingstoke: Macmillan.

Cunnison, S. and Stagemen, J. (1993). *Feminising the Unions.* London: Avebury.

Curtis, P. (2007). '£1000 gap between men and women's pay after graduation'. The *Guardian,* 6 November.

CWU (2006). *Is the Communication Workers Union Representative of its Ethnic Minorities?* London: CWU.

Dale, A. and Holdsworth, C. (1998). 'Why don't ethnic minority women in Britain work part-time'. In J. O' Reilly and C. Fagan (eds), *Part-Time Prospects.* London: Routledge.

Dale, A., et al. (2002). 'The labour market prospects for Pakistani and Bangladeshi women'. *Work, Employment and Society, 16*(1), 5–25.

Daniels, K., and Macdonald, L. (2005). *Equality, Diversity and Discrimination: A student text.* London: Chartered Institute of Personnel and Development.

Davis, A. (1981). *Women, Race and Class.* New York: Random House.

Deem, R., and Morley, L. (2006). 'Diversity in the Academy? Staff perceptions of equality policies in six contemporary higher education institutions'. *Policy Futures in Education, 4*(2), 185–202.

Delamont, S. (2001). *Changing Women, Changing Men.* Milton Keynes: Open University.

Devine, F. (1992). 'Gender segregation in the engineering and science professions: A case of continuity and change'. *Work Employment and Society, 6*(4), 557–75.

Dex, S. (1984). *Women's Work Histories: An analysis of the Women and Employment Survey* (Research Papaer No. 46). Sheffield: Department of Employment.

Dickens, L. (2006). 'Re-regulation for gender equality: from "either/or" to "both" '. *Industrial Relations Journal, 37*(4), 299–309.

DLA Consulting (2000). *Delivering on Equality.* Report of an independent review of equality with the CWU, May.

Donnelly, J. (1992). *Career Development for Teachers.* London: Kogan Page.

Dresser, M. (2007). 'Culture wars? Bristol's colour bar dispute of 1963'. BBC Legacies website http://www.bbc.co.uk/legacies/work/england/bristol

DTI (2006). *State of the Union* website: http://www.dti.gov.uk/employment

Du Gay, P. (1996). *Consumption and Identity at Work.* London: Sage.

Duffy, M. (2005). 'Reproducing labor inequalities: Challenges for feminists conceptualising care at the intersections of gender, race and class'. *Gender and Society, 19*(1), 66–82.

Dumont, J.-C. and Leibig, T. (2005). 'Labour market integration of migrant women: Overview and recent trends'. *Migrant Women and the Labour Market: Diversity and challenges.* Brussels: OECD.

DWP Statistics on low-income families (2002). London: Department of Work and Pensions.

Dwyer, C., Modood, T., Sanghera, G. Shah, B. and Thapar-Bjorkert, S. (2006). 'Ethnicity as social capital? Explaining the differential educational achievements of young British Pakistani men and women'. Paper presented at the 'Ethnicity, Mobility and Society' Leverhulme Programme Conference at University of Bristol, March.

Edwards, S. (1981). *Female Sexuality and the Law*. Oxford: Blackwell.

Ehrenreich, B. (2006). *Bait and Switch: The futile pursuit of the corporate dream*. London: Granta Publications.

Employment Tribunal Service (2006). *Annual Report and Accounts*. London: DTI.

EOC (2004). 'Ethnic minority women and men'. Manchester : EOC.

EOC (2005). 'Outdated assumptions are blighting ethnic minority women's careers'. Press release, 21 October 2005.

EOC (2007a). *The Gender Agenda: The unfinished revolution*. Final Report of EOC, Manchester: Equal Opportunities Commission.

EOC (2007b). *Promote People not Stereotypes*. Manchester: Equal Opportunities Commission.

EOC. (2007c). *Moving on up? The way forward: Report of the EOC's investigation into Bangladeshi, Pakistani and black Caribbean women and work*. Manchester: Equal Opportunities Commission.

European Women's Lobby (2006a). *Strengthening women's rights in a multicultural Europe*.

European Women's Lobby (2006b). *Facts and Figures about Gender Equality in Europe*.

Evetts, J. (1989). 'The internal labour market for primary teachers'. In S. Acker (ed.), *Teachers, Gender and Careers*. Lewes: The Falmer Press.

Evetts, J. (1992). 'When promotion ladders seem to end: The career concerns of secondary headteachers'. *British Journal of Sociology of Education, 13*(1).

Fairbrother, P. (2000). *Trade Unions at the Crossroads*. London: Mansell.

Fawcett Society (2005). *Listening to Black and Ethnic Minority Women's Voices*. Seminar Report.

Fenton, S. (1999). *Ethnicity: Racism, class and culture*. Basingstoke: Macmillan – now Palgrave Macmillan.

Fenton, S. (2003). *Ethnicity*. Cambridge: Polity.

Fenton, S. and Dermott E. (2006). 'Fragmented careers: Winners and losers in young adult labour markets'. *Work, Employment and Society, 20*, 205–21.

Fenton, S., Bradley, H., Devadason, R., West, J. and Guy, W. (2002). 'Winners and losers in urban labour markets: Young adults in Britain'. Report for ESRC.

Fosh, P. (1993). 'Membership participation in workplace unionism: The possibility of union renewal'. *British Journal of Industrial Relations, 31*(4), 577–92.

Fosh, P. and Heery, E. (eds) (1990). *Trade Unions and their Members*. Basingstoke: Macmillan.

Foster, C., and Harris, L. (2005). 'Easy to say, difficult to do: Diversity management in retail. *Human Resource Management Journal, 15*(3), 4–17.

Fox, A. (1966). *Industrial Sociology and Industrial Relations*: The Royal Commission on Trade Unions and Employers' Association, London: HMSO.

Franzway, S. (2001). *Sexual Politics and Greedy Institutions*. Sidney: Pluto Press.

Fuller, M. (1982). 'Young, female and black'. In E. Cashmore and B. Troyna (eds), *Black Youth in Crisis*. London: Allen & Unwin.

Gallie, D. (1998). 'The flexible workforce? The employment conditions of part-time and temporary workers'. Paper presented at ESRC social stratification workshop, Essex University.

Gelb, J. and Palley, M. L. (1982). *Women and Public Policies*. Princeton: Princeton University Press.

Giddens, A. (1979). *Central Problems in Social Theory*. London: Macmillan.

Gilbert, J., Stead, B. A., and Ivancevich, J. M. (1999). 'Diversity management: A new organizational paradigm'. *Journal of Business Ethics, 21*(1), 61–76.

Ginn, J., Arber, S., Brannen, J., Dale, A., Dex, S., Elias, P., et al. (1996). 'Feminist fallacies: A reply to Hakim on women's employment'. *British Journal of Sociology, 47*(1), 167–74.

Glucksmann, M. (1995). 'Why "Work"? Gender and the total social organization of labour'. *Gender, Work and Organization, 2*(2), 63–75.

Goldthorpe, J. (1980). *Social Mobility and Class Structure in Modern Britain*. Oxford: Clarendon Press.

Greene, A. M., Kirton, G., and Wrench, J. (2005). 'Trade union perspectives on diversity management: A comparison of the UK and Denmark'. *European Journal of Industrial Relations, 11*(2), 179–96.

Grey, R. (1994). 'Career as a project of the Self and Labour Force Discipline'. *Sociology, 28*(2), 479–98.

Guest, D. (1992). 'Employee commitment and control'. In J. E.Hartley and G. M. Stephenson (eds), *Employment Relations*. Oxford: Blackwell.

Hakim, C. (1979 December). 'Job segregation: Trends in the 1970s'. *Department of Employment Gazette*, 521–9.

Hakim, C. (1981). *Occupational Segregation by Sex*. Department of Employment Research Paper No. 9.

Hakim, C. (1991 September). 'Grateful slaves and self made women: Fact and fantasy in women's work orientations'. *European Sociological Review, 7*(2).

Hakim, C. (1995). 'Five feminist myths about women's employment'. *British Journal of Sociology, 46*(1), 429–54.

Hakim, C. (1996). *Key Issues in Women's Work: Female heterogeneity and the polarisation of women's employment*. London: Athlone Press.

Halford, S., Savage, M., and Witz, A. (1997). *Gender, Careers and Organisations*. Basingstoke: Macmillan.

Hantrais, L. (2000). 'From equal pay to reconciliation of employment and family life'. In L. Hantrais (ed.), *Gendered Policies in Europe*.Basingstoke: Palgrave Macmillan.

Harrington, J. (2000). *Women's Local Level Trade Union Participation*. PhD thesis, University of the West of England.

Harrington, M. (1999). *Care and Equality: Inventing a new family politics*. New York: Alfred Knopf.

Healy, G. (1993). 'Business and discrimination'. In R. Stacey (ed.), *Strategic Thinking and the Management of Change: International perspectives of organisational dynamics*. London: Kogan Page.

Healy, G. (1997). 'The industrial relations of appraisal – The case of teachers'. *Industrial Relations Journal, 28*(3), 206–20.

Healy, G. (1999a). 'Structuring commitments in interruped careers: The case of teachers'. *Gender Work and Organisation, 6*(3), 185–201.

Healy, G. (1999b). 'The trade union role in career development – A membership perspective'. *Industrial Relations Journal, 30*(3).

Healy, G., and Kirton, G. (2000). 'Women, power and trade union government in the UK'. *British Journal of Industrial Relations, 38*, 343–60.

Healy, G., and Kraithman, D. (1991). 'The other side of the equation – The demands of women on re-entering the labour market'. *Employee Relations, 13*(3), 17–28.

Healy, G., and Oikelome, F. (2006). *Ethnicity, Career and Work in the Health Services*. London: Centre for Research in Equality and Diversity, Queen Mary, University of London.

Healy, G., Bradley, H., and Mukherjee, N. (2004a). 'Inspiring activists: The experience of minority ethnic women in trade unions'. In G. Healy, E. Heery, P. Taylor and W. Brown (eds), *The Future of Worker Representation.*Basingstoke: Palgrave Macmillan, 103–28.

Healy, G., Bradley, H., and Mukherjee, N. (2004b). 'Individualism and collectivism revisited: A study of black and minority ethnic women'. *Industrial Relations Journal, 35*, 451–66.

Healy, G., Hansen, L. L., and Ledwith, S. (2006). 'Still uncovering gender in industrial relations'. *Industrial Relations Journal, 37*(4), 290–8.

Healy, G., Kirton, G., Özbilgin, M. (2006). *Judicial Appointments, Assessment Centres and Diversity*. London: Department of Constitutional Affairs.

Healy, G., Ozbilgin, M., and Aliefendioglu, H. (2005). 'Academic employment and gender: A Turkish challenge to vertical sex segregation'. *European Journal of Industrial Relations, 11*(2), 247–64.

Heath, A. (2001 October). *Ethnic Minorities in the Labour Market*. Report to the PIU, Cabinet Office.

Heath, A. and Cheung, S. (2006). *Ethnic Penalties in the Labour Market: Employers and discrimination*. DWP Research Report 341.

Heery, E., and Kelly, J. (1988). 'Do female trade union representatives make a difference? – Women full-time officials and trade union work'. *Work Employment and Society, 2*(4).

Hibbett, A. (2002). 'Ethnic minority women in the UK'. London: Women and Equality Unit, Department of Trade and Industry.

Hochschild, A. (2000). 'Global care chains and emotional surplus value'. In W. Hutton and A.Giddens (eds), *On the Edge: Living with global capitalism*. London: Jonathon Cape.

Holgate, J., Hebson, G., and McBride, A. (2006). 'Why gender and "difference" matters: A critical appraisal of industrial relations research'. *Industrial Relations Journal, 37*(4), 310–28.

Hoque, K., and Noon, M. (2004). 'Equal opportunities policy and practice in Britain: Evaluating the "empty shell" hypothesis'. *Work Employment and Society, 18*(3), 481–506.

http://www.btplc.com/Careercentre/WhyjoinBT/Morethanjustanemployer/Diversityandequality/Diversityandequality.htm (accessed 14 August 2007).

http://www.cwgl.rutgers.edu/csw0`1/background.htm

http://www.ecu.ac.uk/about/strategy.htm (accessed 14 August 2007).

http://www.tesco-careers.com/home/working/diversity (accessed 14 August 2007).

Hughes, E.C. (1958). *Men and their Work*, Glencoe: Free Press.

Humphrey, J. (2000). 'Self-organisation and trade union democracy'. *The Sociological Review*, 263–82.

ILO (2003). Information base on Equal Employment Opportunities for women and men. *Booklet 6 Alliances and Solidarity to Promote Women Workers' Rights*. Geneva: ILO.

ILO (2004). *Global Employment Trends for Women*. Geneva: ILO.

Institute for Migration and Ethnic Studies, Universiteit van Amsterdam (2006). 'Basic data and information on migration and minorities'.

Jenkins, R. (1986). *Racism and Recruitment: Managers, organisations and equal opportunity in the labour market*. Cambridge: Cambridge University Press.

Jenkins, R., and Solomos, J. (eds) (1987). *Racism and Equal Opportunity Policies in the 1980s*. Cambridge: Cambridge University Press.

Jenkins, S., Lucio, M. M., and Noon, M. (2002). 'Return to gender: An analysis of women's disadvantage in postal work'. *Gender, Work and Organization, 9*(1), 8–104.

Jenson, J., Hagen, E. and Reddy, C. (eds) (1988). *Feminization of the Labour Force*. Cambridge: Polity.

Jewson, N. and Mason, D. (1986). 'The theory and practice of equal opportunities policies: Liberal and radical approaches'. *Sociological Review, 34*(2), 307–34.

Kandola, R. and Fullerton, J. (1998). *Diversity in Action: Managing the mosaic*. London: CIPD.

Kanyora, M. (2001 September). *The intersection of race and gender. Concern.*

Kelly, J. (1998). *Rethinking Industrial Relations: Mobilization, collectivism and long waves*: London: Routledge.

Kersley, B., Alpin, C., Forth, J., Bryson, A., Bewley, H., Dix, G., et al. (2005). *First Findings of the 2004 Workplace Employment Relations Survey*. London: Routledge.

Kingma, M. (2006). *Nurses on the Move: Migration and the global health care industry*. New York City: Cornell University Press.

Kirton, G. (2006). *The Making of Trade Union Women*. Aldershot: Ashgate.

Kirton, G. (2007). 'Alternative and parallel career paths for women: The case of trade union participation'. *Work, Employment and Society, 20*(1), 47–65.

Kirton, G., and Greene, A.-M. (2000). *The Dynamics of Managing Diversity*. Oxford: Butterworth-Heinemann.

Kirton, G. and Greene, A.-M. (2002). 'The dynamics of positive action in UK trade unions: The case of women and black members'. *Industrial Relations Journal, 23*(2), 157–72.

Kirton, G., and Greene, A.-M. (2006). 'The discourse of diversity in unionised contexts: Views from trade union equality officers'. *Personnel Review, 3* (4), 431–48.

Kirton, G., and Healy, G. (1999). 'Transforming union women: The role of women trade union officials in union renewal'. *Industrial Relations Journal, 30*, 31–45.

Kirton, G., and Healy, G. (2004). 'Shaping union and gender identities: A case study of women-only trade union courses'. *British Journal of Industrial Relations, 42*, 303–23.

Kofman, E. (2005). 'Asian women in the labour market'. *Migrant Women and the Labour Market: Diversity and challenges*. Brussels: OECD.

Kolb, D. J. K., Fletcher, D. E., Meyserson, D., Merrill-Sands, and Ely, R. J. (Eds.). (2003). *Reader in Gender, Work and Organization*. Oxford: Blackwell.

Kossek, E. E., and Lobel, S. (eds.) (1996). *Managing Diversity– Human resource strategies for transforming the workplace*. Oxford: Blackwell.

Labour Force Survey (2001). London: HMSO.

Labour Research Department (LRD) (1998). *Hard Work Ahead for the Unions*. London: LRD.

Layder, D. (1993). *New Strategies in Social Research*. Cambridge: Polity Press.

Ledwith, S., Colgan, F., Joyce, P., and Hayes, M. (1990). *The Social Construction of Women's Trade Union Activism.* London: Polytechnic of North London.

Lee, G. (1987). 'Black members and their unions', In G. Lee and R. Loveridge (eds), *The Manufacture of Disadvantage.* Milton Keynes: Open University.

Lees, S. (1993). *Sugar and Spice.* Harmondsworth: Penguin.

Lemos and Crane/ Department of Health (2000). *Tackling Racial Harassment in the NHS: Evaluating black and minority ethnic staff's attitudes and experiences.* London: Department of Health.

Leonard, A. (1987). *Judging Inequality: The effectiveness of the Industrial Tribunal system in sex discrimination and equal pay cases.* London: Cobden Trust.

Levitas, R. (1998). *The Inclusive Society.* Basingstoke: Macmillan – now Palgrave Macmillan.

Levy, A. (2004). *Small Island.* London: Headline Book Publishing.

Liff, S. (1999). 'Diversity and equal opportunities: Room for a constructive compromise?' *Human Resource Management Journal, 9*(1), 65–75.

Lindley, J. and Dale, A. (2004). 'Ethnic differences in women's demographic family characteristics and economic activity profiles, 1992 to 2002'. *Labour Market Trends.* London: ONS.

Lustgarten, L. and Edwards, J. (1992). 'Racial in equality and the limits of law'. In P. Braham, A. Rattansi and R.Skellington (eds), *Racism and Antiracism: Inequalities, opportunities and policies.* London: Sage.

Macpherson, W. (1999). *The Stephen Lawrence Inquiry.* London: HMSO.

Mama, A. (1984). 'Black women, the economic crisis and the British state'. *Feminist Review, 17,* 21–36.

Marsden, P., Kelleberg, and Cook, C. (1993). 'Gender differences in organisational commitment – Influences of work positions and family roles'. *Work and organisations, 20* (1 August).

Marshall, J. (1995). *Moving Managers Moving on – Exploring career and life choices.* London: Routledge.

McBride, A. (2001). 'Making it work: Supporting group representation in a liberal democratic society'. *Gender Work and Organisation, 8*(4), 411–29.

McCrudden, C., Smith, D. and Brown, C. (1991). *Racial Justice at Work.* London: PSI.

McKenzie, R. (2003). 'Black self-organising groups'. *Working Lives Research Institute.* London: London Metropolitan University.

McRae, S. (1993). 'Returning to work after childbirth: Opportunities and inequalities'. *European Sociological Review, 9*(2), 125–38.

Miles, R. (1989). *Racism.* London: Routledge.

Mirza, H (1992). *Young, Female and Black.* London: Routledge.

Modood, T. (2005). *Multicultural Politics: Racism, ethnicity and muslims in Britain.* University of Minnesota Press and Edinburgh University Press.

Modood, T., Berthoud, R., Lakey, J., Nazroo, J., Smith, P., Virdee, S. and Beishon, S. (eds) (1997). *Ethnic Minorities in Britain: Diversity and disadvantage.* London: PSI.

Morris, L. (2002). *Managing Migration: Civic stratification and migrants' rights.* London: Routledge.

Mouzelis, N. (1989). 'Restructuring structuration theory'. *Sociological Review, 37*(4), 613–35.

Murden, T. (2006). 'Women and minorities lag in business start-ups'. *Scotland on Sunday*, 30 April.

Nixon, D. (2006). ' "I just like working with my hands": Employment aspirations and the meaning of work for low-skilled unemployed men in Britain's service economy'. *Journal of Education and Work, 19*(2), 201–17.

Noon, M. (2007). 'The fatal flaws of diversity and the business case for ethnic minorities'. *Work, Employment and Society, 21*(4).

O'Connor, H., et al. (2004). *Why the Difference: A closer look at higher education minority ethnic students.* DfES Research Report RR552.

Office for National Statistics. (2004). *Annual Population Survey, January 2004 to December 2004.* London: OSR.

Oikelome, F., and Healy, G. (2007). 'Second-class doctors? The impact of a professional career structure on the employment conditions of overseas- and UK-qualified doctors'. *Human Resource Management Journal, 17*(2), 134–54.

Pai, H. (2006). 'Taken for granted'. The *Guardian*, 15 February.

Phizacklea, A. and Miles , R. (1992). 'The British trade union movement and racism'. In P. Braham, A. Rattansi and R.Skellington (eds), *Racism and Antiracism: Inequalities, opportunities and policies.* London: Sage.

Phizacklea, A. (1990). *Unpacking the Fashion Industry: Gender, racism and class in production.* London and New York: Routledge.

Pollert, A. (1981). *Girls, Wives, Factory Lives.* London: Macmillan.

Pollert, A.(1988a). 'The flexible firm: Fixation or fact?' *Work, Employment and Society, 2*(3), 281–316.

Pollert, A. (1988b). 'Dismantling flexibility'. *Capital and Class, 34,* 42–75.

Prosser, M. (2006). *Shaping a Fairer Future.* Report of the Women and Work Commission.

Purcell, J., and Ahlstrand, B. (1994). *Human Resource Management in the Multi-Divisional Company.* Oxford: Oxford University Press,.

Reynolds, T. (2001). 'Black mothering, paid work and identity', *Ethnic and Racial Studies, 24*(6), 1 November, 1046–64.

Salway, S. (2006). 'Economic activity among UK Bangladeshi and Pakistani women in the 1990s: Evidence for continuity or change in the Family Resources Survey?' *Journal of Ethnic and Migration Studies, 33*(5), 825–47.

Sassen, S. (2000). 'Women's burden: Counter-geographies of globalisation and the feminisation of survival'. *Journal of International Affairs, 53*(2), 503–24.

Savage, M., Barlow, J., Dickens, A. and Fielding, T. (1992). *Property, Bureaucracy and Culture: Middle-class formation in contemporary Britain.* London: Routledge.

Sayer, A. and Walker, R. (1992). *The New Social Economy: Reworking the division of labour.* Oxford: Blackwell.

SERTUC (2000). *New Moves Towards Equality: New challenges.* London: SERTUC.

Shields, M. A., and Wheatley Price, S. W. (2002). 'The determinants of racial harassment at the workplace: Evidence from the British nursing profession'. *British Journal of Industrial Relations, 40*(1), 1–21.

Sikes, P., Measor, L., and Woods, P. (1985). *Teacher Careers Crises and Continuities.* Lewes: The Falmer Press.

Sinclair, D. (1995). 'The importance of sex for the propensity to unionise'. *British Journal of Industrial Relations, 33*(2): 173–90.

Sinclair, D. (1996). 'The importance of gender for participation in and attitudes to trade unionism'. *Industrial Relations Journal, 33* (2 September), 239–52.

Smart, C. (1984). *The Ties That Bind: Law marriage and reproduction of patriarchal relations*. London: Routledge.

Smith, D. (1977). *Racial Disadvantage in Britain*. Harmondsworth: Penguin.

Social Trends (2005). London: HMSO.

Stamp, P. and Robarts, S. (1986). *Positive Action: Changing the workplace for women*. London: NCCL.

Stratigaki, M. (2000). 'The European Union and the equal opportunities process'. In L. Hantrais (ed.), *Gendered Policies in Europe*. Basingstoke: Palgrave Macmillan.

Straw, J. (1989). *Equal Opportunities – The Way Ahead*. London: Institute of Personnel Management.

Sudbury, J. (1998). *Other Kinds of Dreams*. London: Routledge.

Tattersall, A. (2006 July). 'Bringing the community in: Possibilities for public-sector union success through community unionism'. *International Journal of Human Resource Management, 6*(2–3), 186–99.

Terry, M. (1996). 'Negotiating the government of UNISON: Union democracy in theory and practice'. *British Journal of Industrial Relations, 34*(1), 87–110.

Travis, A. (2007). The *Guardian*, 18 September.

TUC (2006). *Black Women at Work*. London: Trades Union Congress.

United Nations (2001). 'Background briefing on intersectionality'. *Working group on women and human rights, 45th session of the UN CSW*, from: http://www.cwgl.rutgers.edu/csw0`1/background.htm

Virdee, S., and Grint, K. (1994). 'Black Self-Organization in Trade Unions'. *The Sociological Review*, 202–26.

Wacjman, J. (1998). *Managing Like a Man: Women and men in corporate management*. Cambridge: Polity Press.

Waddington, J., and Whitston, C. (1996). 'Collectivism in a changing context: Union joining and bargaining preferences among white collar staff'. In P. Leisink, J. Van Leemput and J. Vilrokx (eds), *The Challenges to Trade Unions in Europe: Innovation or adaptation*. Cheltenham: Edward Elgar, 153–67.

Walby, S. (1997). *Gender Transformations*. London: Routledge.

Walby, S., Gottfried, H., Gottschall, K. and Osawa, M. (2007). *Gendering the Knowledge Economy*. Basingstoke: Palgrave Macmillan.

Walsh, J. (2007). 'Equality and diversity in British workplaces: The 2004 Workplace Employment Relations Survey'. *Industrial Relations Journal, 38*(4), 303–19.

Walsh, M. and Wrigley, C. (2001). 'Womanpower: The transformation of the labour force in the UK and the USA since 1945'. *Recent Findings of Research in Economic and Social History, 31*, 1–4.

Ward, L. (2007). 'On the rise. Young Asian entrepreneurs'. The *Guardian*, 29 September.

Watson, D. (1988). *Managers of Discontent*. London: Routledge.

West, J. and Pilgrim, S. (1995). 'South Asian women in employment: The impact of migration, ethnic origin and the local economy'. *New Community, 21*(3), 357–78.

Wertheimer, B., and Nelson, A. (1975). *Trade Union Women: A study of their participation in New York City locals*. New York: Praeger Publishers.

Westwood, S. (1984). *All Day, Every Day*. London: Pluto.

Wills, J. and Simms, M. (2004). 'Building reciprocal community unionism in the UK'. *Capital and Class, 82*, 59–84.

Wilson, E. (1977). *Women and the Welfare State*. London: Tavistock.

Wilson, E. (1996). 'Managing diversity and HRD'. In J. Stewart and McGoldrick (eds), *Human Resource Development: Perspectives, strategies and practice*. London: Pitman, 158–79.

Wilson, E., and Iles, P. (1999). 'Managing diversity - an employment and service delivery challenge'. *The International Journal of Public Sector Management*, *12*(1), 27–48.

Woo, D. (2002). 'Ethnicity and class as competing interpretations: The socio-economic mobility of Asian Americans'. In S. Fenton and H. Bradley (eds), *Ethnicity and Economy: 'Race and class' revisited*. Basingstoke: Palgrave Macmillan.

Wrench, J., and Modood, T. (2001). *The Effectiveness of Employment Equality Policies in Relation to Immigrants and Ethnic Minorities in the UK*. Geneva: International Labour Office.

Yeandle, S. (2007). 'Ethnic minority women and local labour market disadvantage in England'. Presentation to Sociology Department, University of Bristol.

Young, I. M. (1990). *Justice and the Politics of Difference*. Princeton, NJ: Princeton University Press.

Zoll, R. (1995). 'Failing to Modernize?' *European Journal of Industrial Relations*, *1*(1), 119–28.

Index

Printed in the United States
154299LV00001B/22/P